New Perspectives on
Language Mobility

Bloomsbury Advances in World Englishes

Series Editor:
Alexander Onysko, University of Klagenfurt, Austria

Capturing the intense interest in research on Englishes worldwide, Bloomsbury Advances in World Englishes promotes approaches to the complexities of world Englishes from a multitude of linguistic perspectives. Responding to recent trends in socio-cognitive, critical sociolinguistic, contact linguistic and communication-based research, books in this series investigate the interactions of Englishes with other languages and add new theoretical, methodological and applied perspectives to the field.

Bloomsbury Advances in World Englishes adopts an inclusive understanding of world Englishes and their interactions, which considers all dialects of English, Englishes in multilingual constellations, English-based pidgins and creoles, learner Englishes and the global spread of English as significant manifestations of Englishes in the world. Encouraging methodological and theoretical pluralism, encompassing sociolinguistics, cognitive and psycholinguistics, anthropological linguistics, historical linguistics, pragmatics, literary-linguistics and discourse analysis, this series offers an innovative insight into the manifold instantiations and usages of Englishes in the world.

Advisory Board:
Umberto Ansaldo (Curtin University, Australia)
Suzanne Hilgendorf (Simon Fraser University, Canada)
Allan James (University of Klagenfurt, Austria)
Andrew Kirkpatrick (Griffith University, Australia)
Lisa Lim (Curtin University, Australia)
Christiane Meierkord (University of Bochum, Germany)
Salikoko Mufwene (University of Chicago, USA)
Alastair Pennycook (University of Technology Sydney, Australia)
Mario Saraceni (University of Portsmouth, UK)

Philip Seargeant (The Open University, UK)
Peter Siemund (University of Hamburg, Germany)
Bertus van Rooy (University of Amsterdam, The Netherlands)
Lionel Wee (National University of Singapore, Singapore)

Titles Published in the Series:
Metaphor in Language and Culture across World Englishes,
edited by Marcus Callies and Marta Degani
Research Developments in World Englishes, edited by Alexander Onysko
The Societal Codification of Korean English, by Alex Baratta

New Perspectives on Language Mobility

English on German Radio

Sarah Josefine Schaefer

BLOOMSBURY ACADEMIC
LONDON · NEW YORK · OXFORD · NEW DELHI · SYDNEY

BLOOMSBURY ACADEMIC

Bloomsbury Publishing Plc, 50 Bedford Square, London, WC1B 3DP, UK
Bloomsbury Publishing Inc, 1385 Broadway, New York, NY 10018, USA
Bloomsbury Publishing Ireland, 29 Earlsfort Terrace, Dublin 2, D02 AY28, Ireland

BLOOMSBURY, BLOOMSBURY ACADEMIC and the Diana logo
are trademarks of Bloomsbury Publishing Plc

First published in Great Britain 2024
Paperback edition published 2025

Copyright © Sarah Josefine Schaefer, 2024, 2025

Sarah Josefine Schaefer has asserted her right under the Copyright, Designs and Patents Act, 1988, to be identified as Author of this work.

For legal purposes the Acknowledgements on pp. x–xii constitute an extension of this copyright page.

Cover design: Elena Durey

All rights reserved. No part of this publication may be: i) reproduced or transmitted in any form, electronic or mechanical, including photocopying, recording or by means of any information storage or retrieval system without prior permission in writing from the publishers; or ii) used or reproduced in any way for the training, development or operation of artificial intelligence (AI) technologies, including generative AI technologies. The rights holders expressly reserve this publication from the text and data mining exception as per Article 4(3) of the Digital Single Market Directive (EU) 2019/790.

Bloomsbury Publishing Plc does not have any control over, or responsibility for, any third-party websites referred to or in this book. All internet addresses given in this book were correct at the time of going to press. The author and publisher regret any inconvenience caused if addresses have changed or sites have ceased to exist, but can accept no responsibility for any such changes.

A catalogue record for this book is available from the British Library.

A catalog record for this book is available from the Library of Congress.

ISBN: HB: 978-1-3502-9320-5
       PB: 978-1-3502-9324-3
     ePDF: 978-1-3502-9321-2
    eBook: 978-1-3502-9322-9

Series: Bloomsbury Advances in World Englishes

Typeset by Integra Software Services Pvt. Ltd.

For product safety related questions contact productsafety@bloomsbury.com.

To find out more about our authors and books visit www.bloomsbury.com and sign up for our newsletters.

Contents

List of Figures   viii
List of Tables   ix
Acknowledgements   x
List of Symbols and Abbreviations   xiii

1. Introduction   1
2. Critical Sociolinguistic and Cultural Perspectives on Globalization   23
3. The Diffusion of English from a Contact Linguistic Perspective   45
4. A New Perspective on Language Mobility   63
5. Global Cultural Flows   101
6. Competition and Segmentation   127
7. The Workplace   151
8. The Journalist   173
9. Conclusion   193

Appendices   200
Notes   238
References   241
Index   256

Figures

1	The Media Language Model	84
2	Lexical fields of anglicism lexemes (types) in the overall corpus	120
3	Token frequency of anglicisms per minute for each sector	133
4	Token frequency of anglicisms per minute for each station	134
5	Token frequency of anglicisms per minute in station imaging, news and the rest of the spoken content	135
6	Number of types of non-catachrestic occurrences in station imaging that show diachronic development	146
7	Number of tokens of non-catachrestic occurrences in station imaging that show diachronic development	146
8	Word length of non-catachrestic innovations in number of tokens in the overall content	166
9	Word length of non-catachrestic innovations in number of tokens in station imaging	167

Tables

1 Recording method	90
2 Categories of lexical fields applied in the radio corpus analysis	96
A.1 List of anglicism lexemes	200
A.2 List of catachrestic and non-catachrestic anglicism bases	226

Acknowledgements

This book came about due to my interest in language, media and culture and how these are shaped by the forces of accelerated globalization. My completion of an MA in Journalism at the University of Galway (previously NUI Galway) allowed me to gain insights into the media industry, whose language usage provides a fascinating ground for research. The book has been developed from my doctoral thesis presented to the University of Galway in 2019 and further expands and refines some of the theoretical arguments that emerged from my doctoral research.

Throughout my journey of completing this book, I was supported by many wonderful and inspiring people. The implementation of my doctoral study was made possible by the cooperation of several public service and private radio stations in Germany. I would therefore like to sincerely thank the editors and journalists who generously gave their time to me and volunteered to participate in this project by means of taking part in interviews, which allowed me to get a privileged insight into the workplace and daily working routines of German adult contemporary radio journalists.

Special thanks and heartfelt gratitude go to my two PhD supervisors. To Dr Andrew Ó Baoill for his encouragement and support in relation to critical topics of culture and the media, and to Prof. Alexander Onysko for his intellectual guidance and support on the (socio)linguistic aspects of this book. Further thanks go to Dr John Kenny for his support and encouragement to get started on my doctoral project as well as to Dr Bahareh Heravi and Prof. Kevin Leyden, who gave me valuable insights into quantitative research methods. I would also like to thank Dr Justin Tonra, Prof. Richard Pearson, Dr Tina-Karen Pusse, Dr Frances McCormack, and Prof. Em. Allan James for their valuable comments on individual parts of my project.

In addition, there are many colleagues who have supported me in my early postdoctoral career and deserve special credit. I am particularly grateful to Prof. Helen Kelly-Holmes and Prof. Nicola McLelland for giving me invaluable feedback and advice on the structure of this book. I would also like to express my gratitude to Prof. Angela Creese, who helped me shape my thoughts on various topics in sociolinguistics. Special thanks also go to my friend Dr Olivia Walsh and to Prof. Em. Dirk Göttsche for their advice and support in all areas of academia over the last few years.

Further thanks must go to Prof. Onysko in his role as series editor, to the three anonymous reviewers of the proposal and to the reviewer of my completed draft manuscript, who significantly improved this book through their advice and comments. Equal thanks go to the editorial team of Bloomsbury, in particular to Morwenna Scott and Laura Gallon, for their support throughout the production stages of the book.

Above all, I would like to express my gratitude to the people closest to me. My heartfelt gratitude goes to my parents Josefine and Karl-Heinz. Thank you for your constant support, understanding and love throughout my time of education and throughout all other areas of life! Also, I would like to express my dearest gratitude to my husband Michael for his patience and love throughout the implementation of this project. I would also like to thank Flöckchen, Mia and Tiger for their enduring support.

Some of the arguments made in this book as well as parts of the results presented are adopted, revised or expanded from some of my previous publications. Section 1.2.2 is an expanded version of a discussion of the characteristics of radio language that also appears in the article 'Anglicisms in German Media: Exploring Catachrestic and Non-Catachrestic Innovations in Radio Station Imaging' (*Lingua* 221 (2019): 72–88), published by Elsevier B.V. and available online at https://doi.org/10.1016/j.lingua.2019.01.002. The findings and examples presented in Chapters 5 to 8 regarding the use of catachrestic/non-catachrestic anglicisms in radio station imaging materials (including in Figures 6, 7 and 9) were also previously published in this article.

Parts of the categories of anglicisms in Section 3.2, the conceptualization of novel anglicisms in Section 4.2, the methods for the detection of novel anglicisms in Section 4.4, and the results for the analysis of novel anglicisms in Section 7.2 as well as some interview statements in Chapters 5 to 8 also appear in 'English on Air: Novel Anglicisms in German Radio Language' (*Open Linguistics* 7 (2021): 569–93), published by De Gruyter and licensed under the Creative Commons Attribution 4.0 International License (CC BY 4.0).

Section 2.2 and results and examples presented in Sections 5.1 and 5.4 are derived in part from 'Hybridization or What? A Question of Linguistic and Cultural Change in Germany' (*Globalizations* 18, no. 4 (2021): 667–82), published by Informa UK Limited, trading as Taylor & Francis Group, and available online at http://www.tandfonline.com/10.1080/14747731.2020.1832839.

Example (12) is adopted from the article 'Global Englishes and the Semiotics of German Radio – Encouraging the Listener's Visual Imagination through Translingual and Transmodal Practices' (*Frontiers in Communication* 7 (2022): 780195), published by Frontiers Media S.A. and licensed under the Creative Commons Attribution 4.0 International License (CC BY 4.0).

An earlier version of the discussion of Example (23) appeared as part of the blogpost 'Radio Language: A Transmodal Perspective' (*Strictly Language: Sociolinguistics, Language Attitudes, Language Ideologies*, 27 May 2021), available online at https://strictlylanguage.wordpress.com/2021/05/27/radio-language-a-transmodal-perspective/.

Symbols and Abbreviations

*	hypothetical form
/	aborted sentence (interview statements)
→	derived from / resulting in
AWB	*Anglizismen-Wörterbuch* (Dictionary of Anglicisms)
COCA	Corpus of Contemporary American English
DWDS	*Digitales Wörterbuch der deutschen Sprache* (Digital Dictionary of the German Language)
E.	English
G.	German
I-implicatures	implicatures of informativeness
M-implicatures	implicatures of manner
OED	*Oxford English Dictionary*
P	private (station/sector)
PS	public service (station/sector)
RL	receptor language
SL	source language

1

Introduction

Language has long been conceived and examined in traditional (socio)linguistics as a self-contained entity which is at best affected by processes of globalization but is not inherently part of them. As Blommaert points out,

> many people still believe that the issue [processes of globalization] can be formulated as 'language *and* globalization', in precisely the same way as one would speak of 'language *and* culture', 'language *and* society' and so on. That is, with precisely the same problems, Language itself is seen as essentially unaffected by globalization (culture, society, and so on), and globalization is seen as just another context in which language is practised, a new one at best.
>
> (2010: 2; italics in the original)

This perspective ultimately makes globalizing processes part of a static context that is set apart from linguistic structure rather than an intrinsic element of linguistic practices (see also Canagarajah 2018a). In the pursuit for a critical reconceptualization of language in times of accelerated globalization that overcomes this monolithic orientation to language, critical sociolinguists have introduced the notions of language as a social practice involving various semiotic resources and of linguistic and cultural resources that are described as increasingly mobile (Blommaert 2010; Canagarajah 2013; Fairclough 2006; Li 2018; Pennycook 2007). Similarly, as opposed to the idea of pure and separable cultures, notions of cultural hybridization against the background of global cultural flows, mediatization of societies and increased mobility of resources and people have taken hold in both critical sociolinguistics and critical cultural studies (Appadurai 1996; Nederveen Pieterse 2009). From a sociolinguistics of mobility perspective, it is therefore more important to focus on language in use and to analyse the 'voices' people adopt in social interaction rather than to talk about the abstract structure of individual 'languages'. In addition, instead of thinking in binary terms such as 'monolingualism' and 'multilingualism' to describe people's competence in using separate systems of meaning, concepts such as 'heteroglossia' have been proposed to refer to the different 'voices' that speakers adopt in ever-changing sociocultural contexts. As a result of these theoretical developments, the very connections between nation, culture and language that have long been taken for granted as well as their rootedness in bounded geographical spaces are increasingly regarded as ideological constructs (Appadurai 1996; Blommaert and Rampton 2011; Nederveen Pieterse 2009).

The paradigmatic shift proposed by critical sociolinguistics has, however, not yet been commonly accepted. Instead, a paradigmatic gap has evolved between and within the various disciplines in the study around language. Most sociolinguists and applied linguists whose research is rooted in the critical tradition have adopted theories such as translanguaging (Creese and Blackledge 2011; Otheguy, García and Reid 2015), translingualism (Canagarajah 2013) or metrolingualism (Pennycook and Otsuji 2015) within the mobility paradigm to explain the language phenomena of our increasingly mobile world. Contemporary variationist sociolinguists and traditional linguists, however, including those who are interested in language contact, continue to examine languages as systems fixed in time and space (cf. Kerswill and Torgersen 2017; Kortmann and Langstrof 2012; Thoms et al. 2019). In recent years, we have seen this gap in the study around language solidify, resulting in paradigmatic parallelism. This parallelism often leads to mutual criticism amongst researchers of the individual branches of (socio)linguistics regarding mostly ontological and epistemological considerations around the conceptualization of language (cf. Auer 2022; Canagarajah 2018a). The paradigmatic gap is especially evident in studies that are concerned with the global diffusion of English. English has a vast record of mobility, has remained the dominant example of mobile linguistic resources and is closely tied to transcultural flows of popular culture and the mediatization of societies (see Dovchin 2020; Pennycook 2007; Sharma 2012). While studies examining global Englishes from a mobility perspective such as by Pennycook (2007), Dovchin (2020) and Canagarajah (2013) have set out to highlight the fluidity and local appropriation of English linguistic resources and 'Anglo-American' cultural practices, the field of World Englishes has set out to describe the diversity and development of new local varieties, dialects and hybrid forms of Englishes across the globe (amongst others Kachru 1985; Mair 2013; Onysko 2016; Schneider 2007; Schreier, Hundt and Schneider 2020). Despite the ambition of the Kachruvian World Englishes paradigm to tackle the monolithic conception of a globally hegemonic Anglo-American English and to promote postcolonial Englishes as varieties of their own right in response to the dystopic perspective on the diffusion of English promoted by theories of linguistic imperialism (cf. Phillipson 1992, 2009), the Kachruvian World Englishes paradigm is, nevertheless, unable to escape its structuralist roots (Pennycook 2007; Saraceni 2015). In describing new varieties of Englishes, World Englishes has primarily pluralized a monolithic perspective on Englishes by defining new, independent systems of meaning and fixing these in space and time (e.g. Indian English, Chinese English, Nigerian English, etc.; cf. Kortmann and Schneider 2004; Walker and Meyerhoff 2023). In the same vein, the diffusion of English has been extensively researched in studies on language contact with a focus on what is frequently termed anglicisms. Anglicisms are English words and phrases that are used in many domains in localities of the expanding circle of the traditional World Englishes paradigm (Kachru 1985), which includes localities such as France, Italy, Spain and Germany (see Andersen 2015; Furiassi 2010; Glahn 2002; Gottlieb 2020; Onysko 2007; Picone 1996; Pulcini, Furiassi and Rodríguez González 2012). In this context, the field of contact linguistics traditionally adopts a perspective of English in contact with other languages and thereby focuses on linguistic systems as situated and interfering with each other. In anglicism research, the use of English is therefore again treated as set apart from its spatiotemporal context and hence not much attention is given to the social and cultural contexts that trigger the language contact phenomena that the field sets out to describe.

These different takes in the study around language in our globalized times pose a challenge for scholars in (socio)linguistics which I will take on both theoretically and empirically in this book. While the book joins recent works by scholars in sociolinguistics interested in globalization and a critical reconceptualization of language (amongst others Kubota 2020; Slembrouck 2022), the central aim of my book is an attempt for devising a new perspective on language mobility – a socially grounded spatial approach – which bridges the paradigmatic gap in the study around language by promoting methodological pluralism. In developing a new perspective on language mobility, I will focus on the complex uptake, negotiation and appropriation of English resources in times of increased mobility and will highlight the value of methodological pluralism especially for the study around English in the empirical part of this book. In this part, I will also present the case of the use of English linguistic resources in German radio media – a domain of language shaped by the complexities of both fluidity and fixity and therefore by mobilizing forces of accelerated globalization as well as situated structures and norms. Taking together the global flows of media culture, British and American media practices especially in the post-war years, the acceptance and appropriation of English linguistic resources, and the audiences' expectations towards the broadcasting media in their role as evaluative voices of the public in Germany, the German radio media make for a compelling case that raises significant questions about how we need to rethink and study language. The book thereby offers not only a new perspective on language mobility but also new insights into how the mass media operate within global flows of messages and linguistic resources that characterize our mediated societies in areas where the dynamics of global Englishes can be observed. By exploring the use of English in German radio language, I also hope to persuade readers with a linguistic background and an interest in globalization and global Englishes to pay more attention to the complexities of discursive and distributed media practices that make up media communication.

In the following section, I will elaborate on the paradigmatic challenges in (socio)linguistics and how I intend to address these in the book. I will then present the key theme of the book, the sociolinguistics of mass media, which will guide my line of inquiry (see Section 1.2). Taking the sociolinguistics of mass media as an example of complexity will allow us to understand what a new perspective on language mobility in (socio)linguistics could look like – a perspective that takes the best of both paradigms to overcome ontological and epistemological differences in the conceptualization and analysis of language. I will then give a first glimpse of the complexity of discursive radio practices characterized by both fluidity and fixity.

1.1 Complexity as the challenge

In the advocacy of the mobility paradigm, which acknowledges the mixing and hybridization of languages and cultures as a continuous, long-term process, we critical sociolinguists and critical cultural theorists often focus exclusively on the hotspots of cultural, ethnic and social mixing. We choose these hotspots as loci of research to find strong examples that can help us state our case and ask questions such as 'How do we come to terms with phenomena such as Thai boxing by Moroccan girls in Amsterdam, Asian rap in London, Irish bagels, Chinese tacos, and Mardi Gras Indians in the United States?' (Nederveen Pieterse 2009: 75). We mostly focus on highly complex, super-diverse areas and mixing zones where hybridity flourishes and where people holding vastly different linguistic repertoires interact and are in daily contact, such as in super-diverse migrant neighbourhoods in Antwerp or in Bangladeshi-run stores in Sydney and Tokyo (see Blommaert 2013; Pennycook and Otsuji 2015, 2017). It is especially in these hotspots where traditional structuralist approaches to the study of language produce anomalies and experience a paradigmatic crisis (see Kuhn 2012). To highlight the urgency of stepping away from the monolithic view of language in times of accelerated globalization, we therefore particularly focus on such prime examples of intense translingualism and transculturalism, by which we demonstrate how the constructed boundaries that were set by structuralist linguistics are clearly violated in such localities.

While highlighting the complexities of language as a social practice in times of increased mobility is certainly a vital undertaking, we tend to be less concerned with those areas where the context is 'less' chaotic, where societal structures can be deemed more stable and where more sedimented language resources predominate, such as in the case of German radio media. For a paradigm shift in the sense of critical sociolinguistics to take hold in all disciplines concerned with the study around language, we need to therefore demonstrate that a sociolinguistics of mobility also provides compelling explanations for precisely such cases. This, however, means that we need to focus more on how boundaries are constructed and maintained and how people's lifeworlds are shaped by them. In addition, this includes acknowledging that, despite the vital paradigmatic shift in postmodern linguistics that deconstructs the monolithic view of 'languages', completely discarding the category of 'languages' within the cultural framework of modern European nation-states – even though these are increasingly regarded as in a state of declining authority (Appadurai 1996; Nederveen Pieterse 2009) – does not come without difficulties for the study of language practices especially in more stable language settings.

The national standard languages including English and German that have evolved within the last two centuries certainly are no more than a single set of linguistic resources out of many in their respective national contexts. These varieties, however, were given a special status as institutionalized languages of state and of education. Therefore, the normative force of a standardized 'national language' constitutes part of the social reality of many people in Europe. National languages are the dominant varieties around which other related varieties are grouped together to form imagined communities, namely nations (see Anderson 2016). According to Anderson, the advances in early linguistics and especially the creation of dictionaries of differing print vernaculars throughout Europe in the late eighteenth and early nineteenth century substantially contributed to the formation of national consciousness. 'The lexicographic revolution in Europe ... created, and gradually spread, the conviction that languages (in Europe at least) were, so to speak, the personal property of quite specific groups – their daily speakers and readers – and moreover that these groups, imagined as communities, were entitled to their autonomous place in a fraternity of equals' (Anderson 2016: 84).

Most European nation-states are built on the national consciousness that evolved out of using a common print language in each of the respective territories and, as a result, standard varieties of each language still play an important role in shaping national ideology of these nation-states. Today, the convention to use names such as 'the English language' or 'German' for specific sets of linguistics resources, which originates in this era, shows that the viewpoint of individual and distinguishable languages is still common in public discourse. What is more, national languages are the best researched and documented varieties, which becomes evident through the multitude of grammar textbooks and dictionaries available for the various 'languages' of Europe. Today's education systems still proliferate the categorization into 'languages' from first-level up to third-level education by teaching languages as individual school subjects. Universities even have individual departments for each of the 'languages'. Furthermore, the idea of separate languages is also deeply entrenched in the European Union's language and education policies. According to a European Union communication paper, the European Commission's aim is that 'by 2025 all young Europeans finishing upper secondary education have a good knowledge of two languages in addition to their mother tongue(s)' (European Commission 2017: 7). This way of thinking in individual languages therefore has become one of the basic principles of social organization in modern nation-states, shaping people's understanding of language even against the background of increased mobility.

Researching language use in times of increased mobility therefore proves to be a challenging endeavour. While, as indicated above, the structuralist perspective increasingly struggles to explain the dynamism and complexity of language phenomena in an increasingly connected and mobile world, the theoretical and terminological advances in critical sociolinguistics appear disconnected from the social realities experienced by many language users in Europe and beyond. Both viewpoints, therefore, create not only a paradigmatic gap in research on the worldwide use of Englishes but also a gap between the social reality of many language users and sociolinguistic descriptions thereof. The point I am making here is that it is vital for proponents of the structuralist perspective to view language as a social practice and therefore as intrinsically linked to various historical, social and cultural factors, and for critical sociolinguistics to focus more on how speakers draw and maintain boundaries. Even though boundaries are constructed, they are an intrinsic part of many people's lifeworlds. This means that separate languages are very much present in the social realities of many people, especially those living in more linguistically stable social environments. In our ambition to understand language as a social practice, it is therefore not enough to simply acknowledge the normative forces of monolingual ideologies (cf. Blommaert 2010; Canagarajah 2013; Pennycook 2007), but we must engage more closely with those language practices predominately shaped by standard language norms.

Drawing on critical sociolinguistic and critical cultural theory for my methodological frame and empirical approaches from contact linguistics, the book will demonstrate how the different takes on language from both perspectives, when combined, allow for greater insights into the lifeworlds of actual language users, who often employ language in sociolinguistic settings characterized by a strong presence of standard language norms. The case study of the use of English resources on German radio thereby aims (a) to draw attention to the vital need of ontologically stepping away from the monolithic view of language in times of accelerated globalization in the study around global Englishes and language more generally and (b) to generate an understanding of how we as critical sociolinguists can make use of analytical tools from contact linguistics to better understand how boundaries are negotiated and how the monolingual ideology is sustained by language users especially in more stable language situations. The lifeworlds of German radio journalists are a prime example of this, and the case study, even though referring to a specific case, can be taken as an example of many similar cases in more stable language environments. As Shulman states, 'a case, properly understood, is not simply the report of an event or incident. To call something a case is to make a theoretical claim – to argue that it is a "case of something", or to argue that it is an instance of a larger class' (1986: 11). I therefore follow the reasoning that 'unique and situated events ... can and do indeed reveal a lot about the very big things in society' (Blommaert and Jie 2020: 13).

A pluralistic take on language furthermore requires a refined understanding of the language practices analysed. Viewing media language as a social practice involving various semiotic resources therefore also calls for a long overdue rethinking of analyses of the use of English resources in media content, which I will elaborate on further in the following section. This means to consider the monolithic perspective on languages that was constructed and disseminated by modern linguistics not as the ontology of language but as part of the lifeworlds of language users and in this regard as a fundamental feature of the social organization of particularly Western nation-states and of the sociolinguistics of media. As we shall see throughout the book, the case of the use of English linguistic resources on air by German radio journalists provides a compelling example of how global cultural flows shape language and of how the normative forces of standard language ideologies still very much shape the lifeworlds of language users. To attain a detailed insight into the language practices of radio journalists and therefore into the sociocultural context that is intrinsically linked to how English is used on air, I will focus on a particular type of radio programme and its collaborative production processes: the morning shows of German adult contemporary radio stations. Adult contemporary radio stations play mainly pop music and provide a mix of entertainment and information for a target audience between 25 and 49 years of age. I will elaborate on this specific radio format and the morning show situation in Sections 1.2.1 and 1.2.2. By taking the ontological stance of the mobility paradigm as a foundation and combining it with analytical tools from contact linguistics, the case study explores the specific sociocultural factors that drive the use of English linguistic resources in German radio media. This is also achieved by means of comparing radio stations from both the public service and private broadcasting sector in Germany and paying attention to how competition between these sectors shapes language use on air. The analysis and discussion of the case study are centred around two major questions:

1. Why are English linguistic resources used by German radio journalists on air?
2. How are these English resources embedded in journalists' professional language practices?

The major questions of the case study are examined by combining qualitative and quantitative methods (see Chapter 4). These include an analysis of the frequency of English linguistic resources in a self-compiled radio corpus of 60 hours, a semantic and pragmatic analysis of English linguistic resources in radio content, and qualitative interviews with nineteen journalists responsible for writing and producing the examined radio content. Through qualitative interviews, the case study acknowledges the views of the actual producers of media texts on their use of English in radio broadcasts. This way the book also reaches beyond the scope of previous research in the study of mobile Englishes by giving unprecedented insights into the lifeworlds of the producers of media messages (i.e. radio broadcasts). The case study will show how radio journalists operate within global flows of messages and linguistic and cultural resources. Understanding individual lifeworlds is key to understanding our language practices.

1.2 Towards a critical sociolinguistics of mass media language

In their search for new patterns, structures and varieties of Englishes in the expanding circle, researchers in World Englishes and contact linguistics often base their investigations on large corpora of traditional mass media (amongst others Fiedler 2022; Glahn 2002; Lee 2014; Onysko 2007; Plümer 2000; Smakman et al. 2009; Yang 1990). Mass media language is usually chosen for reasons of practicality since the media provide a vast amount of language material that is readily available. However, in line with the structuralist orientation, the language material under investigation is frequently set apart from its spatiotemporal context and taken as representative of the language use of a whole (imagined) speech community. This is problematic in several ways, as it does not acknowledge media language as an assemblage of historical, social, cultural and material factors that come together in journalists' meaning-making and make this language practice highly specific (Schaefer 2019, 2021a; b). According to Blommaert, language 'cannot be understood as autonomous, but needs to be examined as part of the larger package: as the sociolinguistic side of the larger social system' (2010: 2). Language practices in a given society change and develop in various ways due to different causes. These include conflicts, such as war, or oppression, such as occupation or colonization. Language is also shaped by cultural flows caused by migration, trade, technological development or increasing mediatization of societies. The diffusion of English linguistic resources in Germany and in other European countries is an example for this and needs to be analysed against this background.

At the same time, the materiality of the medium is essential for the social practices of message production and reception. According to Lievrouw, 'devices and systems that exist in a given time and place shape users' practices and larger social expectations about what the artifacts can do, what they are for, and what people might actually do with them (that is, practices are *remediated*)' (2014: 47; italics in the original). Furthermore, the medium as the channel of communication has certain affordances, which need to be acknowledged. According to Hutchby, a medium's affordances refer to how material characteristics of media technology shape the 'possibilities for action that it offers' (2001: 449). This also applies to radio with which only restricted communication is possible since it merely allows for a communication that is within the scope of its technical possibilities. Radio is auditory only and therefore includes other auditory modes besides speech (i.e. music and sounds) to compensate the lack of a visual dimension

(Crisell 1986; Schaefer 2022; Shingler and Wieringa 1998; see also Section 1.2.2). This reminds us of Fairclough, who also acknowledges that each medium has 'particular technical properties which constitute possibilities and constraints for communication' (2006: 98). According to Hjarvard (2004), the way each medium shapes the language used through it leads to new language varieties that he calls *medialects*. 'Unlike dialects, medialects have no geographical province; in contrast to the case of sociolects, the users' social position, etc., is indifferent. Instead, the focus rests on the channel of communication' (2004: 94). While the term 'medialect' in the sense of media-bound language varieties implies a more static take on language, it is nevertheless useful to help us view media language as a specific contextually shaped, practice-based register.

In the context of a medium's affordances, it is also important to note that media language needs to be seen as a complex semiotic assemblage of various semiotic resources. Media language should therefore not be considered in terms of separable modes as individual semiotic systems but rather as semiotic resources that are mixed, blended and entangled with one another in meaning-making practices. As Pennycook states, 'not only are languages not discrete entities in relation to each other but the separation of language from the complexity of signs with which its use is associated has limited our understanding of a broader semiotics' (2007: 49). Therefore, Pennycook prefers the term 'transmodal' to 'multimodal' to describe the entanglement of multiple modes. The notion of transmodality also refers to how semiotic resources are entangled in the spatiotemporal complexities of the material world and thus considers semiotic resources simultaneously as material, social and cultural resources. While I will mostly adopt the term 'transmodal' in this book, I will also occasionally use the term 'multimodal' as proposed by Kress and van Leeuwen (2001). It is important to note that in the specific context of professionally produced media texts, the term 'multimodal' is nevertheless valuable to reflect the meaning-making practices of journalists since their work is so to speak a norm- and routine-based transmodal practice of combining three 'separate' programme elements of speech, music and sounds to create a harmonious flow of the radio programme.

In contrast to studies that take mass media texts merely as a source for large language corpora, a substantial amount of research in sociolinguistics, applied linguistics and related fields such as cultural studies has focused on media discourse and media language as their object of study. These studies mainly follow different research agendas ranging from how media use language and how discourse in society shapes media texts to how media discourse shapes our societies. This includes approaches to analysing media discourse such as semiotic analysis, (inter)textual analysis, cultural analysis and critical discourse analysis. Most prominent works on media discourse and media language (in a wider semiotic sense) include those by Hall (2013) on representation (see also Tuchman 1978), van Dijk's (1988) work on the structures of news texts (for further studies on news texts from a sociolinguistic perspective see Bell 1991; Fowler 1991), Fairclough's (1995) work on critical media discourse analysis, and Kress and van Leeuwen's (2001) work on the social semiotics of media language. Furthermore, there are studies in sociolinguistics that place greater emphasis on practices of journalists in the newsroom, often through ethnographic methods (i.e. newsroom observation), and have investigated language practices of the press (amongst others Cotter 2010; van Hout 2011, 2015) and of television journalists (amongst others Merminod and Burger 2020; Montgomery 2007; Perrin 2013, 2017).

Despite this plethora of research, the complex entanglements of various sociocultural factors, material aspects and semiotic resources that make up language in traditional mass media have not received sufficient attention in previous works around media discourse and media language or on language phenomena in mass media corpora. In other words, taking these aspects merely as contextual background to language, if at all, or only acknowledging some of these as intrinsically linked to media language creates a problematic text–context binary that does not consider the entanglements of professionally produced media language with a complex web of practices, norms, resources and artefacts in both time and space (Canagarajah 2018a).

Adopting a holistic, spatial approach and therefore viewing mass media language as a transmodal assemblage (see Pennycook 2017) of social, cultural, historical and material factors and resources allows us to lift the text–context binary often drawn by traditional (socio)linguistic research. 'Ideally, such an approach would mean that we ... consider how features we may have treated as part of context may constitute an assemblage that is integral to meanings and communication' (Canagarajah 2018a: 34). It is important to note at this point, however, that we also need to consider the journalists' perspectives on their language choices and how these shape media practices within this assemblage. Such a take on mass media language allows insights into how radio language is produced within a dense network of factors that simultaneously push and pull the journalists in various directions during content production and thereby give radio language its specific characteristics (see also Section 1.2.2). As we shall see throughout the book, these factors range from larger processes of globalization to the individual journalists' personal backgrounds. The use of English in German radio media is an example of how the effects of cultural and linguistic flows caused by war, occupation, re-education, reunification, nation building and accelerated globalization shape the language practices of speakers in this locality. I will come back to this in Section 2.2. Furthermore, the German broadcasting system, like broadcasting systems in many other Western European countries, comprises of a public service and a private sector that together form a competitive market and shape media content, which I will explore in Chapter 6. Moreover, the work of journalists behind the scenes of a radio programme is also shaped by the social structures of newsrooms and station policies (see Chapter 7). As a mass medium and influential voice of the public sphere, radio is also subject to legislation and regulation, and journalists have a responsibility to cater for the public interest.

Given the complexity of these assemblages, radio is a highly versatile medium. Radio programmes come in different formats, ranging from news talk to music- and entertainment-oriented programmes focusing on various music genres and thereby catering for different target audiences. It is also a mass medium that is omnipresent in our daily lives – a background medium played to entertain us especially while we are busy doing other things, such as driving, working or doing housework. This omnipresence is also the reason why radio is usually taken for granted. As the consumer of a product, we do not tend to think much about the complex collaborative production processes involved in creating a radio broadcast and what the lifeworlds of professional journalists are like. What matters for us is that we as customers are satisfied with the product. Radio has to entertain, inform and be at our disposal whenever we feel like turning it on. In the following section, I will introduce the case study by shedding light on the format of adult contemporary radio and on why the morning show is the most important programme of the day. I will then provide some first examples of German adult contemporary radio language and its complexity, also in a wider semiotic sense.

1.2.1 Adult contemporary radio and the morning show

In Germany, the radio landscape is divided into different radio formats. These focus mainly on different target audiences and vary in the kind of music they play and in the mix of both spoken content and music throughout the programme. The concept of format radio was established in the 1950s in America, where it quickly gained popularity (Haas, Frigge and Zimmer 1991). According to Goldhammer (1995: 235), the trend to produce formatted radio programmes in Germany in the mid-1980s was driven by the creation of the private radio sector and represented a 'kleine Revolution' (little revolution) on the German radio market. The term 'format radio' refers to the practice of fitting wording, music and all other parts of a radio programme to the taste of the target audience (Gerhards and Stümpert 2017; Goldhammer 1995; Haas, Frigge and Zimmer 1991). According to Haas, Zimmer and Frigge, 'die Wahl eines Formates beeinflusst alle Bereiche des Senders. Sowohl den On-Air-, als auch den Off-Air-Bereich' (the choice of a format shapes all areas of a station. Both on-air and off-air domains) (1991: 160), which includes all parts of the programme, such as station imaging materials – the self-advertisement of radio stations (e.g. trailers, jingles) – news and other radio pieces. In addition, the way in which content is presented and the amount of information provided in the content varies from format to format (Gerhards and Stümpert 2017). Various radio formats have become common in the German broadcasting landscape, including oldies, contemporary hit radio, classic and rock. The most popular format, however, is adult contemporary, which plays mainstream pop music.

As previously mentioned, adult contemporary radio stations in Germany focus on providing a mix of information and entertainment and target a broad listenership between 25 and 49 years of age. Journalists working for adult contemporary stations therefore face the challenge of having to address a linguistically diverse audience as they need to attract not only a wide range of age groups but also all social strata and, depending on the size of their broadcasting area, different regional communities. The profile of each station, which means the design and structure of the station's programme and the journalists' language use, is vital for a station to differentiate itself from other stations of the same format (Gerhards and Stümpert 2017). While the music playlist is similar amongst adult contemporary radio stations, how the listener is addressed by the presenters and hosts varies amongst stations.

The most important time of the day for radio stations is the morning since each station gets most listeners during this time. Hence, self-promotion of the station in the morning programmes is vital, and the amount of spoken content in morning shows is higher in comparison to other segments of the stations' programmes throughout the day. Morning shows additionally contain most genres on radio, such as news including weather and traffic, comedy, service (consumer information and advice) and station imaging. This means that the programme covers a wide range of different topics, such as lifestyle, sports and politics. Providing information and interacting with the listener in an informative and entertaining way is of primary importance in the radio morning show (Buchholz 2017; Gerhards and Stümpert 2017; Goldhammer 1995). The audience wishes to be entertained and informed while waking up with the programme and usually keeps listening throughout the morning until they go to work.

Likewise, the morning show cast represents a wide potpourri of different characters where each member contributes his or her individual part to the language used on air (Buchholz 2017). Each of the journalists working in the morning show team also has a specific role to fulfil, including the main host, the sidekick, the news expert, the weather presenter or the funny comedian. This diverse team of hosts and presenters shall provide a fresh and varied morning programme and together with the before-mentioned complexities of the radio format makes the morning show a highly versatile communicative event. In the following section, I will give a first glimpse at adult contemporary radio language.

1.2.2 Radio language and its characteristics

The language used by the mass media has previously been linguistically defined as a mix of formal and conversational language, which often contains both terminology and slang (Adler 2004; Burger and Luginbühl 2014; Fitzgerald 2006; Nowottnick 1989). This description, however, is too simplistic and needs to be understood in the light of the transmodal and translingual practices of radio journalists and the characteristics of the medium through which communication is made, which mirror both fluidity and fixity in space and time. Against the background of a more stable language situation and the complexities of the adult contemporary radio format, the spatial repertoire available to German adult contemporary radio journalists emerges from a highly specific environment composed of sedimented practices, diverse life trajectories of journalists and mobile resources within global cultural flows. Thus, whenever adult contemporary radio journalists use English mobile resources, they renegotiate and at times transgress linguistic boundaries within a professional environment shaped by standards, norms and fixities. In addition, we will see throughout the book that the tasks of successfully communicating with the target audience are collaboratively accomplished by several media practitioners.

My intention with the following examples taken from the morning show corpus is to provide a first insight into the specific characteristics of adult contemporary radio language and its multifaceted forms. While my discussion in this section is mostly focused on linguistic and semiotic features of radio language and raises several questions about the translingual and transmodal practices of radio journalists, I will answer these questions by addressing this complexity and engaging more deeply with journalistic practices from a wider sociocultural perspective later in the book. In the following, I give examples from radio language on a verbal level as well as two examples in the form of transcriptions of transmodal assemblages to guide us through different features of radio language. Given the limited scope of this book, I will only present an in-depth analysis of examples from adult contemporary radio language incorporating semiotic and material resources at suitable points.[1]

> (1) Königin Maxima stand gestern in pinkem Kleid, mit pinkem Hut bei Sonne in München, mit pinken Tulpen in der Hand und hat Selfies mit Fans gemacht; total nett.
>
> (Yesterday in Munich, Queen Maxima wore a pink dress and a pink hat and had pink tulips in her hands while taking selfies with fans in the sunshine; how nice.)
>
> (Private Station 3, 14 April 2016)
>
> (2) Auf warme 26 kommen die heute noch. ... Diese Woche bleibt der Sommer noch ... und dann wird es leider uselich.
>
> (They [temperatures] will reach a warm 26 today. ... The summer will stay for this week ... and then unfortunately it's going to get ugly.)
>
> (Private Station 1, 9 May 2016)
>
> (3) Gegen die neuen Einschnitte gibt es seit Tagen Streiks und Demonstrationen. Zehntausende demonstrierten am Sonntag in Athen.
>
> (Strikes and protests are going on for days against new cuts. Tens of thousands attended protests in Athens on Sunday.)
>
> (Public Service Station 1, 9 May 2016)

On radio, journalists use a very descriptive and pictorial language that catches the listener's attention, as shown in Example (1): 'in pinkem Kleid, mit pinkem Hut ..., mit pinken Tulpen in der Hand' (a pink dress and a pink hat and ... pink tulips in her hands). As briefly mentioned, this is because the listener cannot see what is going on in contrast to print and television media, where descriptive elements are often perceived visually by the audience through images and footage. Examples (1), (2) and (3) also indicate the above-mentioned mix of formal and informal language used on adult contemporary radio, which is, however, subject not only to the materiality of radio but also to genre conventions and their distinctive communicative aims (see Schaefer 2021b). The verbal resources used in Example (3), taken from a news broadcast, index formality. Short and unambiguous main clauses are used in this example since journalists are particularly careful to make language used in news bulletins easy to understand. This means that journalists only include most relevant facts in news pieces to avoid lengthy news reports and comprehension problems on behalf of the listener. Moreover, the use of the preterite form *demonstrierten* (protested) indexes formality since the use of the German preterite is mostly confined to written language, whereas the use of perfect is more common for referring to past events in colloquial speech. In contrast to Example (3), Example (1) taken from the genre of host talk and Example (2) from a weather forecast contain linguistic resources that are typical for colloquial language used on radio. The dialectal term *uselich* denoting unpleasant weather used as part of the weather forecast as well as the omission of the unit *Grad* (degrees centigrade) indicate adult contemporary radio's conversational character. In the same vein, the intensifier *total* (totally) in Example (1) serves as a marker of colloquial language, which is used to create an informal atmosphere and therefore a sense of proximity between the journalist and listener.

Besides radio language's alignment to the materiality of the medium radio, which becomes especially evident in Example (1), the examples in this section also indicate that journalists combine linguistic resources of different spatiotemporal distribution. Not only does the message of the news opener in Example (5) below illustrate radio's entanglement in both global and local contexts but also the linguistic choices in Examples (1) and (2) signify this entanglement of the global and the local. On the one hand we can find recent expressions of global reach in line with adult contemporary's orientation to popular culture such as *Selfie* (selfie) in Example (1), while on the other hand the dialect term *uselich* (Example (2)) also indicates this adult contemporary station's local rootedness.

Radio language can at times also be quite repetitive. Again, this depends mostly on the communicative aims of each genre. In station imaging, for example, repetition is quite common. Usually, verbal resources are used repetitively here to promote the station's image in trailers and jingles (Schaefer 2021b). Another reason for repetition on radio is that radio is a transient medium where listeners tune in at different times. Journalists try to reach as many members of their target audience as possible by repeating relevant parts of content. These may include, but are not limited to, warnings in weather and traffic reports or important news concerning, for example, public safety. This again shows how sedimented practices align to the materiality of the medium radio. What also needs to be noted in this context is that media language is generally adapted to its target audience. I will come back to this in Chapter 6. Examples (4) and

(5) from station imaging show how radio journalists additionally rely on the semiotic resources of music and sounds to convey their messages.

Example (4)

Time (sec.)	Speech / Lyrics	Music
0.0–5.4	**Station voice 1 / 2:** Das ist der beste Mix, wir spielen das Beste von heute, (This is the best mix, we play the best contemporary music,)	Calvin Harris 'Blame ft. John Newman' (instrumental)
5.2–9.9	... *[chorus of song]* ...	(instrumental + vocals)
10.0–13.4	**gemixt** mit echten Kulthits, (mixed with real classic hits,)	(instrumental)
13.5–21.0	... *[chorus of song]* ...	Kate Yanai 'Summer Dreaming' (instrumental + vocals)
21.1–24.3	für mehr Abwechslung **und mehr Musik.** (for greater variety and more music.)	(instrumental)
24.4–28.7	**Jetzt,** Jamie Lawson, „Wasn't Expecting That". (Now Jamie Lawson, 'Wasn't Expecting That'.)	Jamie Lawson 'Wasn't Expecting That' (instrumental)
28.8–39.6	... *[second verse of song]* ...	(instrumental + vocals)
39.7–43.0	Wir spielen die besten **aktuellen Hits.** (We play the best contemporary hits.)	(instrumental)
43.1–44.8	**Radio X.**	subsequent song: Jamie Lawson 'Wasn't Expecting That' (instrumental intro)

Note: Station voice 1: standard font; Station voice 2: **bold** English translations in parentheses.

(Private Station 1, 14 April 2016)

Example (4) portrays a trailer (a compilation of different music bits) and a claim. This combination of two station imaging elements highlights what kind of target audience the station wishes to reach with their music selection. The use of certain words and phrases in the claim, such as *Der beste Mix* (the best mix) containing *das Beste von heute* (the best contemporary music) as well as *Kulthits* (classic hits), clearly shows that the station belongs to the format of adult contemporary. In addition, the pop music clips played between the claims spoken by the station voice function to present this station's particular music selection. The English-language music clips further illustrate adult contemporary radio's entanglement in global flows of popular culture. Such a multimodal orchestration of different semiotic resources is vital on radio as it evokes an image of the nature of the programme with the listener (for further examples see Section 5.2 as well as Schaefer 2022).

Example (5)

Time (sec.)	Speech	Music
0.0–3.9		ID tune of station's news
4.0–11.2	**Station voice:** Radio X, die Nachrichten. Das Neueste von hier und das Wichtigste aus Deutschland und der Welt. (Radio X, the news. The latest from here and the most important from Germany and the world.)	instrumental background music (urgent rhythm, reminiscent of telegraph pulses; cymbal strike as concluding sound)
Note: English translations in parentheses.		

(Private Station 2, 8 April 2016)

Station imaging elements are mostly used to split different genres of the radio programme (see Lengenfelder 2017). Openers, for example, as illustrated in Example (5), are part of station imaging and are used to highlight the quality of the news service of a station. In doing so, an opener also functions as a promotive slogan for the station's service. In this example, the overall message of the news opener emerges from a complex entanglement of the semiotic resources of background music and verbal language. Like the superlative *wichtigste* (most important), the urgent rhythm of the background music highlights the significance of the news to follow. Moreover, by mimicking the sound of telegraph signals, which alludes to the material ecology of journalism of the past, the background music provides a metaphoric representation of the currentness of the station's news as coming 'straight out of the wire'. Station imaging elements therefore have an important function in the radio programme, which is mainly to highlight what image a station wishes to present to its target audience. As I mentioned above (see Example (4)), station imaging elements also promote the music a station identifies with, other programme elements, the hosts of a programme and listener competitions. Furthermore, the language used in station imaging has an appellative function, which is mostly to persuade the listener to stay loyal to the station. The frequent use of superlatives, as shown in Examples (4) and (5), also functions as a linguistic tool to convey a highly attractive station image to the listener. The language used in station imaging therefore follows a specific purpose, which is to sell a product, the station's programme.

The picture we see emerging from these examples of radio language is one of complexity. This complexity, however, is not the result of a state of chaos or lack of orderliness. Rather it is due to a complex entanglement of structure and fluidity, of the local and the global, of the present and the past, of boundary maintenance and transgression. As this section has highlighted, seeking to understand journalists' language practices and thereby how they use English resources on radio also requires us to acknowledge the materiality of the medium through which language is communicated. We therefore need to bear in mind that, amongst other things, radio is a highly structured language environment consisting of different genres and their conventions and an auditory-only medium which shapes the language used by radio journalists. Furthermore, the wider sociocultural environment and its historicity, which shape on-air language and make it multifaceted and versatile, are crucial for an analysis of media language. I will return to this in Chapter 2.

1.3 Overview of the book

Chapter 2 provides an overview of the current perspective on language as a more fluid and borderless social practice in critical sociolinguistics. It will focus on conceptions of English based on language mobility and will discuss concepts such as mobile linguistic resources and translingualism. To set the wider context of English use on German radio, the chapter will show how linguistic and cultural resources are intrinsically linked and jointly mobilized in globalizing processes. In this context, processes of linguistic and cultural hybridization in Germany are elaborated, and the chapter continues to give a brief overview of the historical context of German radio media and of the evolution of the German broadcasting system. While highlighting the ontological benefits of viewing and investigating language phenomena as mobile resources in a world characterized by linguistic and cultural fluidity, I also point to the difficulties this theoretical perspective poses for the empirical study of language, especially when one tries to apply its terminology in research frameworks involving participants in areas/ domains of greater linguistic stability. In this regard, I draw on Bolton's (2013) notion of 'language world' – an individual's subjective, perceived language reality – and I argue that its consideration is of great importance for studying a speaker's language usage.

Chapter 3 looks at the study of language contact and its paradigmatic foundations, which can be traced back to Saussure's *Course in General Linguistics*. Special attention is given to the linguistic concept of 'anglicism' and the field of anglicism research, which focuses on examining the impact of English on other languages. In this context, I will outline that the field of contact linguistics and anglicism research is far from a state of disciplinary unity as it is characterized by various competing definitions and categorizations of contact processes and their outcomes. Thereby, it is demonstrated that the traditional monolithic perspective on languages as separable entities or systems in contact with each other and exerting a certain influence onto each other is too inflexible to describe the complexities of linguistic phenomena involving English in a world characterized by increasing mobility. However, since the language worlds of the actual language users are often based on the monolithic orientation to language and notions of fixity, I argue that we have to be open to the possibility that traditional contact linguistic terminology and methods can nevertheless provide a key to a better understanding of speakers' language practices.

In Chapter 4, I bring together the previous two discussions on the benefits and drawbacks of the existing paradigms. I argue that, while using a sociolinguistics of mobility as a valuable overarching framework, analytical tools from contact linguistics are useful when applied for specific purposes within the larger framework of language mobility, especially when they are suitable to describe linguistic phenomena along the lines of speakers' language worlds, which still are shaped by perceptions of 'languages' as separable systems and by other normative forces. In this context, I will explain the value of contact linguistic concepts such as codeswitching and novel anglicisms for analysing language practices. In addition, I will outline the specific media-related normative forces that shape journalists' language choice on air.

I will open up some new theoretical spaces by arguing that it is beneficial to combine poststructuralist sociolinguistic theory with empirical approaches from contact linguistics (rooted in structuralist approaches) to overcome the drawbacks of each of the two paradigms as long as we are aware of the limitations and usefulness of each of these. For analysing mass media language, I will present an analytical model based on my theoretical discussion, pulling in useful threads from both perspectives combined with previous approaches from media studies and critical cultural studies on influences on media content (from the global/cultural environment, the media system, the organization and the individual). This model allows a focus on the communicative event as spatially entangled, while paying attention to individual language users and how discursive media practices are influenced by various centres of authority. The final sections incorporate a brief presentation of quantitative and qualitative methods used in the case study. This includes on the one hand the station selection, the sampling method for the radio corpus and the methods used for the detection of anglicisms as examples of mobile English language resources in the radio corpus, and on the other hand the interview methods applied in the qualitative part. I will thereby explain how data for the discussion of findings in Chapters 5 to 8 were gathered and why corpus linguistic methods and interviews with the actual language users giving their opinions are important for understanding media language and journalists' language worlds.

In Chapters 5 to 8, I look in greater depth at the factors that influence media language and at translingual journalistic practices and their embeddedness in spatiotemporal and material environments. Chapter 5 examines the role global cultural flows play for radio journalists' language choices. Special attention is given to the status of English as a world language and to the influence cultural flows from the mediascape in times of accelerated globalization exert on radio language. I demonstrate that an analysis of English linguistic resources in different lexical fields can give indications of where linguistic flows originate and alongside which other cultural flows they migrate. Therefore, this chapter highlights the importance of cultural flows for the mobility of English resources and that especially international flows of media products accompanied by English resources shape German radio language.

Chapter 6 focuses on influencing factors that can be attributed to the media system and investigates competition between the broadcasting sectors and stations to provide insights into how the media system sets the scene and determines the scales on which communication takes place and how this influences on-air language. In relation to competition, it furthermore focuses on the role of a station's image and of the target audience in shaping radio language. Since radio stations of both sectors compete for audience attention, I examine whether the fact that an anglicism has undergone a diachronic development or not (from marked to unmarked lexical choice) affects its use in station imaging materials.

An examination of influencing factors from the journalists' workplace constitutes the theme of Chapter 7. The discussion focuses on the impact that editors and colleagues have on the production of on-air language to show that radio stations have their own social order, which influences language usage. Furthermore, I examine routine practices of journalists and their effects on radio language, illustrated by an analysis of brevity of anglicisms compared to their German equivalents and an investigation of novel anglicisms and how these are made comprehensible. These analyses give insights into possible motivations for journalists to use mobile English resources.

Chapter 8 is devoted to language attitudes and perceptions of journalists and thereby gives an insight into their language worlds, which, as will be demonstrated, are shaped by their personal backgrounds and private lives. Therefore, influencing factors on radio language that are attributable to the individual journalist are the focus of this chapter. A semantic and pragmatic analysis of anglicisms shows how the perception of modernity in a journalist's language world influences their speech behaviour.[2] In addition, I will explain stylistic functions of anglicisms in German adult contemporary radio.

I will give concluding thoughts on my results by stressing the importance of acknowledging mobility and considering the complexity of influencing factors in the discourse on global Englishes in Chapter 9. I stress the value of a combined methodological approach (integrating analytical tools of language contact theory into a sociolinguistics of mobility) to study the language worlds of speakers and to understand their language practices. The conclusion encourages the linguistic community to widen their perspective when analysing language and provides new impulses for future research to study language as a spatially entangled social practice rather than as linguistic systems. Furthermore, I call for the need to place greater importance on the individual's language world and the communicative event in which language is practised and entangled in various social, cultural and material environments.

2

Critical Sociolinguistic and Cultural Perspectives on Globalization

To grasp the complexities of global Englishes in our increasingly mobile world, we need to adopt a critical perspective on language and culture that allows us to consider the diffusion of English as part of larger processes of globalization. As Blommaert reminds us, what we need to develop in this regard is not a new *linguistic* theory of language but a theory that treats language as 'something far more dynamic, something fundamentally cultural, social, political and historical' (2010: 2). Such a theory of language in times of increased mobility ultimately makes sociolinguistics a transdisciplinary endeavour and requires us to look beyond the linguistic level.

In the following sections, I will develop such a more complex vision of mobile Englishes in the context of mass media language for which I will first draw on different critical theories of globalization from both sociolinguistics and cultural studies. This allows us to view English linguistic resources as part of larger sociocultural globalization processes and thereby to widen our understanding of these processes by also incorporating concepts of power and hegemony. The paradigm of a sociolinguistics of mobility, which provides the pivotal tools for the investigation of English on German radio, is first discussed in Section 2.1. I will then sketch out the language–culture nexus that forms the dynamic, expansive context for the use of English linguistic resources on German radio. Based on a discussion of different paradigmatic perspectives on cultural globalization, I will look in greater depth at the cultural developments in Germany following the Second World War (henceforth WWII), with a particular focus on the German broadcasting system. Chapter 2 also builds the foundation for a detailed analysis of more specific, media-related factors that influence media language in Chapter 4, for which I will draw on models of influence on media content from media studies.

2.1 Sociolinguistics of globalization

Blommaert (2010) proposes that a new theory of language in society must be capable of addressing the complex language phenomena associated with globalization that result from mobility, which he explains as the 'dislocation of language and language events from the fixed position in time and space attributed to them by a more traditional linguistics and sociolinguistics' (2010: 21). Although traditional studies in sociolinguistics have focused on language in use in various social contexts (amongst others Labov 1972, 1982; Trudgill 1974), the variationist take on sociolinguistics has, like most studies in linguistics and contact linguistics, not overcome the biases of structuralism and Saussurean synchrony. According to Blommaert, in such studies the 'movement of language resources is seen as a movement in a horizontal and stable space and in chronological time; within such spaces, vertical stratification can occur along the lines of class, gender, age, social status etc. The object of study, however, remains a "snapshot" in which things are in place, so to speak' (2010: 5).

Blommaert's call can be regarded as prototypical of the wider theoretical debates that have occupied and defined the field of critical sociolinguistics for the last two decades. In terms of mobility, Pennycook (2007) argues that we need to understand language use against the background of the complexity of cultural flows and global networks of communication. In his work on the use of global Englishes in hip-hop culture, Pennycook highlights the benefits of moving beyond the traditional conceptions of culture and language that are the legacy of modernism and structuralism. He uses the term 'transcultural flows' to describe the mobility of linguistic and cultural resources as part of accelerated globalization and highlights that these flows should not only be understood as 'the spread of particular forms of culture across boundaries' (2007: 6) but that we need to look at social practices of borrowing, appropriation and blending that are associated with these flows.

Also calling for a greater focus on language practices, Canagarajah (2013) has criticized the ontological concepts underlying linguistic terminology inherited from structuralist linguistics – which includes notions such as monolingual, bilingual or multilingual – as ideologically motivated constructs that do not adequately represent human language competence. Instead, he argues that all speakers are essentially translingual and that language is a social practice in which various semiotic resources are used by speakers in a collaborative, contextually influenced effort to create shared meaning. In his 2013 book, Canagarajah describes translingual practice as neither new nor a phenomenon that has recently arisen in the wake of increased mobility but 'as arising from a common underlying human competence' (2013: 9). Translingualism is therefore considered the primal state of human language practice, which has only been restricted or supressed by monolingual ideologies and language standardization.

In a similar way, the concept of translanguaging has been widely adopted in applied linguistics to refer to the linguistic practices of language users as an 'act of deploying all of the speaker's lexical and structural resources freely' regardless of their competence in named languages (Otheguy, García and Reid 2015: 297). Building on the notion of language as mobile resources, Li argues that 'from the Translanguaging perspective … we think beyond the boundaries of named languages and language varieties including the geography-, social class-, age-, or gender-based varieties' (2018: 19). Translanguaging therefore refers to going between and beyond linguistically defined language systems to make meaning (Li 2011). In their work on heritage language tuition in complementary schools in the UK, Creese and Blackledge (2011) use the term 'flexible bilingualism' to describe how pupils and teachers use language resources from both their heritage language and English in routine classroom interaction. They show that translanguaging is omnipresent in language education and that the language boundaries constructed by monolingual ideologies and target-language-only approaches to teaching, which call for 'separate bilingualism' in the classroom, are frequently crossed in the here and now of social interaction. These fundamental shifts in the ontological conceptualization of language and the associated focus on language practices have ultimately necessitated the development of new analytical frameworks for the study of meaning-making.

Against the background of accelerated globalization, Blommaert (2010) has provided a valuable set of methodological tools for investigating language in social interaction. In his view, language used by people in real-life contexts must be considered as consisting of linguistic resources that are not fixed in time and space but are in motion across various, interacting spatiotemporal frames. This concept of spatiotemporal frames is adopted by Blommaert from world-systems analysis as proposed by Wallerstein (1998), who argues that time and space are inseparable and need to be seen as a single dimension, which he refers to as TimeSpace. Blommaert adapts this idea to a sociolinguistic context when he refers to his concept of *scales*. According to Blommaert, scales are understood 'as levels or dimensions at which particular forms of normativity, patterns of language use and expectations thereof are organized' (2010: 36); it is on these levels where people with similar understandings communicate. Blommaert describes scales as 'phenomena that develop in TimeSpace' and therefore combine the dimensions of space (geographic) and time (historical context) since 'every social event develops simultaneously in space and in time' (2010: 34). He also adds that these phenomena are social phenomena; therefore, TimeSpace is semiotized to social contexts. According to Blommaert, semiotized TimeSpace is also cultural, social, historical and political in nature; therefore, it encompasses different vertical orderings of hierarchy and power. When linguistic resources move across these spatiotemporal frames, they get reinterpreted and appropriated on the scales on which they occur. Therefore, the meaning of identical linguistic forms may differ from one scale to another. This does affect not only language on a lexical level – as in the example of the word 'city' in English and the usage of the word *City* in German to mean 'downtown' – but also the indexical value of various sets of linguistic resources.

To describe such resemiotizations of mobile language resources, Blommaert applies two further conceptual tools to study language usage, *orders of indexicality* and *centres of authority*. According to Blommaert, patterns of normativity are inherent to scales and define what is regarded as appropriate language and what is not. To describe these patterns of normativity, he applies the concept of orders of indexicality, which he defines as a 'stratified general repertoire' (2010: 38) in which *indexical orders* (e.g. registers, dialects, vernaculars) stand in relation to one another according to common standardized values attributed to them by a given social community, depending on the scale on which communication takes place.

Blommaert's concepts of scales and orders of indexicality and the relation between both can also be compared to Fairclough's (2006) *orders of discourse*. Fairclough describes moments of discourse as an interplay of three categories. These include discourses themselves and two further categories he refers to as *genres* and *styles*. Genre, according to Fairclough, can be understood as the type of communicative setting, which together with discourse provides, in Blommaert's terms, the scale for communication. Style is the expression of identity through communication or, in the sense of spoken language, the way we speak, which therefore resembles indexical orders mentioned by Blommaert. As Fairclough states, these three entities are patterned in orders of discourse, and whenever there are several orders of discourse available in a certain situation, one is regarded as most appropriate. The notion of a hierarchical order as given in Blommaert's orders of indexicality is, therefore, also present in Fairclough's concept of orders of discourse. However, Fairclough does not mention in his discussion of categories where this normative power originates from. Blommaert introduces the concept of centres of authority in this context.

These centres of authority shape how language is used in any given context and situation by setting orders of indexicality or, in other words, by determining the value and appropriateness of various language resources. Blommaert (2010) also refers to polycentricity in this context, a term that describes that many centres of authority exist in a given situation, which simultaneously set language standards. It is especially the concept of centres of authority which is useful for the study of mass media language as it allows for an investigation of the various influences that shape the language used by journalists. I will come back to this in Chapter 4.

2.2 The language–culture nexus of globalization

As we saw in the preceding section, the conceptualization of language as a social practice ultimately requires us to acknowledge the wider social, cultural and historical contexts that provide the scales for individual language events. In this section, I will draw from globalization theories from the field of critical cultural studies, which together with a sociolinguistics of mobility allow for an examination of global Englishes in view of the complexities of globalization. Within the field of critical cultural studies various paradigmatic and theoretical positions on globalization have developed in parallel with critical sociolinguistics. These, broadly speaking, complement each other, while one focuses more on language and the other more on culture (see James 2009; Kuppens 2013). A combination of these paradigmatic perspectives of globalization from both critical sociolinguistics and critical cultural studies allows for a deeper understanding of linguistic and cultural flows and of how these are intertwined in times of intensified globalization. This approach for the study of mobile Englishes is also advocated by Pennycook, as he uses 'the term *global Englishes* to locate the spread and use of English within critical theories of globalization' (2007: 5; italics in the original). However, while Pennycook's main intention in this regard is to argue for the need to overcome the traditional dichotomy between discourses of homogenization (e.g. linguistic imperialism) and heterogenization (e.g. World Englishes) in favour of a position that focuses on hybridity, it is important not to overlook the local historical developments that underlie these traditional discourses on the effects of cultural globalization in a given society. In the case of Germany, studies on cultural developments in this locality have mainly focused on the influence of Anglo-American culture especially after WWII with some studies interpreting the effects of globalization as an Americanization of German culture and other works in which global changes on this locality are viewed as processes of hybridization (amongst others Becker 2006; Hepp 2005; Maase 1996, 1997; Willett 1989). Before I move on to look at the case of Germany in greater detail, I will briefly sketch out the relation between the differing voices in the two paradigmatic perspectives of homogenization and hybridization against the background of wider discourses around globalization in both critical sociolinguistics and critical cultural studies.

2.2.1 Different worldviews on language and culture

Beyond disciplinary boundaries, the differing paradigmatic perspectives of homogenization and hybridization in both critical sociolinguistics and critical cultural studies, broadly speaking, show significant similarities in the conceptions of the effects of globalization on language and culture, the latter including new perspectives on language and culture as mobile resources that I mentioned in previous sections (amongst others Appadurai 1996; Blommaert 2010; Canagarajah 2013; Nederveen Pieterse 2009; Pennycook 2007). Theories of cultural homogenization and linguistic imperialism go by the notion that linguistic and cultural flows especially originating from the United States have been having an impact on other cultures and languages throughout the world (Hamelink 1983; Mattelart 1983; Phillipson 1992, 2009; Schiller 1976). Theorists from cultural studies focus particularly on the media here since the media play a central role in disseminating popular culture (amongst others Schiller 1976). According to Schiller (1989), global capitalism, especially stimulated by transnational companies that disseminate their products globally, leads to cultural homogenization (see also Ritzer 2019). Regarding theories of cultural convergence, Tomlinson highlights that there is neither an original cultural imperialism thesis nor a 'unified coherent set of ideas'; as he states, 'a better way of thinking about cultural imperialism is to think of it as a variety of different articulations which may have certain features in common' (1991: 8–9). For him cultural imperialism is discussed in four ways: as media imperialism, as a discourse of nationality, as a critique of global capitalism and as a critique of Modernity.

According to the perspective of hybridization, language and culture are in constant motion. As I previously touched upon, Blommaert (2010) and Pennycook (2007) as well as Appadurai (1996) and Nederveen Pieterse (2009) hold a position on linguistic and cultural developments that is based on the notion of fluidity. Hybridity in sociolinguistics and critical cultural studies goes by the theory that linguistic and cultural resources are mobile, and therefore mixing and crossing of ideologically constructed borders is viewed as a process that has occurred all along. According to this paradigm, the view that globalization has only started in the mid-twentieth century with the extensive use of the mass media across the globe including satellite television and telecommunications neglects that there has always been mixing. What should be rather acknowledged here is that we nowadays experience processes of globalization in a much more accelerated form than hundred years ago, which of course is additionally fuelled by the mass media (see Nederveen Pieterse 2009). In this regard, Appadurai (1996) talks about global cultural flows, which he divides into five dimensions called scapes: *ethnoscapes*, *mediascapes*, *technoscapes*, *financescapes* and *ideoscapes*. Central to his argument is the notion of deterritorialization, which he uses to refer to the mobility of people in times of accelerated globalization that is accompanied by flows of capital, information, technology and ideas. As he states, 'we are functioning in a world fundamentally characterised by objects in motion. These objects include ideas and ideologies, people and goods, images and messages, technologies and techniques' (2000: 5).

While Nederveen Pieterse (2009) and Appadurai (1996), both coming from an anthropology background, focus more on culture than on language in this context, Pennycook (2007) and Blommaert (2010), as outlined in Section 2.1, engage more with how the complexity of globalizing flows shapes language repertoires of speakers. Pennycook (2003) therefore enhances Appadurai's cultural approach by proposing the concept of *linguascapes*, which according to him accompany deterritorialized cultural resources in Appadurai's *scapes*. Linguascapes, Pennycook argues, 'capture the relationship between the ways in which some languages are no longer tied to locality or community, but rather operate globally in conjunction with these other scapes' (2003: 523). Pennycook therefore pleads for not only focusing on the movement of cultural forms but in particular on the 'take-up, appropriation, change and refashioning' of cultural forms in local contexts (2007: 6). A similar position is held by Nederveen Pieterse (2009), who states that whenever cultural elements are transferred between cultures, mixed or hybridized forms are the result.

When put into dialogue, it becomes evident that the difference between the two perspectives of hybridization and homogenization relating to the effects of globalization on language and culture revolves around the notion of 'boundaries'. According to Nederveen Pieterse, 'in the end the real problem is not hybridity, which is common throughout history, but boundaries. … Hybridity is unremarkable and noteworthy only from the point of view of boundaries that have been essentialized' (2009: 96). The nation-state as the most prominent example of such boundaries is either portrayed in the light of the hybridization paradigm as a constructed entity setting borders to the complexity of linguistic and cultural resources, which are crossed in processes of mixing (Blommaert 2010; Nederveen Pieterse 2009); or it is a basis for argumentation of theories of homogenization, for which borders, such as those of nation-states, mark the territories of different cultures, which can be categorized along these boundaries (Phillipson 1992, 2009; Schiller 1989). Here, the different borders attached to each individual nation-state or other boundaries marking regions or towns are regarded as separating one culture from another. Theories of homogenization explain many forms of cultural and linguistic change from the point of view that a dominant culture or language invades another language or culture, and such border-crossing is then often perceived as a form of imperialism.

It should be noted here that, according to theories from both paradigmatic perspectives, there is always a power play involved between dominant and subdominant languages and cultures. Appadurai (1996), for example, states that global cultural flows may be accompanied by homogenizing forces; however, these become hybridized on a local scale. To critically assess the effects of globalization in the light of the impact of linguistic and cultural flows on Germany, it is vital to understand that out of either of the two perspectives the results of these power relations are merely viewed differently. How can one explain these opposing views describing the same phenomena? What we need to take into consideration when explaining these differing conclusions regarding the effects of globalization is that the two paradigms of homogenization and hybridization are based on different spatiotemporal frames. In this context, it is useful to apply Wallerstein's (1998) dimensions of TimeSpace to compare the different viewpoints in the discussion, which are *episodic geopolitical, cyclico-ideological, structural* and *eternal* TimeSpace.[1] These four dimensions range from short-term and local (events are interpreted in the direct context in which these happen) to eternal and global (events are interpreted independent of time and of space).

When we apply Wallerstein's (1998) dimensions of TimeSpace in the context of the differing positions on boundaries such as the nation-state in globalization theories, it becomes evident that theories of hybridization are placed within the frame of *eternal* TimeSpace. As stated above, hybridity theorists consider ongoing mixing and translocalization as processes that are as old as humanity and part of the *longue durée* since, as Nederveen Pieterse states, 'cultures have been overflowing boundaries all along and … boundaries have been provisional and ever contentious superimpositions upon substrata of mingling and traffic'

(2009: 110). The nation-state or other boundaries that mark languages and cultural territories are hence regarded as ideological constructs that divide cultures and languages, which are in fact hybrid. In this sense, hybridization as a long-term process is merely stimulated through flows of travelling linguistic resources and cultural mobility in current times of accelerated globalization. Therefore, the nation-state and other such boundaries, according to Appadurai (1996) and Nederveen Pieterse (2009), are increasingly in decline as a result of accelerated globalization, where the diversity of language resources available to speakers and hybridity of cultures flourish. In line with the hybridization paradigm, other theorists like Blommaert give a more nuanced picture by stressing that due to linguistic and cultural mobility 'the nation may be on its way out, but the state is not' (2010: 153).

National consciousness, however, does not go further back in time than the eighteenth century in Europe and the idea of the nation-state only became prevalent in the nineteenth century. As I hinted on in Chapter 1, the advances in early linguistics and the creation of dictionaries of differing print vernaculars throughout Europe at this time substantially contributed to the formation of national consciousness (Anderson 2016). Theories of cultural imperialism (Schiller 1968) and linguistic imperialism (Phillipson 1992) in a contemporary context are heavily dependent on the era of nation-states and nationalism as well as on the resulting imagined cultural boundaries and notions of otherness. This also limits the space in which such cultural processes are perceived to occur to these bounded cultural spheres. In addition, theorists who argue that a homogenization of culture has been taking place in many countries of the world often pay particular attention to the power exertion of the United States on the rest of the world since the twentieth century, in which predominantly the mass media have been spreading American consumer culture and the English language throughout the world. Therefore, within the homogenization paradigm, processes of globalization and their effects are analysed, in Wallerstein's terms, in a medium-term time frame or *cyclico-ideological* TimeSpace. From this we can conclude that the paradigm of homogenization through Americanization is a theoretical perspective that merely captures a medium-term episode within the *longue durée* of hybridization.

As the discussion of the spatiotemporal frames highlights, the two paradigmatic perspectives of homogenization and hybridization are not as 'fundamentally excluded' from one another as some authors claim (cf. Nederveen Pieterse 2009) but are merely based on different frames of reference. Against the background of this theoretical observation, the following section outlines the complexity of the debate around the effects of globalization on Germany and thereby describes the sociocultural setting for the case study of German adult contemporary radio language. In this context, I will reconsider discourses on linguistic and cultural change in Germany which have led to either views of an Americanization or to a perspective that views changes happening in this locality as a result of hybridization. Since radio broadcasting is a specific social practice with its own historical trajectory, I will then go on to additionally provide a brief overview of the historical origins of the German broadcasting system.

2.2.2 The case of Germany: Americanization or hybridization?

The effects of the English language and Anglo-American culture on Germany have led to various debates in and outside of academia. Long before the occupation time after WWII by the Allied forces in West Germany, many people, according to Lüdtke, Marßolek and von Saldern (1996), looked towards North America as the 'promised land', where one could start a better life than in Europe, which at the time of the early nineteenth century was driven by famine and economic crisis. As pointed out by Maase (1996) and in line with Lüdtke, Marßolek and von Saldern (1996), this way of thinking about North America was often based on stereotypes which had developed in the German population in the sixteenth century and were then strengthened in the nineteenth century. These mainly concerned divided ideas on the American way of life, which was on the one hand admired due to its unconstrained nature but on the other hand perceived as childish and shallow. Lüdtke, Marßolek and von Saldern additionally note that while North America was viewed as a land of opportunities, at the same time it was also feared by many, and people were sceptical about a possible homogenization by means of Americanization of the German culture especially in the early twentieth century. Particularly American 'mass culture' was regarded as homogenizing and commodifying in the early to mid-twentieth century and viewed as a threat to 'high culture' by the critical thinkers of the Frankfurt School. According to them, the cultural industries had the power to deceive the masses by means of producing false consciousness amongst the working classes (Horkheimer and Adorno 1972).

Following the end of WWII in Europe, the occupation of West Germany by the Allied forces led to an intensification of the discourse around the effects of American culture on Germany. Since Germany had been shaped by National Socialism for more than 10 years and the former democratic and civil culture of the Weimar Republic had in many ways vanished, the abuse of the media for propaganda purposes as well as the National Socialistic ideologies had to be overcome for a new democratic political approach in a defeated Germany. For many Germans, particularly the younger generation, the Allied influences, especially the ones originating from the United States, were perceived as a liberating cultural and societal force (Faulstich 2006). However, according to Estel (2014), others believed that these influences originating from the United States posed a threat to German culture and civic norms. This dividedness in public opinion is also mirrored in academic discourse. While many researchers claim that the occupation of West Germany after WWII has had its impact on German culture (amongst others Faulstich 2006; Stephan 2006), we find divided opinions on whether the occupation time has led to an Americanization of the German language and culture (Ermarth 1993; Lüdtke, Marßolek and von Saldern 1996; Willett 1989) or to hybridization (Hepp 2005; Maase 1997). Willett (1989) argues that the West German population was in close contact with American culture due to the occupiers and pleads for an Americanization of the German culture during post-war times. Kellner and Soeffner (2002) state that the extent to which West Germany was subject to the forces of globalization in the period of German separation becomes evident by looking at the cultural differences between the Federal Republic and the former German Democratic Republic at the time of reunification. While the Federal Republic was shaped by Western cultural influences and developed into a liberal democracy and consumer culture, the Democratic Republic was largely shielded by the Iron Curtain against these Westernizing currents.

According to Schiller (1968), this American influence on other cultures did not happen by coincidence since the foreign policy of the United States after WWII was built upon the promotion of freedom. 'Freedom of trade, freedom of enterprise and freedom of speech became the catchwords of American foreign policy' (Schiller 1968: 635). The intention of the US government was the expansion of American influence through building economic relations and getting access to foreign media markets. In this context, however, Becker (2006) highlights that the American influence on the institutions of the young German Federal Republic was far smaller than often presumed. The political, educational and economic systems, for example, are largely based on their German predecessors rather than on an adoption of an American role model. At this time, to be more precise, it was the concept of the 'American way of life' that was spread through American consumer goods and cultural products such as mass media, fashion and food which had a profound impact on German lifestyle. This is in line with Willett, who states that 'the Occupation (and its Americanization potential) succeeded best' (1989: 27) when the Military Government stopped trying to re-educate the German population and when the currency reform introducing the Deutschmark turned West Germany into a consumer society. From this time onwards, American businesses and mass media have had unrestricted access to the German market and were the driving forces of American cultural influence.

As Maase (1996) points out, the cultural developments resulting from the occupation time can also be considered as an 'Amerikanisierung von unten' (Americanization from below) mainly driven by juvenile subcultures whose members were revolting against the stiffness of civic norms and the condemnation of popular taste by cultural elites in the 1950s. By means of adopting American styles in terms of fashion, music and behaviour – with a particular focus on rock 'n' roll culture – the young generation challenged the moral authorities in West Germany, which regarded these American styles as uncivilized and vulgar, and in the end succeeded in shifting the balance within the cultural hegemonial order of the German society to their benefit by means of legitimizing popular culture. This defence of popular culture against the critical judgement of the 'cultured' classes went hand in hand with the transformation of the West German economy into a consumer culture. Popular taste gained its justification out of the democratic principles of the free market, where sales figures of cultural products rather than the judgement of cultural elites became the determining criterion of acceptability. Therefore, according to Maase (1996), the process of Americanization can be regarded as not only having a superficial impact on the German society but as having induced a more profound change to its cultural hegemonial order. Based on this argumentation, Maase (1997) in a later work enhances his discussion by means of interpreting these changes in the light of hybridization. While acknowledging that most changes of German culture stand in connection with American popular culture, he interprets these changes as the result of reinterpretation and resemiotization and thereby calls for the need to look at these changes in greater detail before jumping to conclusions of Americanization as homogenization.

Faulstich (2006), who subsequently to Maase (1996) describes the Americanization of the 1960s and 1970s, states that Americanization should be seen as an enrichment to German culture. In doing so, he gives examples of American rock and pop music, American movies and popular novels, which were easily disseminated throughout the German population. In line with Maase's (1996) observations regarding the immediate post-war years, Faulstich (2006) also notes that the West German youth's attraction to American cultural products allowed the young generation of the 1960s and 1970s to distance themselves from the stiffness of German traditional cultural values.

Beyond the occupation time of West Germany, an imbalance in cultural flows becomes evident through the spread of American popular culture, which has been reaching Germany mainly through the mass media – therefore *mediascapes* – via Hollywood movies and the music industry. This popular culture is associated with a modern way of life by many Germans and the English language also appears as modern and trendy (Onysko 2004; Piller 2003). Many linguists view the 'impact of English on German' as an enrichment to the German language through indigenization and hybridization of English terms (amongst others Knospe 2014; Onysko 2007), while especially some members of the public, including mainly those who are members of purist movements such as the Verein Deutsche Sprache (German language association), decry the usage of English.

Despite these differing viewpoints on the 'impact of English on German', which have remained until today, English has become an integral part of German life. English is the first foreign language taught in German schools and the most frequently used language alongside German in German product advertisements (Gerritsen et al. 2007; Piller 2003). The spread of computer technology throughout the world is another example of cultural products originating from the United States that are now an integral part of German everyday life. Together with *technoscapes*, *linguascapes* again bring along new vocabulary attached to such products; examples include the anglicisms *Radar*, *PC*, *Smartphone* and *Tablet*. Amongst others, Busse and Carstensen (1993) note in their dictionary of anglicisms in German that especially after WWII the amount of anglicisms in Germany had significantly increased.

Despite these examples of imbalanced linguistic and cultural flows, critics like Becker (2006) and Tomlinson (1991) call for a view that replaces the concepts of Americanization and cultural imperialism with globalization in contemporary times. According to Becker, even if products originate from the United States and are available in Germany '– was in manchen Fällen nicht einmal sicher ist – lässt ihre weltweite Distribution dieses Profil doch verschwimmen; mittlerweile zeigen sie eher eine Globalisierung als eine Amerikanisierung an' (– which in some cases is not even certain – their worldwide distribution blurs this profile; by now they indicate more of a globalization than an Americanization) (2006: 67). Likewise, Tomlinson states that globalization stands for 'interconnection and interdependency of all global areas which happens in a far less purposeful way' (1991: 175) than theories of linguistic and cultural imperialism claim (cf.

Phillipson 1992, 2009). Even though Becker and Tomlinson clearly have a point here, the usage of the term 'globalization' alone is not sufficient to explain the complexity of cultural flows that exert an influence on Germany since the term, due to its multifaceted usage, does not give any more clarity on the matter. Rather than covering linguistic and cultural change under the veil of globalization, the task is to identify and critically analyse the often unbalanced global flows and their influences on today's societies. An analysis of all these complex cultural and linguistic influences on Germany clearly exceeds the scope of this book; however, the case study of the German adult contemporary radio media will function as one example out of many other cases in the German context pointed out by previous research (cf. Maase 1996, 1997; Willett 1989). In the following section, I will look at radio in Germany, an example that illustrates the complexity of cultural and linguistic developments from the post-war years until today.

2.2.3 Radio in Germany: German broadcasting media restructured

To better understand the communicative event I will focus on in the case study, this section gives an overview of the German radio market, which includes some historical facts relevant to adult contemporary radio and a description of the current broadcasting landscape in Germany. In post-war times, the Allied powers in West Germany laid the foundation for the contemporary German broadcasting system.[2] During WWII, foreign radio including British and American music were banned and censored in Germany (Dahl 1983). After the war, as part of their re-education plan, the Allied forces were eager to restructure journalism in West Germany since it was so to speak the ambition of the Allied forces to eliminate the manipulative propaganda-driven journalism of former Nazi-Germany. The Allied forces wanted to make sure that the German media were never to be instrumentalized for such purposes again and therefore intended to have new decentralized, federal broadcasting networks in their occupation zones for which the BBC functioned as a role model (see Dahl 1983; Goldhammer 1995; Haas, Frigge and Zimmer 1991).

In 1950, the Arbeitsgemeinschaft der öffentlich-rechtlichen Rundfunkanstalten in der Bundesrepublik Deutschland (Consortium of public service broadcasters in the Federal Republic of Germany), ARD for short, was founded, which consisted of six *Landesrundfunkanstalten* (Land broadcasting corporations) (Haas, Frigge and Zimmer 1991). These 'set the pattern for public broadcasting in Germany that remains operative right through to the present day' (Sandford 1997: 49) and, at the time, gave public service broadcasting in Germany a monopoly position.

Well before the initiation of the private broadcasting sector in the 1980s, the Allied army stations in post-war West Germany introduced a new kind of radio experience including requested programmes and music as well as broadcast greetings by listeners to ensure their loyalty to the station (Rumpf 2007). They also found it of utmost importance to directly address the listener in a friendly, good-tempered and rather easy-going manner to connect with the listener, as Rumpf (2007) describes. Stations like AFN (American Forces Network) and BFN (British Forces Network) in post-war times did not have an educational purpose but merely broadcast to entertain especially soldiers and their families, who were far from home. Rumpf (2007) also notes that the British and American broadcasting model and its concepts were highly popular and regarded as modern. Especially presenters such as Chris Howland and Bill Ramsey and their presenting style quickly gained popularity. These media products hence became dislodged from their original contexts. They were now consumed by an audience of German people, for which they were originally not intended, which led media outlets in West Germany adapt their presentation styles to stay competitive and attractive for their listeners. Gradually, from the 1970s onwards the public service sector broadcast easier-listening programmes which emulated these British and American radio presenting strategies and concepts. This included a varied and appealing radio programme with a show-like character, DJs and call-ins, which created a close connection to the audience and were adopted from UK and US radio broadcasting styles (Rumpf 2007) but remodelled for a German audience. The easy-going informal manner of speech and the radio presenter's DJ-like presentation style have remained the prevailing and most popular styles of radio broadcasting throughout Germany for both the public service and private broadcasting sector.

In the 1980s, the initiation of a dual broadcasting system promised greater variety and pluralism in the German broadcasting landscape. The additional establishment of the private, commercial broadcasting sector, which followed the American example, led to changes in not only broadcasting structures but likewise journalistic styles and practices, especially through the initiation of format radio. When I started my work on the case study of this book in 2016, the private radio broadcasting sector consisted of 283 stations operating throughout Germany including stations that broadcasted nationwide, regionally and locally.[3] The German public service radio sector consists of nine *Landesrundfunkanstalten,* all regional broadcasters; *Deutschlandradio,* a nationwide broadcaster; and *Deutsche Welle*, Germany's international broadcaster. Each of the *Rundfunkanstalten* (e.g. *NDR*, *SWR* and *BR*) consists of individual stations which aim at different target audiences (e.g. for *SWR*: *SWR1, SWR2, SWR3, SWR4, DAS DING*, etc.). These mainly differ in age and music taste of the targeted audience as well as in the amount of information, as opposed to entertainment and music, provided by each station. This means that at present every region in Germany is covered by a public service broadcaster and several local and regional private broadcasting stations aiming at various target audiences, of which most people listen to adult contemporary stations. As a result of this competitive situation, even public service stations have adopted the programme concepts of format radio, especially of adult contemporary, in a process of 'self-commercialization' of their style to face their private competitors (Goldhammer 1995: 233). This has led to theories of a possible convergence between the two broadcasting sectors (see Schatz, Immer and Marcinkowski 1989). I will return to this in Chapter 4.

2.2.4 Germany: A case of asymmetrical hybridization

Where does this leave us in terms of the sociocultural environment of the case study? The cultural situation that had developed in post-war Germany remaining until today is characterized by an imbalance of linguistic and cultural flows, which has often been interpreted as an Americanization (see also Maase 1997). As previously stated, homogenization as Americanization is a theoretical perspective that merely captures a medium-term episode within the *longue durée* of hybridization. This gives room to adopt a perspective that allows to overcome the major pitfalls of both paradigms. The theory of cultural synchronization (or homogenization) (Hamelink 1983; Schiller 1989) is, for example, criticized by Nederveen Pieterse for being 'fundamentally incomplete', as he claims that 'it downplays the ambivalence of the globalizing momentum and ignores the role of local reception of western culture – for example, the indigenization of western elements' (2009: 75). On the contrary, Morley (2006) argues that the concept of hybridization must be taken with a certain caution. According to him, despite new centres of cultural influence having emerged (e.g. China for Asia, or Brazil for Latin America), the United States remain the most influential source of cultural imports in many of the world's regions including Europe. In addition, Morley (2006) makes reference to the negligence of the function of media power in these claims and argues that an overly optimistic view of the active recipients of culture downplays that many hybridized forms are based on American role models. Due to the role of the United States as the liberator and occupier, as an ally and protecting power throughout the Cold War, and as the most influential producer and disseminator of pop cultural products, there has been a continuous influence of cultural flows originating in this locality on Germany. While at times this influence was politically motivated and deliberately imposed by the United States – as was the case during the re-education phase following WWII – the identity crisis of the German nation after the reign of National Socialism made German society long for cultural goods that provided them with alternative lifestyles. The interplay of the dominant political and economic position of the United States, the light-heartedness of American popular culture and the particular 'way of life' associated with it, as well as the cultural void that had to be filled within the German society, therefore, has led to Germany being predominantly affected by cultural flows originating from the United States.

Therefore, rather than viewing the current situation in Germany from the perspective of homogenization or hybridization, I propose the term 'asymmetrical hybridization' in the context of Germany. This term is not to be misunderstood as a combination of Americanization and hybridization but as hybridization that in itself flows asymmetrically and therefore is driven by unbalanced or one-sided cultural and societal developments in the world. The presence of English in German can therefore not simply be regarded as threat to language and culture in Germany but has to be considered as a phenomenon that is part of the *longue durée* of linguistic and cultural hybridization in this locality.

2.3 Limitations for empirical research

The paradigmatic shift towards a sociolinguistics that acknowledges the complexities of globalization and the associated mobility of people and linguistic and cultural resources allows new ways of engagement with linguistic, social and cultural diversity in present-day societies. In this chapter, I have sketched out how a sociolinguistics of mobility in combination with the concept of hybridization from critical cultural studies offers us the analytical tools for an analysis of the use of mobile Englishes in complex social practices, such as in the case of German radio language. By proposing the concept of asymmetrical hybridization in the German context and by describing the sociocultural environment of radio media, I also have discussed the cultural and historical contexts that form the scale on which this language event takes place.

In line with the conception of language as a social practice, the task at hand for developing an understanding of how English linguistic resources are used on radio is now to explore language in use and therefore the language practices and the voices of media practitioners. This, however, is where we encounter some difficulties. As I hinted on in Chapter 1, the perspective of mobility- and fluidity-based approaches in critical language studies, deconstructing the notion of separate languages and their connection to ethnic or (imagined) national communities, has not remained uncriticized. Kubota (2016), for example, has discussed at length the risks and drawbacks that the wider field of linguistics is subject to in what she calls the 'multi/plural turn', which is based on hybridity or fluidity thinking. She draws on the field of postcolonial studies, which already in the 1990s has discussed the notion of hybridity and the issues associated with this paradigmatic shift. One of the issues that was raised then is that postcolonial scholars create a gap between theory and practice, for example by describing cultural developments in postcolonial societies along the lines of theoretical concepts that the formerly colonized populations would not have access to. Kubota transfers this argument onto the theoretical debates in applied linguistics and thereby highlights the issue that postmodern and poststructuralist linguistics is based on concepts that appear as abstract to non-academic language users and are hardly suitable to describe their lived everyday experiences. Referring to the adoption of concepts of hybridity such as Bhabha's *Third Space* in applied and sociolinguistics, Kubota and Miller state that 'the intent is to question the conventional understanding of language and language use, which has viewed them as normative and bounded, and to legitimate linguistic practices of minoritized language learners or users. However, this discussion tends to be caught in an abstract and idealistic trap, creating also a theory–practice gap' (2017: 139). In this way, the theoretical advancements in critical language studies run the risk of becoming more a 'self-serving academic activity' (Kubota 2016: 485) than being directed to social issues since these approaches to language not only remain abstract and largely inaccessible to language users but also distance the researcher in the field from the research participants whose language is investigated.

Even in complex settings that are shaped by dislocated language resources, such as language teaching involving migrant children or heritage language tuition, the monolithic orientation to language often provides the ideological basis for people's self-perception of their linguistic practice. D'warte's (2014) study into the lifeworlds of a diverse group of Australian secondary school students with mostly migratory backgrounds presents an example of such complex social settings. As her discussion of the results of her ethnographic fieldwork shows, the lived language experiences of her participants are very much shaped by the notion of separate languages. Participating students gave descriptions of how they make use of their linguistic repertoires, which indicated that they perceive their own language practices as separate bi/multilingualism. D'warte's (2014) interview quotes show, for example, that having to translate for members of their families (e.g. official documents, or in social encounters at banks, shops, doctor's appointments) is a regular part of students language practices. Their experiences are therefore very much shaped by social conventions regarding the value and appropriateness of one 'language' rather than another in certain social activities.

Creese and Blackledge (2011), as discussed earlier, have shown that engaging in translanguaging in practice does not mean that people do not think along the lines of traditional nationalist identities and value the separateness of their linguistic and cultural repertoires. As Creese and Blackledge (2011: 1201) state, their fieldwork at heritage language schools has revealed that while teachers engage in translanguaging to deliver their lessons, they also 'expressed their fear that the young people would lose their language and identity unless they insist on separate bilingualism' in classroom tuition. This shows that the metalinguistic discourses people engage in, which are also expressions of their conceptualization of language and therefore the foundation to their linguistic practice, do not necessarily correspond with postmodern linguistic discourse in academic settings.

As these examples show, the monolingual orientation does not only constitute part of the lifeworlds of speakers in settings of greater stability such as in the case of radio in Germany, where mostly sedimented language resources are used in social practice. Instead, fixity also plays a part just as important as mobility in areas of greater complexity in people's everyday lives (Otsuji and Pennycook 2010). In addition, the fixity of bounded languages is not always perceived as a constraint by language users who not only ascribe a certain value to Language A or Language B but also benefit from their command of a standardized set of resources. The complete deconstruction of named languages (cf. Otheguy, García and Reid 2015), which mainly intends to overcome oppressive language standardization ideology, therefore also runs the risk of undermining the positive effects of fixity in social practice, such as the protection of the language rights of speakers of minority languages (MacSwan 2020) or the pride of learners when they achieve competency in another (standard) language (Slembrouck 2021). The critical poststructuralist attempt to abandon the structural conception of language, therefore, overlooks that these boundaries are not always perceived by speakers as imposed or as having no social meaning.

Blommaert calls for accepting 'that abandoning a structural notion of language (a linguists' construct, as we know) compels us to replace it by an ethnographic concept such as *voice*, which embodies the experiential and practice dimensions of language and which refers to the way in which people actually deploy their resources in communicative practice' (2010: 180). In this statement by Blommaert we can identify two key aspects of the theory–practice gap that Kubota refers to. First, from a critical sociolinguistic perspective, it appears necessary to 'abandon' the structuralist, monolithic concept of separate languages not only on an ontological level. As Slembrouck (2021) points out, however, categorization is an essential part of our everyday social practices and therefore ultimately also of our language practices. Therefore, 'the nature and dynamics of boundary drawing is something that needs to be looked at "in practice". It requires empirical examination in its own right' (Slembrouck 2021). Second, critical sociolinguists are 'compelled' to adopt new terminology that is suitable to describe how 'people actually deploy their resources in communicative practice'. Acknowledging 'the experiential and practice dimensions of language', however, also requires us to acknowledge structuralist thinking and its associated vocabulary as important concepts for an analysis of language. In the context of Germany, for example, Spitzmüller (2005) has shown that public metalinguistic discourse is shaped by the perception of neatly separable languages. When engaging in and analysing metalinguistic discussions of research participants as part of ethnographic studies, interview-based research or focus groups, we need to use terminology that is as close as possible to research participants' linguistic experiences as part of their lifeworlds. This is where some structuralist terminology can retain its raison d'être, especially in more stable language situations (see Chapter 4).

Since simply abandoning structuralist notions of language in empirical research involving participants forms the core of the theory–practice gap, it is necessary to reconceptualize the role of structuralist language ideologies within a critical sociolinguistics of mobility. A valuable approach that supports the argument I am making here is offered by Bolton's (2013) notion of *language worlds*, which acknowledges the language perceptions of speakers and the values, emotions, practices and social capital they associate with certain languages or varieties thereof. This also enables us to understand the relation between speakers' language worlds and the normative forces of standard languages in a way that can be compared to Habermas's (1981) lifeworld–system duality. The system's continued existence is only maintained if it is supported by people's lifeworlds. If we take constructed standard languages as part of the system, then their continued existence must be based on their acceptance in people's language worlds and on the value that is ascribed to them in these language worlds. This ultimately means that the 'system' created by structuralist language ideologies in society is not immutable but always open to negotiation.

Returning to Slembrouck's (2021) argument above, if we conceive of language boundaries as social constructs, it is also important to look at the social practices involving such boundaries. Canagarajah (2013) states that translingualism involves that people in less advantaged positions can renegotiate power relations in communicative interaction. This also applies to the normative forces of standard languages. While societies provide various contexts in which more standardized or more hybrid language forms are perceived as appropriate, this must not be taken as a mere limitation of people's linguistic competencies by structuralist language ideology. People can negotiate the value of standard languages depending on social situations and can deliberately move into and out of standardized language forms, for example, for stylistic reasons. While the monolingual bias can be conceived as a part of larger social structures and therefore as given from above (the system), people negotiate it from below in their everyday language interactions, at times adhering to its norms and enjoying the rewards (think about language learners who receive a high grade for good performance in a standardized variety), at times dismissing its conventions in successful cultural productions such as hip-hop, comedy or peer group talk. While not denying the social inequity and injustice that is associated with limited access to standardized language forms, I argue that in linguistic and cultural settings such as the German radio media we are required to rethink whether constructed language boundaries are necessarily a limitation of speakers' practices in all cases. Rather, seeing the construction of these language boundaries as a social practice allows us to acknowledge practices of boundary maintenance, redrawing, deliberate crossing, or even parodization of such boundaries.

3

The Diffusion of English from a Contact Linguistic Perspective

Much of the prominent research on the diffusion of Englishes that has been put forward has emerged from the field of contact linguistics and has its roots in the structuralist linguistic tradition (amongst others Haugen 1950; Thomason and Kaufman 1988; Weinreich 1953). Since linguistic structuralism has become a feature of people's language worlds in Western societies and therefore of public metalinguistic discussion, overcoming the issue of the theory–practice gap in critical sociolinguistics and critical applied linguistics requires addressing the very issue of the paradigmatic gap between structuralism and poststructuralism in the study of language. If concepts based on structuralist thinking such as *foreign word*, *anglicism* or *Denglisch* (a perceived mixture of the two entities *Deutsch* (German) and *Englisch* (English)) form part of public discourse, we should not simply discard them based on poststructuralist ontological considerations but need to acknowledge their social meaning and function. As I outlined in Chapter 2, there is a need, as I see it, to recognize and acknowledge the fixities that are part of social practices and the basis of social organization. At the same time, it is necessary to apply concepts in participant-based research that are best to describe people's language worlds as perceived by speakers themselves. Since structuralist linguistics has shaped the language worlds in Western societies over many years, we must consider that the analytical toolkits and concepts of structuralist linguistics, when integrated into the larger paradigmatic frame of a sociolinguistics of mobility, can provide a key to a better understanding of people's language practices.

This chapter sets out to give an overview of the origins of the monolithic orientation and of the vast amount of research into language contact in this context. It will thereby outline the different viewpoints on how to define the phenomenon of anglicisms from a contact linguistic perspective. Chapter 3 closes with a discussion on the limitations of the structuralist paradigm and how it is challenged by language mobility. The intent of the following section is to be illustrative rather than exhaustive about structuralist-oriented thinking in language contact research to allow us to better understand the sedimentation of English linguistic resources in Germany from a more traditional perspective, which will also inform the case study in later chapters.

3.1 The paradigmatic foundations of contact linguistics

To understand the foundations of contact linguistics, it is useful to look at its connection to the conception of monolingualism as a widely accepted norm of linguistic competence – a norm that is deeply entrenched in our contemporary Western societies. The monolingual orientation has a long-established history, and its arguments are often described as going back to Herder and other thinkers of romanticism for whom language, community and territory are said to have formed a unified triad: one language, one culture, one territory (Bauman and Briggs 2003; Blommaert 2006). Although this view is not unequivocally accepted as an appropriate representation of Herder's thought (see Piller 2016), the so-called Herderian triad has served as a foundation for a range of other discourses, such as around language purification and ownership of language, and their political consequences (for a detailed account see Canagarajah 2013). The origins of the monolingual orientation therefore need to be conceived as closely related to the advent of European nationalism and print capitalism.

Not only the mass production of print material and publishers' ambitions to enlarge their markets were the drivers of language standardization (Anderson 2016) but also the developing forms of democratic governance and the resulting need to effectively communicate with the electorate led to the emergence of shared written codes amongst people speaking related dialects and vernaculars (Wright 2012). These fixed written languages became languages of power and prestige that were used by societal elites to communicate their ideas and eventually adopted by nation-states as languages of education and administration. Most importantly, however, the ability to exchange ideas in written format created an ideological perception of a relatively homogenous community in (one single) language or, as Silverstein (1996) puts it, created the ideology of a monoglot standard. As Wright states, 'all nationalists believe that the nation-state is ideally a monolingual entity: ideologically, nationalism requires the citizen to use the national language to display loyalty; practically, economic, political and cultural life organized on a national scale is more easily managed in a monolingual setting' (2012: 64).

In line with this monolingual orientation and against the socio-political background of modern nationalism, modern linguistics has played an important part in the definition of standard languages (e.g. English, French, German, etc.) particularly in Western societies and has endeavoured to scientifically describe these individual languages. The conception of different, bounded languages, however, ultimately has required linguists to also devote attention to cases of mixing resulting from contact between individual languages. Going back to early works of historically oriented linguists of the nineteenth century, we already find debates on the notion of contact effects between languages and its implications for the *Stammbaum* theory of language evolution through internal language change (Winford 2003). The essential base of today's contact linguistic research, however, was laid in the early twentieth century by the advent of linguistic structuralism. A key figure in this emerging tradition was Ferdinand de Saussure, whose theories and ideas of languages as self-standing systems of meaning have served as the foundation of structuralist linguistics up until today. Saussure's work included two important distinctions concerning the study of language which influenced most of twentieth-century linguistics. First, Saussure distinguished between the study of language as an abstract system (*la langue*) and language as actually used (*la parole*). Second, according to Saussure, there are two dimensions to the study of language: the synchronic, descriptive study of language that, so to speak, takes a snapshot of the linguistic system at a given moment in time and the diachronic study of language describing language change as a succession of (synchronically describable) language events in a historical dimension (Culler 1986). According to Saussure, linguistics concerns itself with the synchronic study of *la langue* to explore how meaning is created within the system of language (Holdcroft 1998). In line with this Saussurean synchrony, the structuralist linguistic tradition has popularized the notion of languages as self-defined and self-standing systems of signs and thereby formed the basis for early contact linguistic studies such as by Weinreich (1953) and Haugen (1949, 1950), which are considered key works in this field. Based on the Saussurean legacy, we find many phrases like 'we will be looking at examples from clear cases of separate languages in contact' (Thomason 2001: 2) or 'the impact of English on German' (Knospe 2015: 99; see also Fiedler 2022) in studies within the contact linguistic tradition. This again clearly highlights the language-as-a-system as opposed to language-as-a-social-practice approach in the study around language.

The structuralist contact linguistic view on language also involves a different take on what I have called the language–culture nexus in critical sociolinguistics in Chapter 2. Even though contact linguistics traditionally has interdisciplinary roots drawing from various fields such as historical linguistics, sociolinguistics, psychology and studies on bi-/multilingualism – resulting in different research foci on matters of contact between language systems in the field – language contact is perceived as being affected by language-internal and -external factors, and therefore culture and globalization are set apart from linguistic structures (Canagarajah 2018a). According to Winford, the objective of contact linguistics 'is to study the varied situations of contact between languages, the phenomena that result, and the interaction of linguistic and external ecological factors in shaping these outcomes' (2003: 5). In other words, contact linguistics is concerned with the linguistic and sociocultural contexts shaping contact situations internally and externally, the processes of language contact itself and the results of contact (see also Onysko 2016).

Intra-linguistic factors, according to contact linguistic theory, for example, include the typological distance between receptor language (into which the language material is integrated) and source language (the language material is taken from), which has been described as affecting the likelihood of transfer of different types of linguistic material and structures. Peripheral elements of a language (e.g. nouns) are said to be more susceptible to transfer, even across larger typological differences, than core features (e.g. grammatical structures such as affixes) that require greater typological overlap between languages (see Aikhenvald 2007; Thomason 2010). Based on this theory, several borrowability scales or hierarchies of borrowability have been proposed (Field 2002; Haugen 1950; Matras 2007; Muysken 1981). The general validity of such and similar intra-linguistic constraints that are said to restrict or even inhibit the transfer of certain linguistic features, however, has remained a debated topic in contact linguistics (cf. Heine and Kuteva 2008; Sankoff 2002). In this context, early contact linguistics especially emphasized the need to look beyond the linguistic processes of language contact since 'a full account of interference in a language contact situation ... is possible only if the extra-linguistic factors are considered' (Weinreich 1953: 3). In line with Weinreich's position, other scholars such as Thomason and Kaufman (1988) and Thomason (2001) argue that social factors external to linguistic structure are decisive for the outcomes of language contact and that there are no linguistic constraints that cannot be overruled if social pressures are large enough.

In terms of extra-linguistic factors, Thomason (2001) states that the various social, cultural and historical contexts that facilitate transfer between languages can be categorized on a scale ranging from *casual contact* to *intense contact*. Based on this categorization, Thomason (2001) proposes a borrowability scale in which the likelihood of certain linguistic outcomes of language contact is tied to social predictors rather than solely dependent on linguistic constraints. While situations of casual contact – as in the case of French in the UK with low levels of bilingual competence amongst speakers – are characterized by occasional borrowing of peripheral vocabulary, intense contact involving extensive bilingualism within a population leads to heavy lexical and structural borrowing. This division of extra-linguistic and linguistic factors again reminds us of the text–context binary and that these external factors, if acknowledged at all, are regarded as set apart from linguistic structures (Canagarajah 2018a; b).

Concerning the processes of language contact, the locus of research is usually the mind of the individual speaker (see amongst others Onysko 2016; van Coetsem 2000) rather than the social interaction that brings different language resources into contact. While early studies focused largely on contact phenomena that are part of the language produced by speakers categorized as bilingual (Haugen 1949; Weinreich 1953), later studies devised more general models of transfer processes that acknowledge that bi/multilingual competence is not necessarily a prerequisite for language contact. A widely recognized model is proposed by van Coetsem (2000) in his general and unified theory of transmission processes. This model distinguishes between two types of transfer from a source language (SL) to a receptor language (RL), which are governed by a speaker's level of competence in RL and SL. Cases in which the RL is a speaker's linguistically dominant language are, according to van Coetsem, shaped by RL agentivity and result in borrowing from the SL. In cases of the SL being a speaker's linguistically dominant language, SL agentivity results in the imposition of linguistic features of the SL in a speaker's RL output. In addition, van Coetsem's (2000) model recognizes linguistic and extra-linguistic factors as shaping the transfer process and determining its outcome through the notions of inherent and subsidiary stability. Inherent stability means that certain domains of a language are more stable than others, which in cases of RL agentivity goes along the lines of the borrowability hierarchies mentioned above (i.e. content items are most likely borrowed, structural elements largely resist borrowing). Subsidiary stability relates to contextual factors, such as the language attitudes of speakers, the typological affinity between the SL and the RL, and the social prestige of SL and RL.

The outcomes of language contact have been investigated at various linguistic levels, such as phonology, lexicon, syntax and pragmatics, and morphological and grammatical categories (Sankoff 2002). The research foci regarding the outcomes of language contact can range from the language practices of a collective of language users, such as in works on the global diffusion of English (Kachru 1994), to an individual speaker's repertoire as in Matras's (2009) work on the linguistic development of children in multilingual environments. On the level of linguistic communities, Winford (2003) categorizes the linguistic outcomes of contact along three general types of contact situations. Firstly, language maintenance, which means that a language is passed on from generation to generation and only slow change occurs due to internal processes and/or limited contact. This refers to cases of relatively stable language communities where transfer processes are characterized by borrowing of words and phrases, codeswitching in stable bilingual communities and, in cases of close, long-term contact, structural convergence. In situations of language shift, in which a linguistic community partially or completely abandons their native language to adopt another language, imposition of linguistic features of the shifting speakers' L1 onto the RL takes place, especially when language learning of the RL is imperfect (Thomason 2001). Lastly, the emergence of new contact languages (such as pidgins and creoles) involves the creation of new language systems by mixing and combining lexical items and grammatical structures of various languages in contact to varying degrees.

Regarding the use of English in Germany, we will find that from a contact linguistic point of view Germany is a linguistic area characterized by German as the socially dominant RL, a majority German-speaking population and English in the role of a subdominant SL (see Onysko 2007). Speakers of German largely encounter English in institutional settings of education, where English is usually taught as a first foreign language, and through media content, while contact with English L1 speakers in Germany is rare for most people. This ultimately means that German is also the linguistically dominant language for most speakers and that bilingual competence is rather limited. In van Coetsem's (2000) terms, the transfer process in German–English language contact is hence shaped by RL agentivity and resembles a borrowing process. In line with Thomason's (2001) borrowability scale, the *slightly more intense* contact situation between German and English in Germany leads to frequent borrowing of content words as well as some structural borrowing, as in the retention of s-plural for many English loanwords. The various contact phenomena and linguistic changes which result from these transfer processes have been closely observed by German contact linguists and have been grouped into several categories such as borrowings, codeswitches, hybrid and pseudo-anglicisms, which I will return to in the next section.

As I outlined before, fixity plays a part just as important as mobility in people's everyday lives and social practices (see also Otsuji and Pennycook 2010). Many people especially in the Western world perceive language change and development against the background of the monolithic orientation to language, which forms the ideological basis for people's self-perception of their linguistic practice. As researchers and observers engaging with people's language practices, we therefore need to adapt our line of inquiry to acknowledge people's multifaceted experiences with language. This means to first and foremost refrain from solely thinking in terms that appear as abstract to non-academic language users and to adopt an emic perspective. To consider that analytical toolkits and concepts of structuralist linguistics, when integrated into the larger paradigmatic frame of a sociolinguistics of mobility, can provide a better understanding of people's language practices is a good place to start. In the following, I will therefore further engage with the contact linguistic toolkit by outlining the concept of anglicism and its various categories to later demonstrate how these can support an analysis of language practices around the use of English linguistic resources on German radio (see Chapter 4).

3.2 What constitutes an anglicism?

The use of English linguistic resources in German has been the object of a variety of research in contact linguistics (amongst others Carstensen 1965; Fiedler 2017; Fink, Fijas and Schons 1997; Hunt 2019; Onysko 2007; Viereck 1986; Yang 1990). This discourse around what is frequently called anglicisms involves many debates in both academia and the public focusing in particular on what anglicisms are, their function in the German language, and their dissemination and quantity. These debates range from early investigations of anglicisms in the context of language purism (Dunger 1882; for a discussion of later works see Pfalzgraf 2009) and debates by the general German society on the radicalization against the use of English in German – mainly supported by the Verein Deutsche Sprache – to studies on global English in Europe more recently (Duszak 2004; Gerritsen et al. 2007; Martin 2006; Zenner, Speelman and Geeraerts 2012). In addition, the term '*Anglizismus*', as used in German contact linguistic research, has also aroused attention by the German media and has become widely known amongst the German society as a representation of a perceived impact of English on the German language and culture (Spitzmüller 2005).

Despite the long-standing research tradition of investigating the use of English in German, the very definition of the term 'anglicism' remains subject to debate in contact linguistics (see Busse and Carstensen 1993; Busse and Görlach 2002; Duckworth 1977; Onysko 2007). According to Onysko:

> As far as the international impact of English is concerned, the term anglicism is often used as a generic name to describe the occurrence of English language elements in other languages. However, a closer analysis of the concept of anglicism unveils the existence of fuzzy boundaries between linguistic and cultural influences and between changes imposed from the outside on the RL and changes happening within the RL.
>
> (2007: 10)

Many traditional classifications of anglicisms are based on Betz's (1959) typology of loan influences – originally developed to categorize Latinate loans in German. This typology has often been used and further developed in anglicism research but has also been criticized in so far that 'indirect loan influences' appear as anglicisms, although these words are not formally marked by lexical elements of English origin (see Glahn 2002; Schelper 1995). An example for such a word that has been categorized as an anglicism in several studies, based on Betz's typology, is German *Wolkenkratzer* (skyscraper) (see Busse and Carstensen 1996). According to Onysko (2007) such words are conceptual transmissions since an English influence can only be attributed, if at all, to the concept they represent rather than their word form.

In his study on anglicisms in *Der Spiegel*, Onysko (2007) does not go by Betz's classification but makes a more analytical approach to lexical borrowing in relation to language contact theory by placing a specific focus on the transmission processes involved between the SL (English) and RL (German), largely drawing on van Coetsem's (2000) model of transfer processes. He makes a clear distinction between what he considers as a lexical transfer into the RL, as lexical/syntactic productivity within the RL and as instances that are of a rather speculative nature, such as conceptual transmissions and certain loanwords that qualify as borderline cases due to their international use or unclear origin, such as *Sport*, *Radio* and *Video*. Onysko's method for the detection of anglicisms is mainly based on synchronic criteria, which he prioritizes over diachronic criteria in the search for anglicism occurrences since diachronic criteria can often be ambiguous due to conflicting etymological information for lexical items in different reference works. He therefore mainly considers those lexical items as anglicisms that show clear graphemic and/or phonological markedness in German. When an anglicism is graphemically marked, it deviates from German spelling conventions, as can be seen in the examples of *Baby* (*y*) and *Hightech* (*gh*). Phonological marking applies to those cases of anglicisms that deviate from German pronunciation conventions, such as *Beauty* [ˈbjuːti] and *Job* [dʒɑːb]. In particular the /dʒ/ phoneme in *Job* is a typical example for such kind of marking in German.

According to Onysko, in addition to this lexical markedness, an anglicism is 'any instance of an English lexical, structural, and phonological element in German that can be formally related to English' (2007: 90). Similarly, Görlach states that 'an anglicism is a word or idiom that is recognizably English in its form (spelling, pronunciation, morphology, or at least one of the three), but is accepted as an item in the vocabulary of the receptor language' (1994: 224). Onysko (2007) refers to such marked occurrences containing English lexical material in German as core anglicisms. This term includes borrowings such as *Boom*, *Team*, *Song* and *Service*; hybrid anglicisms such as *Computerspiel* (computer game) and *Teilzeitjob* (part-time job); and pseudo-anglicisms such as *Dressman* (male model) and *Oldtimer* (vintage car). I will come back to these core anglicisms in the following sections. Furthermore, Onysko refers to all other formally unmarked lexical items as borderline cases, which include unobtrusive borrowings such as *Test* and *Hit*, and interferences such as *klicken* (to click). An interference is a lexical item for which a similar word form exists simultaneously in both languages (German and English). In one of the two languages, in this case German, an additional meaning is adopted from the other language (English). Borderline cases, according to Onysko (2007), need to undergo an additional diachronic analysis to verify whether these show strong etymological evidence of being of English origin.

When spoken language such as on radio is analysed, Onysko's approach appears as the most appropriate to identify and categorize anglicisms since journalists producing radio content most probably are only aware of using an anglicism if the linguistic resource is recognizably English in its pronunciation or spelling. Applying a definition of anglicisms that is as close as possible to speakers' language perceptions allows us to better grasp journalists' language worlds. While I will give an overview of the core anglicism types, as categorized by Onysko (2007), that we will come across again in this book in the following sections, how these are relevant for the case study will be explained in Chapter 4. What I would like to mention briefly in this context, however, are the different notions of fluidity and sedimentation that come with these anglicism categories. From a structuralist perspective, mobility is perceived by speakers in two different ways: as novelty to language or as otherness. Some categories therefore seemingly express more fluid elements of language use (codeswitching and novel anglicisms), while others convey greater fixity (established borrowings, hybrid and pseudo-anglicisms). Speakers can also deliberately use specific resources to create these effects of novelty and otherness, which I will further explore in the context of journalists' language use in this book.

3.2.1 Borrowings

In the case of direct loans, according to contact linguistic theory, a borrowing process from the SL to the RL takes place where both concept and word form are transferred as one unit and become established in the RL (Onysko 2007). This means that most aspects of the meaning of such borrowed lexical items are retained in the RL. Examples of borrowings from the radio corpus include *Hit*, *Airport* and *Stop-and-go*. Like most anglicisms, borrowings often undergo processes of assimilation in the RL or, in other words, processes of appropriation and hybridization. These processes include orthographic assimilation in German, which mainly concerns capitalization and Germanized spellings (G. *Tipp*; E. tip), as well as morphological assimilation. In the latter case, German inflections are added to the English stem (G. *checken*; E. to check) or other derivational processes can take place (G. *Kick* (kick) → G. *Kicker* (soccer player)). Lastly, phonological assimilation of borrowings means that these anglicisms become adapted to German pronunciation conventions (G. *Stress* [ʃtrɛs]; E. stress [stres]). Borrowings can appear in all lexical categories and either introduce a new concept in the RL or expand the RL by means of adopting additional pragmatic meanings (see my discussion on catachrestic and non-catachrestic anglicisms in Section 3.2.4).

3.2.2 Hybrid and pseudo-anglicisms

Hybrid anglicisms have given rise to various definitions and classifications (amongst others Allenbacher 1999; Carstensen 1965; Haugen 1950; Onysko 2007). According to Onysko (2007), the category of hybrid anglicisms is based on a purely formal/structural criterion, namely that the lexical unit consists of both SL and RL material. It is important here to note that the term 'hybrid' should only be applied to processes of word formation (i.e. compounding and affixation) and not to the mere inflectional integration of a borrowing. Hybrids can be of various kinds; they can be productively created by combining an English borrowing with RL terms or morphemes, or they can be the result of a partial translation of an SL compound. For contact linguists, the latter process is not considered as creative as the former since it involves a conceptual role model and lexical transfer. Hybrids can appear in all German word classes. Examples of hybrid compounds include *Babypause* (baby break), *Teilzeitjob* (part-time job) and *Konzert-Tickets* (concert tickets).

Like in the case of hybrid anglicisms, various definitions (amongst others Duckworth 1977; Furiassi 2010; Galinsky 1963; Onysko 2007) and classifications (amongst others Carstensen 1980; Glahn 2002; Görlach 2003) of pseudo-anglicisms have been put forward. Onysko (2007) defines pseudo-anglicisms as any product of language-inherent creation using English lexical material to create a new sign within the RL that is unknown in English. Examples of pseudo-anglicisms are *Handy* (mobile phone) and *Beamer* (digital projector). Unlike Yang (1990), Plümer (2000) and Glahn (2002), for whom pseudo-anglicisms can be identified and split according to a categorization of three types of pseudo-anglicisms – namely lexical pseudo-loans such as *Twen* (person in his or her twenties), morphological changes such as *Pulli* (pullover) and *Profi* (professional), and semantic pseudo-loans such as *City* (city centre) – Onysko (2007) only regards anglicisms as pseudo-cases if these cannot be found in English reference works and additionally cannot be understood by native speakers of English.[1]

3.2.3 Codeswitching and novel anglicisms

Another core anglicism according to Onysko's typology is codeswitching. Codeswitching describes the act when a speaker switches between different languages or codes in a stretch of discourse. It can occur in the form of intrasentential and intersentential switches in the RL (Onysko 2007). Intrasentential switching occurs within sentence boundaries whereas intersentential switches are independent sentences where the switch occurs at sentence boundaries. Further distinctions in this context are drawn between single- and multiword switches. Multiword codeswitching is defined as cases where full sentences or phrases from an SL are used in a matrix language (RL). These multiword units are internally consistent with English morphological and syntactical as well as sometimes also phonological rules (Poplack 1993).

Previous research has shown that distinguishing between single-word codeswitching and borrowing is a rather difficult task (Haspelmath 2009;

Onysko 2007). A repeatedly held position amongst researchers in contact linguistics is that there exists a continuum between single-word codeswitching and borrowing (Clyne 2003; Myers-Scotton 1993). According to Matras, 'such a continuum would ... be dynamic rather than strictly linear: It represents not just the length of time during which a lexical item has been in use, but various constraints and preferences conditioning its employment in a variety of interaction contexts and settings' (2009: 110–11). In his prototype approach, Matras (2009) lists seven dimensions of this continuum for the distinction between borrowing and single-word codeswitching. These are bilinguality (bilingual vs. monolingual speaker), composition (elaborate utterance/phrase vs. single lexical item), functionality (special conversational effect, stylistic choice vs. default expression), unique referent/specificity (lexical vs. para-lexical), operationality (core vocabulary vs. grammatical operations), regularity (single vs. regular occurrence) and structural integration (not integrated vs. integrated). According to Matras, items from another language that match all criteria at either end of the multidimensional continuum can be classified as prototypical instances of either codeswitching or borrowing, while 'in-between the two we encounter fuzzy ground' (2009: 114). Haspelmath (2009), who disagrees with the assumption of an existing continuum, however, calls for the need of a new term for instances of borrowings that enter the RL as a new lexical item. He therefore proposes to refer to such cases of novel borrowings as 'incipient loanwords', 'regular switches' or similar.

Against the background of increased mobility, it is certainly useful to agree with the theory that there exists a continuum between single-word codeswitching and borrowing rather than considering these as neatly separable instances of language use. However, focusing on the practices around perceived linguistic boundaries requires us to particularly cast an eye on the 'fuzzy ground'. In this context, the term 'incipient borrowing', as proposed by Haspelmath (2009), allows for labelling an intermediate stage between single-word codeswitching and borrowing. Haspelmath, however, neither provides his reader with a detailed definition of his proposed terms nor describes how to distinguish incipient loanwords from codeswitches. Additionally, part of the processes of language development that lead to the appearance of new anglicisms is lexical creation within the RL. In previous research the term 'creation' has referred to different phenomena of word formation (Betz 1959; Galinsky 1963; Onysko 2007). These are conceptual transmissions; pseudo-anglicisms, also known as false anglicisms; and hybrid anglicisms. Like in the case of incipient loanwords, novel creations have not been sufficiently investigated by previous research. It is, however, valuable to explore the dynamic use of novel anglicisms and therefore of mobile resources that are not yet fully sedimented in the context of radio language since these express more fluid elements of language use and allow to better understand how journalists negotiate linguistic boundaries and thereby make use of greater linguistic mobility for communicative purposes. I will therefore further develop some of the existing arguments and theoretical concepts outlined in this section in Chapter 4. This involves that I will propose a categorization of novel anglicisms that is distinguishable from other anglicism categories and at the same time mirrors journalists' language perceptions.

3.2.4 Catachrestic and non-catachrestic anglicisms

What has often been discussed in linguistic analyses is whether lexical borrowing enriches the RL or is unnecessary, which has previously resulted in the traditional division into *necessary* and *luxury* loans (Carstensen 1965; Tagliavini and Meisterfeld 1998; Tesch 1978). This distinction has been applied by many researchers including Zenner, Speelman and Geeraerts (2012) and Șimon (2016); however, it does not provide reasons for why luxury loans are borrowed at all since the term 'luxury' implies that these are redundant (Onysko and Winter-Froemel 2011). Furthermore, it does not acknowledge the additional pragmatic effects of some of these anglicisms in the RL. In a similar distinction, Myers-Scotton (1993) divides borrowings into cultural and core forms. Despite using a more neutral terminology for her classification, she states that 'core loans meet no real lexical needs and may be largely or entirely redundant' (1993: 169). Given these drawbacks, a more pragmatically oriented perspective therefore allows for a better insight into language practices and perceptions of speakers. By building on Levinson's (2000) theory of presumptive meanings, Onysko and Winter-Froemel (2011) redefine the traditional distinction of necessary and luxury loans and develop the classification of catachrestic and non-catachrestic innovations as a new distinction.[2] The term 'catachresis' as used by Onysko and Winter-Froemel (2011) is not to be misunderstood here as a misapplication of a word – the more common meaning of the term – but needs to be seen in its classical rhetorical sense, in which the term 'relates to the naming of a concept for which there is no pre-existing expression in language' (Onysko and Winter-Froemel 2011: 1553n6).

According to Onysko and Winter-Froemel's (2011) alternative terminology, the term 'catachrestic anglicism' relates to those anglicisms that are new lexical items which have not existed in the German language before and have appeared in the RL along with a new concept. These new lexical items over time become conventionalized in the RL and then function as standard terms in German. This differs from the concept of non-catachrestic anglicisms, where the innovation at the time of its first appearance in the German language already has a semantic near-equivalent in the RL. The difference between the German term and the non-catachrestic innovation from the SL is mainly that the latter has additional pragmatic meaning in the RL. An example of a non-catachrestic innovation from the radio corpus that in comparison to its German counterpart has a different pragmatic value is the anglicism *Show*, which was used as part of the hybrid compound *Morgenshow* (morning show). Its lexical equivalent *Sendung* connotes a meaning of a programme that is more conservative and reputable, while *Show* connotes a light entertainment programme. Non-catachrestic innovations may also become standardized over time in a process described by Onysko and Winter-Froemel (2011) as diachronic development from M- to I-implicatures. This means that the non-catachrestic innovation partly loses M-implicatures (of manner) and gradually adopts I-implicatures (of informativeness). An example is the anglicism *Test*, which is used without an additional pragmatic meaning alongside its near-equivalents *Prüfung* and *Probe* in German.

3.3 Increased mobility as a challenge for contact linguistics

Viewing language as a social practice means to acknowledge speakers' language worlds. Especially in localities where the monolingual bias predominates, even against the background of increased mobility, this requires finding ways to better understand how people use language to address the socially constructed fixities and boundaries that shape people's lifeworlds. While the terminology used in traditional contact linguistics brings us closer to the phenomena of boundary acceptance, crossing and negotiation, we nevertheless need to be aware that, ontologically speaking, increased mobility poses a challenge to traditional contact linguistics. This becomes evident in the fact that the field of contact linguistics and especially anglicism research is far from a state of disciplinary unity as it is characterized by various competing definitions and categorizations of contact processes and related outcomes. Looking in greater detail at the drawbacks of the structuralist orientation, we find that reaching a common ground in the conceptualization of language in traditional contact linguistics is an issue that has also been repeatedly raised by contact linguists themselves (see Clyne 2003; Winford 2007). As van Coetsem puts it, contact linguistics still lacks 'an adequate conceptual basis on which a synthesis can be built that is theoretically well founded' (2000: 5). What underlies this struggle in the search for a common ground is the structuralist foundation of traditional contact linguistics. As has frequently been discussed in related disciplines, the traditional concepts of language contact and language change based on structuralist conceptions of fairly static, monolithic language systems lose their explanatory power in the light of increasing complexity of social interactions fuelled by the worldwide mobility of people and resources (see Blommaert 2010; Canagarajah 2013; Pennycook 2007). Although I have touched on the relevant arguments in this context in Chapter 2, I will briefly recall some of the main points for my discussion in this section.

The monolithic take on language has produced an artefactualized image of language (Blommaert 2010) and has set language apart from its spatiotemporal contexts. In this way, modern linguistics has created an artificial binary distinction between text and context and largely ignores that language is essentially a social activity (Canagarajah 2018a). Every language event is part of a dense network of social, cultural and political factors and is discursively entangled with other (language) events across both space and time. It is these discursive connections that Silverstein (1985) has flagged as essential for a comprehensive analysis of what he called the *total linguistic fact*. Scollon and Scollon, in a similar way, call for the need to acknowledge the 'relationships among text, action and the material world through what [they] call a "nexus analysis"' (Scollon 2008: 233). In addition, language is not limited to verbal meanings but takes the form of semiotic assemblages that combine various modes of meaning-making (Pennycook 2017, 2020b). Within the structuralist paradigm, linguistic structures have been abstracted from these social, temporal and material contexts to reduce complexity and attain a scientifically analysable object (see Blommaert 2010; Canagarajah 2013). As a result of the conceptualization of language as a self-contained entity, historical, cultural and social contexts are often regarded as the mere background to instances of language use and are not part of linguistic structures themselves. We can find this simplifying analytical approach throughout various research topics of contact linguistics. Especially in many analyses of Englishes in media texts of the expanding circle we hardly ever see these contextual factors addressed. Through focusing on themes such as the borrowability of individual words/features, the stability of grammatical structures or the typological distance of distinct languages, contact linguistics prefers to look for the 'laws' of language mixing in the abstract, bounded systems of language instead of focusing on social interaction and the emerging power relations that facilitate the contact of different resources. An exemplary endorsement for this orientation is given by Winford, who states that 'it is of prime importance for us [contact linguists] to seek explanations as far as possible in linguistic structure' (2003: 25) while he relegates sociocultural factors to a regulatory function. Similarly, efforts to differentiate between contact-induced language change and language-inherent changes within a linguistic community (cf. Léglise and Chamoreau 2013) tend to overlook that against the background of ongoing mixing and mobility no community can ever be considered sufficiently homogenous and unaffected by global cultural and linguistic flows as to allow for internal change free from external factors to happen. In the end, the many simplifications that are part of the structuralist attempt to describe language as a system entail that the complexities of language practices often present counterexamples which do not match theoretically proclaimed rules, constraints or prototypes. The ongoing debates that occupy the field and therefore are also part of the study of English–German language contact can perhaps be best summarized by Thomason's observation that 'all the specific constraints on contact-induced change that have been proposed have been counterexemplified' (2001: 85). This means that, ontologically speaking, we need to acknowledge language as mobile and fluid in times of increased mobility and treat contact linguistics merely as the key to people's language perceptions and daily encounters with normativity and structures in more stable language settings such as on German radio.

As I outlined in Section 3.1, it must be acknowledged that there have also been attempts to move the field of contact linguistics into a more sociolinguistically oriented direction. Thomason and Kaufman (1988), for example, argue for considering social factors as decisive for the outcomes of language contact. However, they nevertheless do not overcome the idea of linguistic constraints and therefore the structuralist biases that separate language practices from other social activity (see Blommaert's (1990) review of Thomason and Kaufman 1988). Similarly, Lim and Ansaldo (2016) call for a greater focus on the sociohistorical contexts of language contact situations and state in their introductory book on language contact that they are 'particularly interested in making connections between what goes on *in* the language and what is happening *around* it' (2016: 25, my emphasis). Despite their extensive account of globalization-related cultural, political and economic phenomena that have implications for language contact, they treat these factors as constituting the external background to language contact and the text–context binary is maintained.

The paradigmatic issues discussed above have also sparked some theoretical reorientations towards a more practice-based approach to language contact. In relation to the individual speaker's cognitive processes as the locus of language contact, Matras (2009, 2013) has, for example, moved beyond the traditional conception of bi/multilingualism as based on a speaker's command of separate and closed-up cognitive language systems. Instead, he proposes that speakers have 'a complex repertoire of linguistic structures at their disposal' (2009: 4) and thereby acknowledges that individual 'languages' are a construct of linguistics. Matras also calls for a functionalist perspective on language use which views the choice of linguistic resources from this unified repertoire against the background of social activity and the pursuance of social goals. However, despite these valuable advances, Matras does not escape from the structuralist bias of separating language from social activities when he describes language use as adapted to and therefore as a consequence of social activity rather than as a social practice in itself.

As we have seen, both paradigms, a sociolinguistics of mobility and linguistic structuralism, have their benefits and drawbacks. The question then is this: What is needed to make use of the valuable tools that both contact linguistics and a sociolinguistics of mobility provide for the study of speakers' language worlds? In the following chapter, I will propose a framework for an investigation of media language that brings together the benefits of the two existing paradigms to overcome their drawbacks in explaining language use in a world shaped by an increasingly complex interplay of fixity and mobility.

4

A New Perspective on Language Mobility

This chapter brings together the benefits of both perspectives, a sociolinguistics of mobility and traditional contact linguistics, to argue for an emic perspective in the study around language that acknowledges speakers' language worlds in the context of mobility and fixity and thereby overcomes the paradigmatic gap between structuralist and critical poststructuralist (socio)linguistics. In Section 4.1, I will outline the main points for this new perspective and will thereby bring together previous discussions of Chapters 2 and 3 on the benefits and drawbacks of these opposing paradigms.

In Section 4.2, I will then demonstrate what such an emic perspective in the case of media language can look like. I already discussed how critical cultural studies can help us to understand the global and cultural background that is intimately linked with journalists' lifeworlds in Chapter 2. However, globalization is not the only shaping factor on media language. Rather, there are more specific influences rooted in media organizational structures and media practices that go beyond the general phenomena of language mobility. To get a better understanding of journalists' professional environment, I will draw from previous research in media studies on factors that shape media content production and therefore the professional lifeworlds of radio journalists. I will start by looking at competition and segmentation in the German broadcasting system, which shapes the everyday working lives of journalists in Germany. Then, I will move to the radio journalists' workplace and what we can learn from media studies in this regard. From there, I will engage with the individual journalist and what we know so far about his or her role understanding and self-perception. Looking at these factors, pointed out by previous research, will allow us to get a first glimpse on the fixities and structures that shape journalists' multifaceted social practices, which I will examine by the example of German adult contemporary radio language in Chapters 5 to 8. Acknowledging the multifaceted social practices that are part of a journalist's professional environment is crucial for our understanding of a sociolinguistics of mass media.

In Section 4.3, I will introduce the Media Language Model, an analytical model which allows for a holistic, spatial approach to the analysis of media language as an assemblage. Against the background of the previous discussion on the two paradigmatic perspectives, the model considers the material ecology (i.e. the arrangement of matter in space and time) journalistic practices are embedded in, the spatial repertoire of verbal and non-verbal resources, and the sociocultural and historical factors that shape media language. It also allows to explore normative forces and structures affecting media discourse that evolve from sedimentation of reoccurring practices, while at the same time it considers these as emerging in interaction and open for renegotiation in practice. At this point it is important to note that a model will always depict the multitude of influencing factors that shape journalists' language use in a simplified manner. My intention here, however, is not to make the complexity less chaotic but to provide a guideline for future research that gives possible impulses, ideas and suggestions for how we can produce more complex interpretations of professionally produced media language that better account for the complexities of meaning-making practices in times of increased mobility.

Sections 4.4 and 4.5 focus on the methods I applied for the case study. Here, I will show what we can take from contact linguistic methods to help us explore the phenomenon of anglicisms as an example of the structures in journalists' language worlds. I will also highlight the importance of speaking to the actual producers of radio broadcasts to get their opinions and statements on their language choices and meaning-making on air.

4.1 A socially grounded spatial approach for acknowledging speakers' language worlds

As we have seen in the previous chapters, each of the two paradigmatic perspectives on language has its benefits and drawbacks. While the mobility paradigm suffers from the theory–practice gap that complicates participant-based empirical research, the structuralist tradition is challenged by its ontological stance. Against the background of accelerated global flows of cultural and linguistic resources, it is especially this ontological stance that makes a paradigmatic shift towards acknowledging linguistic mobility inevitable. A sociolinguistics of mobile resources acknowledges that communicative events are entangled simultaneously in both space and in time. By viewing language from a spatial perspective, a sociolinguistics of mobility overcomes the ontological issues of structuralism. This spatial perspective is crucial for an understanding of language as an assemblage of material and non-material, verbal and non-verbal resources rather than as set apart from its context. A spatial perspective also calls for the need to adopt what has been termed a 'flat ontology'. A flat ontology allows us to go beyond human exceptionalism and view all entities, whether animate or inanimate, cultural or natural, and symbolic or physical, as possessing equal ontological status (Bryant 2011). In relation to language, a 'flat ontology would go beyond the binary of text/context and consider how diverse semiotic resources of different scales of space and time are "entextualized" to constitute the communicative activity' (Canagarajah 2020: 301). This perspective therefore allows us to consider human agency in communication as qualified. Humans interact with other agentive (human and non-human) entities within the wider spatial ecology while strategically aligning semiotic resources in communicative practice (Canagarajah 2018b). A view on language as a spatially entangled social practice allows us to focus more on the social aspects of language use, rather than being caught up in constantly redefining language boundaries or categorizing the results of ongoing change. However, instead of constituting a mere antithesis to the structuralist paradigm, as currently promoted in critical sociolinguistics and critical applied linguistics (Canagarajah 2020; Pennycook 2020a), the spatial approach to language also allows us to consider linguistic structuralism as part of the assemblage of language. Abstract concepts are materially embodied in various everyday objects and thereby become part of the material ecology (see Barad 2007). Linguistic structuralism, for example, is embodied in various material arrangements such as dictionaries, teaching curricula, multilingual public signage or in the social fabric at large, which affect our discursive practices. A spatial approach to language therefore does account not only for the fluidity of linguistic resources and the creative language practices that transgress traditionally defined language boundaries and fall outside the alleged orderliness of structured language systems but also for the role structures play in the overall assemblage. In particular the concept of scales as proposed by Blommaert (2010) is useful in this context as it allows to describe such (embodied) normative patterns of fixity, sedimentation and structuralist language ideologies that shape speakers' language worlds.

Bridging the paradigmatic gap between structuralist and poststructuralist approaches to language – and therefore ultimately the theory–practice gap in critical sociolinguistics that complicates participant-based fieldwork – hence requires us to acknowledge how normative forces in each communicative event shape speakers' strategic alignment of linguistic resources from a spatial repertoire. Such normative forces include constraining language ideologies, standard language norms and representational models of language competence. However, adopting a flat ontology that acknowledges speakers' language worlds also makes it necessary to consider the social affordances connected to structuralist language ideologies, such as the strengthening effects that labelled languages can have on the identity construction of certain social groups (see Canagarajah 2013; see also Section 2.3). Foregrounding all these complex social aspects of language ultimately requires us to focus on the participants in social interaction, to understand the practices of individual language users and to better engage with how language is perceived by its users. Essential for this is not only an emic perspective that acknowledges that terms based on monolingual ideology – such as English, German, monolingual, bilingual, borrowing or codeswitching – have their raison d'être for many speakers but a perspective that goes further and allows to analytically grasp speakers' language perceptions and practices. This means for critical sociolinguists not only to acknowledge and 'contend with the possible monolingual, hierarchical, and structuralist understanding of others' (Canagarajah 2020: 311) but to step outside of our comfort zone and consider structuralist linguistic methods and concepts as a key to understanding speakers' language worlds.

In the case of the use of English mobile linguistic resources on German radio, this means to view media language as an assemblage of material, verbal and non-verbal resources shaped by sociocultural and historical factors that are bound up in constellations of both fluidity and fixity and become entextualized in each moment of journalistic meaning-making. In addition, we need to acknowledge journalists' language worlds to attain an emic perspective, which I will elaborate on in the following section.

4.2 Acknowledging journalists' language worlds

To attain an emic perspective against the background of fluidity and mobility, we need to consider the role that bounded languages and other language norms play in the social realities of speakers. Contact linguistic concepts can help us to better understand the role that fixity plays in speakers' language worlds and how it affects their language practices once we detach these concepts from a structuralist ontology and move them into the realm of social practices. The fact that separate standard languages are social constructs does not mean that they do not have real social effects or linguistic features that are empirically observable (Pennycook 2020a; Slembrouck 2021). I have already outlined in Chapter 2 how structuralist language ideologies have shaped language education and speakers' everyday language experiences. In this way, not only labels like 'English' and 'German' have become socially meaningful for language users but also the concept of 'anglicism' bears socially constructed meaning. Therefore, the analytical concepts of contact linguistics allow us to better grasp people's language worlds and their social experiences of English mobile linguistic resources.

Onysko's (2007) typology of anglicisms, for example, provides a categorization of anglicisms based on formal criteria and therefore on linguistic features recognizably of English origin even for non-linguists. We can then move on to study how speakers make use of such linguistic resources and their associated sociocultural meanings in communicative practices. In the following, I will give a few examples in relation to German radio language to make my point clearer.

My first example draws on the distinction between catachrestic and non-catachrestic anglicisms (see Chapter 3), which becomes a measure for how the socially constructed fixities in language shape language practices. Whenever speakers have the opportunity to choose between different linguistic forms to express an intended meaning, language choice ultimately becomes an act of envoicing identity (Canagarajah 2013). By drawing a line between 'standard' terms (I-implicatures) and pragmatically marked terms (M-implicatures), we can investigate whether journalists make use of deviations from expressions perceived as standard to construct their on-air identity and the station image. I will come back to this in Chapter 6.

Moreover, against the background of journalists' language worlds shaped by different structures and normative forces (see Chapters 5 to 8), the concept of codeswitching remains a valuable tool if we take it to describe a social practice instead of a linguistic outcome. Codeswitches then resemble a speaker's deliberate choice to cross socially constructed language boundaries for stylistic purposes. Codeswitching as a practice means performing a scale jump. Journalists can use a part of their repertoire that in a given situation is out of place, dislocated, or has a different social value to adopt another voice, or to index or mimic a different kind of identity (see examples of single-word codeswitching below).

In this context, I will now also return to the concept of novel anglicisms. I touched upon this already in Chapter 3 and outlined how this concept is not clearly defined by previous research. Novel anglicisms, however, are especially relevant for an examination of radio language. Examining the use of incipient borrowings and novel creations in the case of media language can give us insights into how journalists apply those English mobile resources that are not yet part of locally sedimented language practices and therefore perceived by them as novel. This gives further indications on how journalists are challenged with negotiating and refashioning linguistic boundaries and how they take the opportunity to make use of increased language mobility for communicative purposes. In the following paragraphs, I will therefore show what a contact linguistic definition of novel anglicisms that mirrors journalists' language perceptions could look like.

The larger debate surrounding neologisms in German, of which English linguistic resources are part, is quite controversial in terms of defining when a word can be regarded as new (amongst others Busse 1996; Elsen 2011; Klosa-Kückelhaus and Wolfer 2020). While some scholars define neologisms as 'lexical units or meanings which emerge in a communication community in a specific period of time of language development, which diffuse, are generally accepted as language norm, and which the majority of speakers perceive as new for some time' (Klosa-Kückelhaus and Wolfer 2020: 151), others additionally include words that are one-off creations and nonce formations (amongst others Elsen 2011), therefore, words that are used spontaneously for a particular occasion. According to the definition above, a neologism is a novel lexical item that is commonly accepted as such in German (for example *nice*, *Powerbank* and *Lockdown*). To focus specifically on practices of boundary negotiation, I will investigate those anglicisms that are not yet commonly accepted as neologisms by speakers of German since these cases show an even lesser degree of sedimentation but are used for different purposes by journalists than codeswitches. I will therefore regard an anglicism as novel and not yet commonly accepted in German if it (a) is a distinctive combination of word form and meaning not detectable in a common dictionary or even in its more current online version and (b) can only scarcely be found in regularly updated online corpora. Novel anglicisms are therefore not yet part of general language usage by the broader population and include one-offs and ad-hoc formations.

What needs to be noted in this context is that in the case of novel creations (i.e. novel hybrid and pseudo-anglicisms) speakers of German are generally highly productive in terms of compounding (Onysko 2007), and novel anglicisms created based on an established anglicism combined with a German element are therefore not exceptional. The formation of such words will hence not be perceived as a creative practice around the boundaries of standard languages by radio journalists. While I acknowledge that such hybrid anglicisms are novel if these are not listed in common dictionaries and do not appear frequently in large corpora, I consider only those hybrid anglicisms as novel anglicisms in which the English element either is not an established borrowing in German, or if this is the case, the English element does not bear its established semantic meaning. Examples of hybrid compounds that I do not consider as novel anglicisms in the radio corpus are *Bikerparadies* (bikers' paradise) and *Polizei-Email* (police email), in which the semantic meanings of the anglicism elements *Biker* and *Email* do not deviate from their established meaning in the RL.

The discussion on how to define novel anglicisms also brings us back to the issue of how to define incipient borrowings and how to distinguish these from single-word codeswitching to attain a distinction that also acknowledges journalists' language practices in relation to perceived linguistic boundaries. From a contact linguistic perspective, the prototype approach by Matras (2009) can be of help here. The basic characteristics of incipient borrowings on two levels of the continuum are predetermined since the objects of study are single lexical items (composition) of low frequency (regularity). Three further levels of distinction are not applicable to the case of English linguistic resources on German radio. The dimension of structural integration (cf. Poplack 1993) cannot make a valuable contribution to the identification of incipient borrowings since 'today, the majority of English borrowings have retained their original orthography and are pronounced in close imitation of their English models' (Onysko 2007: 62). In addition, single-word codeswitches may adopt inflectional affixes in the RL (Myers-Scotton 1993). Furthermore, the degree of 'bilingualism' of a speaker is not an insightful criterion since already the slightest degree of 'bilingualism' enables the individual to codeswitch, as pointed out by Matras (2009) himself. Due to their constant contact with English language resources and Anglo-American culture at their workplace through mostly pop music and interviews with celebrity guests, German adult contemporary radio journalists can be considered to be able to perform codeswitching at least on the level of single lexical items. For a distinction between single-word codeswitching and incipient borrowing in the case of this study, the dimension of operationality does not provide insightful criteria either. Matras's (2009) line of argumentation on this level is that occasionally bilinguals non-consciously use grammatical elements of their pragmatically dominant or default language while speaking in another language due to selection errors, which he regards as closer to the borrowing end of the continuum than the conscious selection of core vocabulary. However, the default language for automated routine speech production of journalists on German radio is German. Therefore, both the use of English grammatical operators and core vocabulary would have to be considered an act of conscious codeswitching in cases where these cannot be regarded as established anglicisms.

This leaves the levels of functionality and unique referent as providing the crucial factors for distinguishing between incipient borrowing and single-word codeswitching in the radio corpus. According to Matras (2009), prototypical codeswitches are conscious, discourse-strategic choices made to achieve special conversational effects, while prototypical borrowings are used to refer to their associated concepts. In terms of specificity, English lexical items that show a high degree of specificity are more closely located to the borrowing end of the continuum. According to Backus, 'highly specific means both that the word has a highly specific referential meaning, and that its matrix language equivalent, if there is one, conjures up quite different connotations' (2001: 132). A prototypical codeswitch, however, would be the substitution of a core lexical element in German by using a quasi-synonymous expression of low specificity from English that is merely used for special conversational effects. Adding to my previous discussion on codeswitching, single-word codeswitching is used in the radio corpus either as a discourse marker, to highlight the cultural authenticity of a certain situation, to mark an emotional state of the speaker or to give an event an additional original and authentic undertone (see Onysko 2007), as shown in the following examples.

(6) Host A: In London, Herr X, werde ich an den Feierlichkeiten zum Geburtstag von Prinzessin Charlotte teilnehmen.

(In London, Mister X, I will participate at the celebrations for Princess Charlotte's birthday.)

Host B: Die Tochter von Kate und William, die heute ein Jahr alt wird?

(The daughter of Kate and William, who turns one today?)

Host A: *Exactly*. Nun stellte sich mir die Frage, was schenke ich einem einjährigen Kind.

(Exactly. Now the question is, what do I give as a gift to a one-year-old child.)

(Public Service Station 2, 2 May 2016)

(7) Oh, wie schön wäre es, wie *splendid*, eine Villa zu haben in Großbritannien.

(Oh, how beautiful it would be, how splendid, to have a mansion in Great Britain.)

(Private Station 2, 25 May 2016)

Both single-word codeswitches are used as part of host talk for emblematic purposes to mainly highlight the cultural authenticity of the scene and stand out since they are additionally pronounced in imitation of a posh English accent by the journalists to create a typical English atmosphere (or local colour, according to Galinsky (1963)).

What remains to be noted for a categorization of novel anglicisms is that these cannot be categorized as the result of either lexical transfer processes or lexical productivity in the RL in the sense of two discrete entities since often both processes are involved in lexical innovation to varying degrees. Novel hybrid anglicisms, as previously outlined, may be the result of a lexical creation within the RL or of a borrowing process including partial translation. This includes the fact that incipient borrowings, like established borrowings, can serve as the basis for productive processes within the RL, which means that they can be part of hybrid compounds in German. Overall, the concept of novel anglicisms provides us with a useful tool that helps to describe mobile, non-sedimented English resources along the lines of journalists' language perceptions. This, as I outlined before, allows us to better understand how journalists negotiate and reshape linguistic boundaries to make use of greater linguistic mobility for communicative purposes.

As this discussion has shown, against the background of a flat ontology, integrating contact linguistic concepts into the paradigmatic frame of a sociolinguistics of mobility provides us with valuable tools for an emic perspective – a perspective that acknowledges the negotiation, reshaping and maintenance of boundaries and the relevance of these for people's lifeworlds including their language worlds and language practices. Bearing in mind what I said in Chapters 2 and 3, to arrive at a new perspective for the case of media language, we need to draw several threads together that are intrinsically linked to the communicative event. This means we need to consider the global cultural environment – which was already discussed in Chapter 2 – and, to get a better picture of journalists' professional practices, we need to be aware of the sociocultural structures that are part of journalists' language worlds. In the case of media language, these structures and fixities can be found, for example, in media regulation, genre conventions, the organizational structures of newsrooms and work routines. In the following three sections, I will cross disciplinary boundaries to draw on previous research in media and journalism studies on the sociocultural structures that shape media content production. My intention is not to provide an exhaustive list of previously identified factors influencing media content production but to shed light on those factors that are especially relevant for the case study of German adult contemporary radio. This includes factors such as a competitive German media market including its regulatory framework and, more generally, the media organization, and the journalist and his or her role understanding and self-perception.

4.2.1 Competition amongst German broadcasting media

At the time of the corpus compilation of the case study in 2016, public service broadcasters operated 70 radio stations in Germany,[1] which had to compete with 283 stations operated by private organizations. In addition, statistics from 2017 show that the private broadcasting sector had 42 per cent in audience shares.[2] This illustrates the extent of private media ownership in the German radio broadcasting landscape and therefore the competitive situation between the private and public service broadcasting sectors as well as amongst private radio broadcasters that is part of radio journalists' everyday work experiences. Previous studies on competition between the two broadcasting sectors in Germany often refer to a convergence between the two sectors (Kleinsteuber 2012; Schatz, Immer and Marcinkowski 1989), the function of the public service sector in Germany and its survival strategies to exist alongside an ever-growing private sector (Flügge 2009). In addition, some studies examine different types of competition in the German broadcasting landscape. According to Gundlach (2010) and Hoffmann-Riem (1991), competition on the German broadcasting market needs to be examined on two levels. The first is economic competition, where stations that operate in competitive markets have to achieve economic success to stay competitive and survive. The second motivation for competition is understood as editorial competition. This kind of media competition is regarded as necessary for the free formation of individual and public opinion as well as for the plurality of opinions in society. Editorial competition therefore can be regarded as a competition of opinions and ideas which does not serve economic but societal aims by constituting the foundation of the democratic process in the *Bundesrepublik* (Gundlach 2010).

When examining the German dual broadcasting system, the two concepts of competition need to be applied to each sector quite differently. Private radio stations mainly enter economic competition. Mostly financed through advertising revenue, private stations aim at reaching the largest audience possible since the larger their audience, the more revenue advertising generates. The primary aim of private broadcasters in Germany is therefore to attain maximum market shares by providing a programme that attracts a large audience. Public service broadcasters are almost completely fee-financed and therefore are only minimally engaged in economic competition (6 per cent revenue through advertising).[3] This is because their continued existence is not market-dependent but guaranteed by their duties, such as to provide a certain quality of broadcasting and a 'basic provision' of information necessary for democratic and social needs of the population, as defined by decisions of the German Federal Constitutional Court.[4] Hoffmann-Riem (1991) states that the public service stations merely have editorial competition amongst each other whereas private stations experience both types of competition amongst one another. This dichotomy of competition, however, does not mean that stations only experience these kinds of competition within their own sector. The broadcasting market in Germany is not split and hence must be regarded as a single competitive market where both types of competition cannot be clearly separated (Gundlach 2010). According to Hoffmann-Riem, no direct economic competition exists between the public service and private sector; however, editorial competition is evident. The public service sector therefore has the resources to focus mainly on editorial competition and on fulfilling its duty, which is to proliferate plurality of opinions and support the 'formation of free individual and public opinion'.[5] In contrast to Hoffmann-Riem, Weischenberg (2004) states that the public service sector is not economically independent of the media market since, although broadcasting time for commercials is limited by regulation, public service broadcasting still generates a substantial amount of advertising revenue. In turn, for the market-driven private sector, editorial competition is motivated by economic considerations since, as mentioned above, their continued existence is subject to their economic success. To achieve this, the private broadcasting sector has on offer what sells best to the listener. It is therefore important to consider that both modes of competition lead to broadcasters striving for the attention of their target audiences, regardless of the motives behind these efforts, either commercial or editorial (Gundlach 2010). This mainly creates a competition for listenership between the sectors since both have to reach the largest audience possible to pursue their aims, although for each of the two sides the main motivations are different.

Additionally, the public service sector, as stated in the decisions of the *Bundesverfassungsgericht* (Federal Constitutional Court), has a role model function, which makes it obligatory for public service broadcasting to deliver high-quality content (Flügge 2009). The German dual broadcasting system was built on the foundation of a public service sector that serves as a balanced platform in which 'die Vielfalt der bestehenden Meinungsrichtungen unverkürzt zum Ausdruck gelangt' (the variety of opinions held is brought to expression undiminished).[6] This function of public service broadcasting is the necessary basis for the establishment of a private broadcasting sector, as stated by the German Federal Constitutional Court in its so-called fourth broadcasting decision. A completely balanced representation of the plurality of opinions in the programme offers of the private sector cannot be guaranteed due to its dependency on advertising revenue and its extensive market orientation. Therefore, the court states that the public service sector is a necessary counterpart for a private sector with lesser duties to fulfil and hence more deficiencies. The unfitness of private commercial media organizations operating on a free media market to provide a balanced forum for debate necessary in a democratic society has also been highlighted by Curran (2002), who at the same time proposes an ideal media system consisting of a public service sector at its core, surrounded by other media sectors.

In the German system, both sectors underlie a regulatory agreement between all federal states in Germany, which was called *Rundfunkstaatsvertrag* (Interstate Broadcasting Treaty) at the time of the case study in 2016. Each of the *Länder* (federal states) has its own broadcasting law based on the treaty. Even though, as outlined in the convergence theory by Schatz, Immer and Marcinkowski (1989), a convergence between the two sectors is possible to a certain extent, the public service sector is still obliged to fulfil its duties and therefore cannot devote its programme completely to what is regarded as popular in society, namely popular culture. Certain elements of education and *Kultur* (culture)[7] as well as high-quality news have to be part of public service programmes, which generally affects journalists' language use and content choice.

Despite the obligation to fulfil their duties, public service broadcasters had to react to the competitive environment created by the establishment of the private broadcasting sector by adapting their programmes with a particular focus on specific age groups or certain niche markets (Goldhammer 1995; Lilienthal 1991). This included the public service broadcasters establishing, for example, news talk and classic music stations that aim only at specific target audiences. This process is also observed by Hesmondhalgh (2019), who states that since 1980 market segmentation has increasingly led to more and more media content being produced for specific audience groups, which, he concludes, may be partially caused by the media adapting their products to the social fragmentation occurring in modern consumer societies.

Public service broadcasters can fulfil their obligations by running several radio stations of different formats. This means that some stations may focus more on education and others more on entertainment. Even though this is permissible, entertainment, as statutory regulation postulates, 'should also be provided in line with a public-service profile of offers'.[8] Hence, as already mentioned above, the competition between the two sectors involves different motivations on both sides, as well as different requirements for each of the sectors, which in turn inhibits a complete convergence of the sectors that might result from competition. Competition between the public service and the private sector therefore has only led to a certain convergence in terms of programme structures in German radio broadcasting since to stay competitive, public service broadcasters have largely adopted the programme formats that were initially introduced by private radio stations. Considering all this, it is obvious that both sides will have to approach the audience differently in terms of language and content choices, even if they have similar target audiences and broadcast in the same radio format.

According to studies by Peiser (2000) and Schneider, Schönbach and Stürzebecher (1993), there are significant differences between journalists working for the German public service sector and journalists working for the private sector. These differences concern the personal agendas, backgrounds and professional values of journalists, which affect the content they produce. Peiser (2000), for example, in his study on the journalist's personal agenda, examines how the personal issue importance of news-workers is shaped by different factors. Peiser discovers that German broadcast journalists of the two broadcasting sectors make different judgements when rating the importance of news topics to them. 'It appears that private broadcasting journalists tended to assign less importance to social and human problems (asylum-seekers, violence against foreigners) while they emphasized ecology, as compared to their colleagues working in public-service organizations' (Peiser 2000: 249). In Chapter 6, I will elaborate on the differences between the two broadcasting sectors regarding anglicism usage and how the different types of competition affect this use on air.

4.2.2 Radio workplace

The work environment of journalists has been extensively researched. Key works in this area include those by Breed (1955), Gans (1979), Weaver and Wilhoit (1991) and Weischenberg (2004). The focus of these studies is mainly on the impact the workplace surrounding has on the content journalists produce. Breed (1955) analyses how American newspaper publishers implement policies on staffers regarding their content production. He also mentions the role of the editors and how their actions, which function mainly as controlling guides, influence the work of reporters and other journalists. As Breed's (1955) findings show, most journalists are not briefed on such policies and usually tend to learn what the publisher or editor expects along the way. In fact, according to him, there is no overtly implemented policy regarding news coverage in newsrooms since this would be taken as an admission that a news outlet biases its reporting. Breed (1955) also talks about the influence of newsroom conferences in which staffers discuss their stories with editors, who give feedback on what angle the story should have. The importance of editorial conferences has also been highlighted in a more recent study by Weischenberg (2004), who states that such conferences are an important tool to exert control over a newsroom and to keep the staff 'in line'. Weischenberg (2004) also points to the organizational structure of a newsroom and how it shapes the content produced. He mainly distinguishes between two basic models of organizational structure: on the one hand, a hierarchically structured newsroom, in which the main authority emanates from an editor-in-chief, and on the other hand, an organizational structure that is governed by all members of staff, where important decisions are made collectively. Since both types of organizational structure have their advantages and drawbacks for the workflow in the newsroom, in most cases hybrid organizational forms tending more to one or the other side are implemented by news outlets. As Weischenberg (2004) points out, the power of the editor-in-chief must not be underestimated in such mixed forms of organization. Even if not exerted directly, the power of the chief editor to make definite decisions as a latent source of authority shapes the content produced by journalists.

In addition to the editor's power to shape content, Breed (1955) also highlights the importance of the journalist's colleagues as a reference group with which journalists tend to align. This is in line with Weischenberg, Löffelholz and Scholl, who state that 'the newsroom itself – superiors as well as colleagues – define the limits of the coverage' (1998: 248). Journalists, when entering the workplace environment as a new member of staff, will tend to comply with the style and norms given by the example of their fellow journalists' work. Hence, according to Breed, a 'staffer must be seen in terms of his status and aspirations, the structure of the newsroom organization and of the larger society' (1955: 329). Therefore, depending on the position a journalist holds in a newsroom, he or she may have more freedom or less freedom over the content he or she produces. The lower a journalist's position within the hierarchy of a newsroom, the more his or her work is influenced by professional roles and norms at the expense of their personal beliefs and attitudes. In Chapter 7, I will explore how German adult contemporary journalists' work environment shapes a journalist's language practices and whether there are policies on language usage and restrictions on anglicism usage in German radio newsrooms.

4.2.3 The journalist

The journalist as a professional language user and individual as well as his or her role in the processes and structures of media content production have received much attention in journalism and media studies. How journalists view their professional role has been investigated by various studies, including by Fjaestad and Holmlov (1976) in their work on Swedish journalists and their role as a watchdog and educator, and more recently by Plaisance and Skewes (2003), who look at news journalists in their role as adversaries. In addition, in a comprehensive study of American journalism, Weaver et al. (2007) examine how journalists perceive their functions in society. They point out that journalists' self-perception is centred mainly around four different roles: the disseminator, the adversary, the interpreter and the populist mobilizer. Such role perceptions do not only impact the content that journalists produce but also affect their language use on air, which I will return to in Chapter 8.

Media content is influenced not only by a journalist's self-perception but also by a journalist's own imagination of their target audience. In an early study on the influence of imagined audiences on communicators, Bauer (1958) found out that the potential audience a communicator has in mind while producing content has an impact on how a journalist retains and organizes information intended for communication. According to Bauer (1958), in most cases a communicator does think not only of the actual target audience but also of secondary audiences or reference groups, which might not even take part in the act of communication. While Bauer's results are based on experimental data, for which participants were given a hypothetical audience, Pool and Shulman (1959) investigate how reference groups actually are present in journalists' minds while producing texts. The results of their study show that journalists either have a rather positive image of their audience and aim at being rewarded for pleasing the audience or they imagine their audience in a rather negative light and therefore write aggressively to 'punish and offend individuals they disliked' (1959: 156). In both cases, the communicative behaviour of journalists, according to Pool and Shulman (1959), depends on expected reactions to their content by those imagined audiences. Furthermore, since Pool and Shulman found such images to be consistent over time, the results of their study indicate that the image journalists have of their audience seems to be a factor related to their personalities.

A journalist's background can be divided into the personal background and the professional background (Shoemaker and Reese 2014), which however are interrelated and shaped by each other. In line with findings by Breed (1955),

Shoemaker and Reese (2014) state that although both types of background shape a journalist's attitudes, beliefs and values, the extent to which the content produced by journalists is affected by the personal background depends on the power and autonomy a journalist possesses within an organization. More influential journalists therefore enjoy greater freedom in incorporating their personal attitudes and beliefs. In this context, Burger and Luginbühl (2014) state that hosts and presenters are selected to match the image of the radio station – especially for morning show programmes, where most listeners tune in – or need to adapt to the roles they have to play in the team of presenters. In terms of character of each host and their sidekicks, this includes that they usually take on different roles shaped by their differing personalities in a journalistic team to appeal to a broader audience (Buchholz 2017). This may be a funny, more serious, or even 'your best friend' type of character. Chapter 8 is devoted to the journalist and how his or her language attitudes and perceptions as part of his or her language worlds shape the use of anglicisms in journalistic texts.

The following section combines what I have so far discussed in this chapter in an analytical model that can be used as a guideline to explore how the normative patterns of linguistic structuralism and the structures in journalists' professional environments described by media studies research are part of the assemblage of media language within the paradigmatic frame of the sociolinguistics of mobility.

4.3 Modelling influences on media language

Previous frameworks for an analysis of media language which have emerged out of the linguistic tradition have several limitations for an analysis of the spatial entanglement of discursive media practices. Since my intent here again is to be illustrative rather than exhaustive, I will briefly refer to two of the more prominent and widespread approaches: critical discourse analysis (CDA) as proposed by Fairclough (1995, 2010) and van Dijk (1988, 2015), and social semiotics as proposed by Kress (2010) and Kress and van Leeuwen (2001).

Fairclough's (1995) framework for analysing media discourse contains three distinct concentric levels of analysis with media texts at the core of his framework. These texts are embedded within discourse practices of media production and consumption, which are again embedded in wider sociocultural practices (e.g. privatization and marketization as part of neoliberal capitalism). According to Fairclough, 'the link between the sociocultural and the textual is an indirect one'

(1995: 60) where discursive practices are considered to have a mediating role. It is in this indirect link that the text–context binary remains unchallenged in his approach.

The problematic distinction between text and context is also upheld in van Dijk's (1988, 2015) approach to CDA, according to which discourse or text can have 'general, abstract, or context-free properties' (van Dijk 1988: 24). Van Dijk explicitly refers to the possibility in CDA to examine 'text and context separately, and once a feature of context has been observed, postulated or otherwise identified, CDA may be used to explore whether and how such a feature affects, or is affected by, structures of text and talk' (1999: 460). This detachment of language from the complexity of context is also referred to as CDA's linguistic bias. According to Blommaert (2005: 35), CDA's emphasis on linguistic analysis limits its scope to 'discourse which is there' as part of text (see also Shi-xu 2023).

A further issue arises from van Dijk's socio-cognitive approach to CDA. In contrast to Fairclough, van Dijk (2015) considers cognitive processes as the link between text/language/discourse, and sociocultural processes and structures. In addition, 'context' is presented as a subjective mental model of individuals that controls production and uptake of discourse (van Dijk 2008). This locates discursive practices exclusively in the human mind rather than in social interaction.

A different approach to meaning-making that aims to overcome the linguistic bias has been put forward by the schools of multimodality and social semiotics. Kress and van Leeuwen (2001) have emphasized in their work that language has no primacy over other modes of communication, such as colour or facial expression, and that language 'may now often be seen as ancillary to other semiotic modes' (2001: 46). However, shaped by social semiotics' linguistic legacy, multimodality scholars look for common patterns and general principles of semiosis across different modes – the 'grammar' of modes, so to say – which presupposes the definition of rather strict boundaries between different modes that can be upheld across various contexts in communication. Ontologically, drawing boundaries between what are considered different modes, however, is equally as problematic as defining the boundaries of linguistic codes since predefined modes often do not easily accommodate signs occurring in actual communication (Bezemer and Cowan 2021).

A further issue is that multimodality studies were traditionally based on the assumption that humans actively make use of various (passive) material/semiotic resources available to them to construct meaning. According to Kress, 'in a social-semiotic account of meaning, individuals, ... using socially made, culturally available resources, are agentive and generative in sign-making and communication' (2010: 54). Due to this theoretical position, social semiotics also does often not consider the agentivity of other (non-)material resources in the production of multimodal ensembles (see Caronia and Mortari 2015). Moreover, although regarding multimodal signs as motivated calls for close analysis of the practices of sign-makers, these practices are seldom looked at in social semiotic analyses of texts (see Bezemer and Cowan 2021; Iedema 2003). As in the case of CDA, this focus on the multimodal text often prevents insights into journalists' lifeworlds from being gained.

Both approaches, CDA and social semiotics, lack a holistic, spatial approach that overcomes the text–context binary in the sociolinguistics of mass media. Drawing on critical sociolinguistic and critical cultural theory as a methodological frame, the analytical Media Language Model I propose in this section allows for a holistic, spatial analysis of professionally produced media language as an expansive assemblage. While a sociolinguistics of mobility and critical cultural theories of globalization – in the case of Germany of asymmetrical hybridization (see also Chapter 2) – provide valuable approaches for the analysis of discursive media practices on a metatheoretical level, a critical sociolinguistics of media language further requires an integration of these two theories in a more specialized framework. Such a framework also needs to acknowledge the socially defined fixities and structures in professional mass media work and must function to identify which factors have an influence on the language used by journalists. In Blommaert's words, it must be able to identify the authority centres that set orders of indexicality for media language and shape the language worlds of journalists. According to the concept of polycentricity, there are always multiple centres that shape the language used by mass media. Viewing polycentricity from the perspective of a flat ontology, we can conceive of authority centres as the nodes of a rhizomatic network in which all points are ontologically of equal status and connected with each other (Deleuze and Guattari 1987). When adopting the metaphor of the rhizome, however, care must be taken not to fall into the trap of insufficiently addressing the powers of norms, categories and structures (Pietikäinen 2016) and to conceive of the rhizomatic metaphor as neglecting stratification and order. Deleuze and Guattari (1987) state that there are potentials for stratification within the rhizome which allow for stability and order to develop. To acknowledge the sedimented structures, norms and practices that journalists encounter in their daily professional media work, it is therefore useful to group these authority centres along the lines of boundaries of social organization that have become meaningful for media work. In the field of media studies, a substantial amount of research has been undertaken by various scholars to identify such sedimented factors of influence on media content (Esser 1998; Preston 2008; Shoemaker and Reese 2014; Weischenberg 2004). Before developing a framework for an investigation of mass media language as a spatial repertoire, my intention in the following section is to provide a basic overview of key works from media and journalism studies that have previously proposed models of influences on media content production. I will focus on describing those models that are relevant for the development of the Media Language Model introduced in Section 4.3.2.

4.3.1 Models of influencing factors from journalism and media studies research

The most common arrangements of influencing factors on media content in previous models of influences on media content production are based on concentric circles or several overlapping clusters, placing the personal influences of the individual journalist at the centre and then moving outwards to address larger contexts (Esser 1998; McQuail 2010; Preston 2008; Shoemaker and Reese 2014; Weischenberg 2004). Although the rhizomatic arrangement of authority centres within a flat ontology decentres the individual and instead 'treats meanings as emerging in activity in the interstices of people, objects, and the environment' (Canagarajah 2020: 304), these previous models from a media-sociological perspective nevertheless help us to understand the structures in journalists' lifeworlds.

In a comparative study that explores similarities and differences in journalism practices and news making in different European countries, Preston (2008) develops a model of influencing factors on news media production. In his model, Preston (2008) identifies five different dimensions or clusters: individual influences, media routines and norms, organizational influences, political-economic factors, and cultural and ideological power. These five levels represent, according to him, 'explanatory perspectives or research traditions which offer distinct but complementary sets of concepts and ways of understanding the influences on journalism and news culture' (Preston 2008: 6) and therefore are depicted as partly overlapping and partly opposing clusters. Preston's model (2008) is noteworthy for going beyond the media structure level to include culture, ideology and power. However, in particular the two macro spheres 'political-economic factors' and 'cultural and ideological power' are depicted as opposing clusters on the same level in his model, a structure that does not adequately address the notion of cultural flows accompanying processes of globalization since these shape political-economic factors as much as other spheres.

In contrast to Preston's (2008) cluster model, other studies that identify various levels of influences apply multi-levelled circular models as a 'theoretical umbrella' for their analyses (Esser 1998; Shoemaker and Reese 2014; Weischenberg 2004). When introducing his model and explaining its structure, Weischenberg (2004) makes use of the metaphor of an onion consisting of multiple layers encompassing each other. Holding a constructivist position, Weischenberg argues that the media provide their audience with *Wirklichkeitsentwürfe* (drafts of reality), and he furthermore states that journalists are constructing these drafts by offering their interpretations of everyday events. This process of reality construction is shaped by the four levels incorporated in his framework – the media system, media institutions, media statements and media actors. What Weischenberg's model does not consider, however, are influences situated beyond what he defines as the outermost level of his model, the media system. In his approach, globalizing forces that have an impact on societies and their media systems are not acknowledged, and by not giving credit to these, Weischenberg therefore also does not specifically refer to omnipresent global cultural flows.

In contrast to Weischenberg's model, these influencing factors coming from the larger societal background are taken into consideration by Shoemaker and Reese (2014), who propose five dimensions of influences on media content in their model.[9] These levels according to them are the individual at the centre of the multi-levelled model, followed by – moving outwards – routine practices, media organizations, social institutions and social systems. On the level of social systems, Shoemaker and Reese consider the interconnectedness of the media with societies and cultures on a global scale. The level of social institutions, according to Shoemaker and Reese (2014), is mainly focused on the relation of the media with other social institutions relating to politics, education or religion. On the level of media organizations, the focus mainly lies on the properties of media outlets, such as organizational structures, ownership or organizational policies. Shoemaker and Reese's model, however, does not acknowledge the influences that different media systems exert on the production of media content. The dual broadcasting systems of many European countries, for example, constitute different regulatory and economic environments for media organizations than largely market-driven media systems, such as in the United States. For the case study on factors that influence language use by German radio journalists, it would therefore prove difficult to analyse influences that can be ascribed to the structure of the German broadcasting system on the levels of social institutions and media organizations.

Esser (1998) deploys a model similar to Shoemaker and Reese; however, he incorporates the media system as a separate level. Likewise, also in contrast to Weischenberg (2004), Esser (1998) places particular importance on societal, cultural and historical influences when he refers to the outer level of his model as the societal system. However, since he deploys his framework in a comparative study of the German and English press and therefore analyses influences on journalism and how it is practised in two different countries, his outermost sphere covers only these national societies and like Weischenberg's model lacks a more global perspective.

Within a spatial approach to the study of media language in times of increased mobility, the complex, polycentric web of both local and situated, and global and dynamic influences needs to be acknowledged. Centres of authority can be broadly attributed to the individual journalist, the media organization, the media system and the global/cultural environment and determine orders of indexicality that shape the language used by journalists. In the following, I will develop a framework that acknowledges this complexity of mass media language.

4.3.2 The Media Language Model

As opposed to taking the text as the locus of study when investigating media discourse (Fairclough 1995; cf. van Dijk 1988), previous models from media studies concerned with influences on media content as proposed by Esser (1998) and Shoemaker and Reese (2014) shed more light on the individual and his or her content production practices governed by socially constructed fixities and structures. Although this is valuable in the context of media language, what we need is a more holistic, spatial framework that combines notions of fluidity and fixity and allows us to investigate the collaborative translingual and transmodal social practices of journalists' meaning-making. Against the background of a flat ontology, I therefore combined the levels of influences on media content production from previous media studies models and the concept of hybridization from critical cultural studies with the theoretical framework of the 'sociolinguistics of mobility' by Blommaert for the Media Language Model (see Figure 1). However, to avoid implying an *a priori* existing hierarchy by using the term 'levels', I prefer to refer to the socially conditioned patterning of authority centres as groupings of influencing factors and have

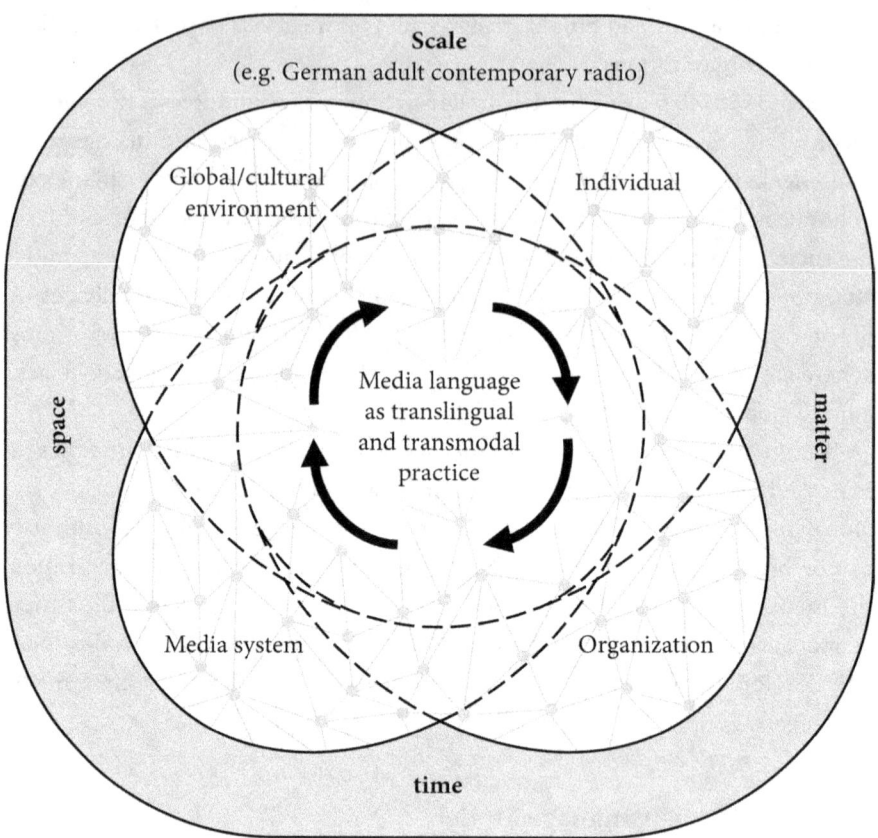

Figure 1 The Media Language Model.

arranged these as partly overlapping instead of as concentric circles (see also Canagarajah 2021). In line with the perspective of a flat ontology, this arrangement of groupings of influencing factors also decentres the individual and thereby allows us to treat human agency as qualified. In addition to these influencing factors on the production of media content, Blommaert's (2010) sociolinguistics of mobility provides the tools for an investigation of media language as a distributed social practice entangled in wider spatial repertoires (Blommaert 2010; Pennycook 2020b).

As mentioned in Chapter 2, language use is governed by normative patterns on various scales of different spatiotemporal extent, which are layered and stratified (Blommaert 2010). For analysing the normative patterns which shape the language of German adult contemporary radio media, it is therefore necessary to focus on authority centres that assemble and are therefore relevant on this particular scale. While some of these authority centres are exclusive to the scale of *German adult contemporary radio*, others emerge from higher-order scales 'invoking practices that have validity beyond the here-and-now' (Blommaert 2010: 35). All media content, for example, must meet the general expectations of authority centres such as the state towards a given medium. For the case study, normative patterns that originate from the superordinate scale of *German radio media* (such as the requirements to use inclusive language and child-friendly language) are also present as centres of authority on the more specific subordinate scale of *German adult contemporary radio*. Centres of authority from lower-order scales such as an individual journalist's language attitudes can also become part of the assemblage and therefore relevant on the scale of *German adult contemporary radio*.

The Media Language Model I propose encompasses four groupings of authority centres: the individual, the organization, the media system and the global/cultural environment. While this framework shows sedimented structures of social organization that journalists encounter in their daily professional media work through the grouped arrangement of influencing factors, the broken lines between the overlapping groupings indicate the possibility for change in the structures of the spatial ecology of media practices. Since sedimented normative forces and structures affecting media language have evolved out of previous, reoccurring interactions, they are often reproduced but are also always open for renegotiation in practice. As indicated by the circular arrows around media language as translingual and transmodal practice (see Figure 1), I therefore consider hierarchies and power relations within the assemblage of media language as negotiable and as emerging in interaction during meaning-making processes (see Canagarajah 2020, 2021).

In line with Blommaert's (2010) concept of polycentricity and the notion of a flat ontology, the model also goes by the basic premise that authority centres across all groupings of influences are part of a complex, rhizomatic network and affect each other. Therefore, any instance of language production by the mass media is shaped by a complex interplay of factors from all four groupings of the model. Not only do factors from the global/cultural environment (which also includes authority centres from a national scale) shape and define the media system and its objectives, but also factors from the media system contribute their part to what is considered as the cultural setting.[10] The same applies to influencing factors within the individual and the station groupings, which on the one hand are shaped by the media system and the global/cultural environment but on the other hand constitute part of these and therefore ultimately can induce change onto them. In this sense, the proposed model is also in line with other critical sociolinguistic approaches to complexity, such as Scollon and Scollon's (2004) nexus analysis or Silverstein's (1985) analysis of the total linguistic fact, while at the same time it offers an opportunity to make both linguistic and social structure part of my methodological framework. How much individual centres of authority – whether specific to the scale of adult contemporary radio or of a lower/higher scale – shape the language used by journalists remains an empirical question and depends on each individual case and moment-to-moment emplacement of the journalist with his or her sociocultural environment (see Canagarajah 2018a), which requires a close examination of the respective medium and its larger sociocultural context.

Taken together, these centres of authority produce orders of indexicality that shape how journalists use transmodal resources available in the wider spatial repertoire when producing language for a particular medium. In this context, the material affordances offered by a medium become an essential element of the network and permeate all groupings of influence. They do not only shape global and national media consumption patterns and cultural production forms but also shape the formation of media systems, media regulation and workplace routines, and the possibilities of expression for the individual journalist.

The framework presented in Figure 1, exemplarily illustrating the case of *German adult contemporary radio* language, can be used as a guideline to investigate mass media language on all scales, which includes different media and media formats. It can also be used to zoom further into the numerous lower-order scales, which in the example of radio include the genres of station imaging, news or comedy, or even individual topics discussed on air. By providing a guideline for exploring both fluidity and fixity in journalists' language worlds, the model proposes a possible way of bridging the gap between the two perspectives on language in the case of mass media language as a translingual and transmodal practice.

In the light of the Media Language Model, I will undertake a holistic, spatial investigation of authority centres setting orders of indexicality in radio journalists' language worlds in Chapters 5 to 8. Several themes relevant for discussion emerged from the empirical data of the case study. To describe the effects of cultural mobility and fixity within the established structures of the media profession, I will explore journalists' language worlds in view of the concept of asymmetrical hybridization, which connects the case of English linguistic resources on German radio to global cultural flows. Furthermore, I will examine themes such as competition in the media system, the journalistic workplace, the journalists' language perceptions and how journalists participate in collaborative meaning-making practices within the assemblage of media language.

As part of the results from the case study, I will examine station imaging in greater detail. Previous research has shown that anglicisms are used frequently in advertisements to attract attention and convey a sense of modernity (Gerritsen et al. 2007; Piller 2003). Examining station imaging elements in relation to language use gives indications as to what image a radio station wishes to present to its audience to attract listeners in a competitive market. I will only briefly address other genres and topics where relevant to my discussion around English linguistic resources. A thorough additional analysis of each of these scales is beyond the scope of this book but can be considered as a subject of investigation for future research in this field.

Before moving on to the results of the case study, I will explain the methods I used to examine journalists' language choices regarding English resources. As previously outlined, the normative forces of monolingual and standard language ideologies are part of the complex assemblage of authority centres. Therefore, to uncover the effects of the structuralist ideology on speakers' language practices, we need datasets that allow us to get an insight into socially meaningful categories of language use as well as into the voices and opinions of language users who navigate these complex waters. The following two sections show a possible approach that allows such an insight. I will combine corpus-based quantitative and qualitative contact linguistic methods with qualitative interviews to demonstrate the value of looking more closely at the language worlds of journalists and getting an insight into speakers' experiences of using language in their professional environments.

4.4 Using corpus linguistic approaches to explore language worlds

In search for anglicisms in the radio corpus, I applied both quantitative and qualitative methods. This mixed methods approach allowed for a comprehensive analysis of media language and has provided new empirical findings on the use of global Englishes in the expanding circle (see Chapters 5 to 8). Quantitative methods helped to identify the number of English linguistic resources used by journalists from each of the stations and broadcasting sectors in the radio corpus. This allowed for a first comparison of stations and broadcasting sectors and provided a valuable basis for further investigation of journalists' linguistic choices in the radio corpus via linguistic qualitative methods. By revealing the scope of anglicism use on adult contemporary radio, the quantitative analysis also made a comparison with previous research on the use of English linguistic resources in media texts of the expanding circle possible. According to Ivankova and Stick, 'the rationale for mixing both types of data is that neither quantitative nor qualitative methods are sufficient by themselves to capture the trends and details of situations. ... When used in combination, quantitative and qualitative methods complement each other and provide a more complete picture of the research problem' (2011: 304). This is certainly the case for the analysis of English resources on German radio, in which the quantitative comparison of the stations' anglicism use later also informed questions for the qualitative interview-based part of the case study, which sheds light on journalists' experiences of using anglicisms in radio morning shows.

The interviews also later revealed that 'quantity of anglicisms' is a meaningful category for journalists as they repeatedly used quantifying expressions such as *viele* (many) and *weniger* (less) when talking about their use of anglicisms on air. This seems to be partially connected to the larger public discourses on language change in Germany and partially to the constraints of the channel of communication (for a discussion on comprehensibility see Chapters 5 and 7). In addition, this shows that a quantitative analysis can give us further valuable insights into the language worlds of journalists. The quantitative analysis also shed light on the language that journalists use in different parts of the programme shaped by genre conventions and their communicative aims, and the target audience's language use (see Chapter 6). In this regard, the quantity of anglicisms used in station imaging, news and the rest of the spoken content (see detection of anglicisms in Section 4.4.2) gave first indications of possible strategies relating to the use of anglicisms by radio journalists working in the competitive German dual broadcasting system.

4.4.1 Corpus selection

The benefit of focusing on one radio format instead of several is that one format can be examined more thoroughly, for example, by digging deeper into matters of competition for the same age group of listeners and routine practices of journalists that stem from a particular radio format (see Chapters 6 and 7). Unlike previous studies on global Englishes in broadcasting media of the expanding circle (cf. Adler 2004; Glahn 2002), I give a comparative overview of the German dual broadcasting system by focusing on three pairs of competing adult contemporary stations in Germany. To make a well-founded comparison, I selected stations aiming at roughly the same target audiences in overlapping broadcasting areas.

Based on their average size in listenership per hour on weekdays from 6.00 am to 6.00 pm (taken from marketing research), I selected the three largest adult contemporary stations from both the public service and private radio sector in Germany. These stations, as outlined above, target an audience of approximately 25 to 49 years of age. I then selected the strongest competitor, which means from either the public service or private sector, in the broadcasting areas of each of the three stations based on the same listenership statistics. I will use the pseudonyms *Public Service Station* (*PS*) and *Private Station* (*P*) in combination with the numbers *1*, *2* and *3* to represent the three pairs of competing radio stations throughout the book.[11] For ease of readability in the excerpts from the radio corpus, I additionally use the pseudonym *Radio X* where journalists refer to their own station name.

I took a representative sample of radio language comparable in size with Glahn's (2002) study, in which he analysed occurrences of anglicisms in German television content in a corpus of approximately 18 hours. Radio is more closely relatable to television than to print because radio as a spoken medium is partially spontaneous. The radio corpus analysed in the case study therefore consists of 20 hours of radio stations' self-produced spoken radio content. While Glahn (2002) selected different television programme types during different hours of the day over a period of 45 days, I focused on the specific hours of the morning where radio stations broadcast their morning programmes. These morning shows, as previously mentioned, are the flagship of both public service and private stations and the most popular programmes on radio, especially since most people tune in during commuter times in the morning. Based on the marketing study *Radionutzung im Tagesverlauf 2016* (Mediendaten Südwest n.d.), content was recorded during the commuter hours of weekdays from 7.00 am to 9.00 am, where a peak in listenership is evident. Since the figures in this marketing study showed a decrease in average listenership for adult contemporary programmes if Saturday and Sunday are included in the analysis, I excluded the weekend morning programmes, which additionally have a different structure than the morning shows during the week.

To decide on further strategies concerning sample choice, I undertook a first exploratory recording of one private and one public service station's morning programme. One hour of material of each of the stations was taped simultaneously and then cut appropriately to isolate spoken content, which resulted in approximately 20 minutes of spoken content per station. Therefore, to get 20 hours of spoken content as a representative corpus size, 60 hours of recording time were necessary. These 60 hours of radio content recordings resulted, due to the chosen number of six stations, in 10 hours of recording time per station. To attain a representative corpus and variation in topics, 10 hours of radio content per station were taped on 10 days in a period of 10 weeks, which meant the recording of 1 hour on 1 weekday per week. The corpus size and samples were selected within a manageable time frame, which was from the first week of April to the second week of June 2016.

With the aim of reaching further variation in content and topics across the week from Monday to Friday, 2 composite weeks from Friday to Monday and Monday to Friday were chosen as a recording method. The recording of radio content therefore started from Friday of 1 week, Thursday of the following week and so on, over a period of 10 weeks. As depicted in Table 1, for the purpose of examining both hours where there is a peak in listenership and to avoid taping the same morning show parts throughout the entire sampling period, the first composite week was taped from 7.00 am to 8.00 am, and the second composite week was taped from 8.00 am to 9.00 am. The samples were recorded using MP3 audio streams provided by the chosen stations. Each of the samples was then cut appropriately with the audio editing software Adobe Audition to isolate spoken content. Excluded from the analysis of quantity and frequency of anglicisms are commercials and songs produced by third parties as well as music and station imaging segments containing no spoken content.[12] Additionally, to undertake a search for anglicism occurrences, all samples were transcribed. For further investigation of different radio genres and possible differences in anglicism frequencies amongst genres, the recorded corpus of 20 hours of spoken radio content was split into several parts. These are news produced by the selected radio stations (including traffic and weather), station imaging materials, comedy, service pieces providing consumer advice and host talk including interviews. English content played in audio clips or produced by third parties that did not function as a multi- or single-word codeswitch was excluded from the quantitative analysis.

Table 1 Recording method.

Week	1	2	3	4	5	6	7	8	9	10
Day	Fri	Thu	Wed	Tue	Mon	Mon	Tue	Wed	Thu	Fri
Hour	7.00–8.00 am					8.00–9.00 am				

4.4.2 Detection of anglicisms

Anglicisms in the radio corpus were detected with the help of the corpus linguistic software WordSmith Tools 7.0. This software was chosen as it provides word lists of all word forms in a corpus (including further data such as type-token ratios) and has a concordancing function for further in-depth analysis. Each station was examined separately to allow for a comparison of results from the three public service and the three private stations not only between broadcasting sectors but also individually within their broadcasting areas and sectors. With WordSmith Tools 7.0, I generated a decontextualized list of all words in the corpus including figures of frequency (number of tokens), which supported the process of identifying anglicisms. In line with Onysko's (2007) detection method for anglicisms, a synchronic analysis of this word list was conducted aided by the *Anglizismen-Wörterbuch* (*AWB*) (Busse and Carstensen 1993, 1994, 1996) to identify word forms that are formally equivalent with English lexical material. As a first stage of elicitation, words that clearly showed graphemic and phonological markedness were identified. The remainder of lexical items on the word list was then checked for words that, despite being phonologically and graphemically unmarked in German, formally resemble English lexical items. These borderline cases were double-checked for a possible English origin by means of using etymological information available in several reference works, including the *AWB* (Busse and Carstensen 1993, 1994, 1996), the online version of the *Oxford English Dictionary* (*OED*), the etymological dictionaries *Duden Herkunftswörterbuch* (2014) and *Kluge* (Kluge and Seebold 2011), and a digital edition of the *Duden Fremdwörterbuch* (2015).

Following the identification of anglicisms according to synchronic criteria (see Onysko 2007), I also examined whether these words are established in the RL to identify novel anglicisms. First, anglicisms were checked for their appearance in common dictionaries. For this I used the *Duden online*, the *Duden – Die deutsche Rechtschreibung* (2013), the *AWB* (Busse and Carstensen 1993, 1994, 1996), the *IDS Neologismenwörterbuch* (2006ff), the *Kluge* (2011), the *Duden Fremdwörterbuch* (2015) and the *Duden Herkunftswörterbuch* (2014). Second, I used the *ZDL-Regionalkorpus* (approximately 6.1 billion tokens from 1993 to 2019) of the *Digitales Wörterbuch der deutschen Sprache* (*DWDS*) for a diachronic analysis in July 2020 to check for occurrences and frequency of all anglicisms that were not listed in common dictionaries, considering the meaning of each anglicism as used in the radio corpus. The *ZDL-Regionalkorpus* was chosen because it is a continuous corpus that covers a relatively long period of time (cf. Gottlieb 2015; Klosa-Kückelhaus and Wolfer 2020) and has a representative size. Like most large corpora, the *ZDL-Regionalkorpus* is based on media texts, in this case regional German newspapers. Even though this corpus represents the language used by print media, such large corpora that allow a diachronic analysis can be taken as an indicator of whether an anglicism is established in general language usage if the medium additionally aims to reach a broad audience. Newspapers usually target a large portion of the population and therefore their selection of topics and the language they use is fitted to the taste of this broad audience.

Based on a study by Gottlieb (2015), a frequency of 0.008 ppm (parts per million) was taken as the threshold below which anglicisms were considered as not established. In his study on established pseudo-anglicisms in Danish, Gottlieb (2015) determined this threshold value since some rare Danish pseudo-anglicisms which are known to most adult Danish speakers appear as seldom as once in 125 million tokens. For the *ZDL-Regionalkorpus*, containing approximately 5 billion tokens (in July 2020) for the relevant period from 1993 to 2016, this equals a maximum of forty occurrences for anglicisms to be included as novel in this study. Anglicisms that were identified as not yet established were examined for transfer and language-inherent processes involved in their word formation. Therefore, all novel items were checked in the *OED Online*, the *Corpus of Contemporary American English* (*COCA*) (Davies 2008) and the largest contemporary English corpus on Sketch Engine (*Timestamped JSI web corpus 2014–2020*) to look for possible usages of these items or possible role models in English.

4.4.3 Anglicism frequency

For the quantitative analysis, anglicisms were counted as units of meaning. This means that all multiword anglicisms were taken as one occurrence (e.g. *Public Viewing* and *made in Germany*) to give an actual account of anglicisms as used and most likely perceived by radio journalists in context. Since radio is a spoken medium, I determined the frequency of anglicisms in relation to the time recorded (anglicisms per minute). For this, all data and word lists gathered via WordSmith Tools 7.0 were transferred to Microsoft Excel for further analysis. For the determination of the frequency of anglicisms per minute, radio content of each recorded hour was cut appropriately to isolate spoken content, which then was evaluated for length with the audio editing software Adobe Audition. In addition to determining the frequency of anglicisms for the overall corpus and the six radio stations individually, I undertook further frequency counts per minute for station imaging, news and the rest of the spoken content including the genres of host talk, service and comedy. As previously mentioned, I will pay greater attention to the genre of station imaging in the analysis of anglicisms as it allows for insights into the image a radio station wishes to present to its audience to attract listeners in a competitive market. For comparison with other anglicism studies using broadcast media corpora, I will also briefly look at the frequency of anglicisms in adult contemporary radio news. Furthermore, to compare my results with previous studies on anglicisms in print media, I additionally calculated the overall frequency of anglicisms per 100 words.

4.4.4 Catachrestic/non-catachrestic analysis

For the catachrestic/non-catachrestic analysis, the radio corpus was split into station imaging materials and the rest of the spoken content (including the genres of news, service, comedy and host talk) in which anglicism occurrences were examined separately. The separate analyses were undertaken to give an unprecedented insight into the use of anglicisms in radio station imaging and to examine whether anglicisms are used differently by radio journalists in this genre. This includes an examination of self-promotional elements produced by radio stations, such as jingles, drop-ins, bumpers and image slogans. These promotional elements are worthy of our attention since they show, as I previously mentioned, how a station wishes to present itself to its target audience and therefore reveal a lot about a station's identity. The language used in station imaging materials therefore gives valuable insights into not only the promotion of a station's image but also how competition is dealt with amongst the different stations and sectors in the broadcasting system.

Following the basic detection of anglicisms in the corpus via synchronic criteria, various reference works were used for the identification of catachrestic and non-catachrestic anglicisms. These reference works include the *AWB* (Busse and Carstensen 1993, 1994, 1996), the *Duden Herkunftswörterbuch* (2014) and the *Duden Fremdwörterbuch* (2015) as well as the *OED Online*. For each of the anglicisms categorized as non-catachrestic, the *DWDS* and the *Duden Online* were used to identify appropriate semantic near-equivalents. Since many anglicisms occur in hybrid constellations, it was necessary to extract the base from all anglicisms (except for the analysis of lexical field; see below). If a compound contained more than one English element, each part of the occurrence was listed as an individual base anglicism. This rule was used only if the resulting lexical items, following this process of extraction, still represented a meaningful unit in German. According to this rule, an example of a catachrestic innovation from the corpus which was not split is *Public Viewing*.

Winter-Froemel, Onysko and Calude (2014) measure the success of anglicisms in terms of relative frequency by comparing non-catachrestic anglicisms with their semantic near-equivalents used in German. They use a top 100 list of anglicisms from a previous study by Onysko (2007) containing frequent English lexical types and their equivalents in German. In a large print corpus, they then determine the number of tokens of these anglicisms and their counterparts. In contrast to Winter-Froemel, Onysko and Calude (2014), I examined each anglicism in its actual context of usage in spoken content, which allowed for a thorough analysis of how these words are used on radio. In addition, I analysed the actual semantic and pragmatic effects of these innovations to investigate what equivalent could have been used for substitution of the non-catachrestic loan. Furthermore, in contrast to Winter-Froemel, Onysko and Calude (2014), it therefore was not necessary to exclude polysemous, homonymous and homographic English lexical items.

To acknowledge people's language worlds, I again applied both qualitative and quantitative linguistic methods in the analysis of the use of catachrestic and non-catachrestic anglicisms. In addition, I asked journalists about their use of these anglicisms and included statements from the qualitative interviews in the analysis. This allows for an exclusive insight into the language worlds of journalists that goes beyond focusing on structural patterns of language or *la langue* (cf. Winter-Froemel, Onysko and Calude 2014). Furthermore, the sociocultural contexts intimately linked to radio language and the characteristics of radio language are thereby acknowledged. To get a better understanding of why and how anglicisms are used on German radio, I investigated whether facilitating factors that, according to a study by Winter-Froemel, Onysko and Calude (2014), influence the success of some non-catachrestic anglicisms in German print corpora are also relevant in the context of radio language. Factors I will pay attention to are brevity, semantic reasons, lexical fields and diachronic development. This will also allow for an understanding of journalists' practices in relation to non-catachrestic anglicisms, and I will show how an analysis of these facilitating factors allows us to better grasp the complexities of journalists' language worlds.

Brevity is always a crucial factor for journalists when writing content for radio since long sentences and words can cause comprehension problems. As spoken language was analysed, word length of non-catachrestic anglicisms was determined via a syllable count. In Chapter 7, I show how a tendency towards brevity in expression affects the use of non-catachrestic anglicisms on radio. According to Winter-Froemel, Onysko and Calude's (2014) results, it seems that word length is less significant than semantic reasons. An analysis of semantic reasons in Chapter 8 gives insights into whether these are also a relevant factor for the use of anglicisms on radio and into the difference between the use of anglicisms and their German equivalents. It also sheds light on the use of anglicisms on radio in relation to modernity. In particular the qualitative interviews and a spatial approach acknowledging the materiality of the medium radio shed new light on the functions of anglicisms also in orchestration with other semiotic resources (see also Chapters 5, 7 and 8).

An analysis of lexical fields gives an insight into the connection between linguistic and cultural flows and how these are part of journalists' everyday work. All anglicisms found in the radio corpus, both catachrestic and non-catachrestic, were therefore put into different lexical fields. The list of lexical fields developed for the case study draws on a previous list of lexical categories by Busse (1993). I further refined this list to get a selection of lexical fields in the context of contemporary radio language. The refinements largely concerned the omission of obsolete categories such as *Brand names/Institutions*, which were not counted as anglicisms in this study, as well as the addition of further categories such as *Journalism* to address journalism-related terms. These refinements were made since Busse's list of categories, despite providing a useful and comprehensive overview of basic lexical fields, was rather outdated and at the time designed by him for the purpose of analysing the editions of the German general language dictionary *Duden Rechtschreibung* published between 1880 and 1986.

I determined a total of nineteen lexical fields, which allowed for a categorization of all anglicisms in the radio corpus (see Table 2). When the same anglicism appeared in two or more lexical fields, it was categorized as *General Language*. This is also consistent with the methods used by Winter-Froemel, Onysko and Calude (2014).

Previous studies have found many anglicisms in the lexical field of *General Language* (see Schaefer 2019; Winter-Froemel, Onysko and Calude 2014), which is mainly due to categorizing abstracted anglicism bases instead of words as actually used in context into lexical fields. Since hybrid anglicisms occur quite frequently in German (see Glahn 2002; Knospe 2014; Onysko 2007), an anglicism base can appear in various contexts and lexical fields depending on the German part of a hybrid compound. Hence, to minimize

Table 2 Categories of lexical fields applied in the radio corpus analysis.

Art/Culture/Education
Biology
Business/Employment
Consumer Goods
Food
General Language
Geography
Journalism
Law
Lifestyle/Fashion/Leisure
Media/Communication/Entertainment
Medicine
Music/Dance
Politics
Science
Sport
Technology
Transportation/Infrastructure
Travel/Tourism

the number of anglicism occurrences in the lexical field of *General Language* in the radio corpus, I undertook an investigation of anglicisms in different lexical fields according to lexemes of anglicisms and their meanings in context. This furthermore allowed for a thorough investigation of which lexical fields have experienced most shaping from transcultural flows. As part of this analysis, I undertook a separate examination of lexical fields of anglicism lexemes in station imaging materials.

In addition to the above-named factors, I checked all non-catachrestic innovations for whether they have undergone a diachronic development from marked to unmarked lexical choices or not (see Onysko and Winter-Froemel 2011). Anglicisms that have experienced diachronic development from M- to I-implicatures, as exemplified in Chapter 3, partly have lost their pragmatic markedness. As a result, these anglicisms are as pragmatically unmarked as their closely synonymous lexical equivalents in German. What is additionally characteristic for such pragmatically unmarked anglicisms is that they share

I-implicatures with their semantic near-equivalents and are close to default terms in German. Diachronic development compares to the notions of sedimentation (Canagarajah 2013) and entrenchment, which makes a shift in implicatures a measure of sedimentation. My intention with this analysis is to show whether the fact that an anglicism has experienced diachronic development or not impacts its use on radio. I will present the results of the analysis of brevity, lexical field, semantic reasons and diachronic development in relation to the use of anglicisms in Chapters 5 to 8.

4.5 Exploring language worlds: Interview-based research

The interview-based part of this research is informed by the linguistic quantitative and qualitative analysis of anglicisms in the radio corpus. Qualitative interviews give valuable insights into the language worlds of people and, in the case of this research, allow to speak directly to the hosts and presenters and other journalists working in editorial positions responsible for the content produced by the selected radio stations. All interviews were undertaken in a semi-structured format and face to face with each of the interviewees individually. This means that even though questions were prepared prior to the actual interviews, the interview questions only served as a basis. This way, the interviews were more flexible and turned into conversations that shed light on not only how radio content is produced but also, from the individual's point of view, how journalists talk about anglicisms and what shapes their word choice on air. Especially the possibility to ask follow-up questions for further clarification, which is a benefit of semi-structured interviews in contrast to structured interviews where the sequence of questions is predetermined (see Brennen 2017), allowed to get an understanding of each participant's individual experience of using English on air. These personal experiences of interviewees are essential for understanding their language choices.[13]

I conducted a total of nineteen interviews for which the quantity was determined partly by the availability of participants and partly by the scope and feasibility of the case study. This resulted in an interview phase of a period of over 3 months. Each interview was scheduled to be approximately 1 hour in length, and to avoid possible language barriers that could affect the interview data, I conducted all interviews with journalists in German. Furthermore, all interviews were conducted on location in Germany, either at each station or at a public meeting place where I met my interviewees at the close of their working hours. Since one of the three private stations (Private Station 3) decided not to participate in the interview part of the research project, interviews were conducted with professional journalists working for five out of six stations of which content was searched for anglicism occurrences. Each interview was taped and later transcribed.

Interviewees were selected based on their participation and function in the morning shows and in the morning show teams of the radio stations chosen in this study. To get a wide range of perspectives and a deep insight into practices at the station, the aim was to get both the writers and producers of the content broadcast for interview as well as the people working in the background responsible for the decision-making of what content gets broadcast. Therefore, journalists who present content on air including hosts; sidekicks; news, weather and traffic presenters; content producers; and journalists who work in positions with editorial responsibilities for all elements of the morning show content, including station imaging, were chosen as potential interview partners. All interviewees were over 18 years of age, and no preferences were given to gender, age or other characteristics which could have biased the results.[14]

The key themes of the interview questions were determined according to the research questions and aims of the case study as well as guided by the influencing factors on media language and journalistic practices as outlined in Sections 4.2 and 4.3. In addition, all questions for the interviews were based on the findings from the quantitative and qualitative data analysis. The thematic questions aimed to explore the spatiotemporal context of radio language and content production and therefore focused on the role of broadcasting in society, on journalistic practices and working routines, and on competition between sectors and stations. In addition, further questions were asked on the topics of globalization, language change and language contact, and on popular culture to develop an understanding of journalists' language worlds. In all cases of the nineteen interviews, participants were asked similar questions, except where not applicable for a journalist's specific role at a given station and where additional questions came up in conversation with each interviewee.

4.6 Acknowledging complexity

In this chapter I have covered quite a lot of important ground, starting from what a new perspective on language mobility – which is to view language as a spatial repertoire that includes socially constructed language ideologies – can mean for overcoming the gap between the two paradigmatic perspectives and therefore ultimately for overcoming the theory–practice gap. I have suggested that a spatial approach – instead of constituting a mere antithesis to the structuralist paradigm, as it is currently promoted in critical sociolinguistics and applied linguistics (Canagarajah 2020; Pennycook 2020a) – allows us to consider linguistic structuralism as part of the assemblage of language, as part of the social resources within the spatial repertoire. The result of this is not mere fluidity or fixity but complexity – complexity of mobile resources on various spatiotemporal scales that permeate our lifeworlds and come together in a single moment of meaning-making.

Furthermore, I suggested that such an approach requires us to adopt a flat ontology, which goes beyond the binary of text–context and considers how diverse actors and resources including human and animal, animate and inanimate, cultural and natural, or material and cognitive stemming from different scales of space and time become 'entextualized' in communicative activity. Again, such a flat ontology, however, should not exclude structure, fixity, hierarchy, boundaries and limitations but acknowledge these as an intrinsic part of socially constructed realities and therefore of the language worlds of people.

Against the background of these considerations, I then offered some ideas on what such a holistic, spatial approach could look like in the case of media language, and I proposed an analytical model for an investigation of media language as a spatial repertoire. Finally, by the example of anglicisms in media language, I outlined possible methods for a socially grounded spatial approach to language that includes people's language perceptions. For this, I drew on a combination of corpus-based quantitative methods, qualitative contact linguistic methods and qualitative interviews with the actual language users. In this context, I iterated the value of gathering and examining data that give us an insight into socially meaningful categories of language use as well as into the voices and opinions of the actual language users.

So what do the language worlds of actual language users such as German adult contemporary radio journalists look like? How do journalists make meaning on air and what spatial and temporal factors shape this social practice? We will now embark on a journey into the lifeworlds of German adult contemporary radio journalists and will discover the depths of a socially grounded spatial approach in Chapters 5 to 8. In this context I would like to highlight that the themes presented in Chapters 5 to 8 do not represent the groupings of influences of the Media Language Model. Instead, against the theoretical background of a complex interplay of influencing factors, these four themes emerged from the case study as the major themes we need to draw our attention to in the case of German adult contemporary radio. These themes therefore illustrate the complex entanglement of various factors from the four groupings of influences in the Media Language Model.

5

Global Cultural Flows

The focus of this chapter is on how the global/cultural environment shapes the use of English linguistic resources by journalists on radio and therefore on the intrinsic link between Englishes and globalization. Previous studies in critical sociolinguistics have shown that the processes of accelerated globalization are important factors that need to be acknowledged when phenomena of language development are analysed (Blommaert 2010; Fairclough 2006; Pennycook 2007, 2020b). I will join this current discourse and make my argument by acknowledging increased mobility as a major cause for the frequent appearance of English linguistic resources on German radio. My intention with this chapter is therefore to give insights into how global cultural flows become embedded in radio language. For this, I discuss journalists' use of anglicisms on radio in the light of asymmetrical hybridization in Germany in Section 5.1 (see also Chapter 2). The analysis of the global/cultural environment as a source of authority centres that shape the language worlds of journalists will include viewpoints of journalists on matters of cultural and linguistic mobility in times of accelerated globalization and their language attitudes and opinions on the present situation of language development in Germany. In addition to journalists' opinions on the matter from the qualitative interviews, the effects of transcultural flows on German adult contemporary radio language are further investigated through an analysis of lexical fields of anglicisms in the radio corpus (see Section 5.3).

5.1 Why English?

Looking at globalization and how it is intrinsically linked to language in the case of English requires us to look not only at the global but also at the local. In this chapter, I argue that asymmetrical hybridization is very much present in the lifeworlds of German radio journalists. I will show that while the omnipresence of English is viewed differently amongst journalists, whenever English is used on radio it is locally appropriated. As taken from the interviews, cultural, social and historical contexts play a crucial role when it comes to language choice on radio, especially regarding the use of English linguistic resources. One journalist of Public Service Station 2 answered the question of why English terms are used in German as follows:

> Dadurch, dass die Engländer die größte Kolonialmacht waren, dadurch dass … Engländer und Amerikaner Alliierte in Deutschland waren und dass die Amerikaner seit dem 2. Weltkrieg das gesamte Kulturleben weltweit so massiv beeinflusst haben, dass jeder dahin wollte und dass jeder das cool fand. Das fing wahrscheinlich nach dem 2. Weltkrieg mit irgendwelchen Stockings an und Chewinggum und Lucky Strike … und das hat halt so eine Markenwelt geprägt. Also Jeanshosen, wie man früher noch sagte, waren dann cool und dadurch haben die Leute das dann als modern und fortschrittlich begriffen.

> (Due to the fact that the English were the biggest colonial power, due to the fact that … the English and Americans were Allies in Germany and that the Americans after the Second World War have influenced the entire cultural life so greatly around the world that everyone wanted to go there and thought of that to be cool. That probably started after the Second World War with stockings and chewing gum and Lucky Strike … and that has shaped the brand environment. Thus, jeans trousers, as one used to say back then, were cool and hence people conceived this as modern and progressive.)

This statement is in line with other comments made by many interviewees from both broadcasting sectors, who stated that the post-war period and in particular American consumer culture have since had an effect on language and culture in the locality of Germany (see Faulstich 2006; Stephan 2006; Willett 1989). Some journalists additionally mentioned a widely prevailing perception in the German society that America stands for a guiding culture and that the Hollywood film industry still affects language and culture in Germany.

As discussed in Chapter 2, especially when it comes to German journalism, the BBC and American journalism in general functioned as role models in Germany after WWII. The resulting radio formats and broadcasting styles, professional terminology, and the commercialization of journalism in the Federal Republic all shaped the kind of journalism that is practised in Germany today. This clearly supports notions of asymmetrical hybridization in the case of Germany. Proximity was also mentioned in this context by a journalist who stated that if something happens in America, it is automatically of greater importance to Germans than if something happens outside of the Western world. This asymmetry of cultural flows in the context of Germany is explained by a public service journalist as follows:

> Das ist eine Kulturfrage. Wir haben seit 1945 eine ganz stark westwärts gewandte Kultur. Immer noch empfinden wir viele Dinge ... die von dort kommen als weit vorne, als trendsetzend. Ich wüsste nicht welchen Trend wir aus Bulgarien, aus der Mongolei oder aus Sibirien in den letzten Jahren hier integriert hätten. Also das ist komisch. Und die Sachen gelten auch oft als uncool. Ich meine, wir hätten ja auch die Chance gehabt nach der Wiedervereinigung Begriffe aus der DDR zu übernehmen, die zum Teil auch lustig waren, auch mit einem gewissen Witz in der Alltagssprache. Nichts, das galt einfach nicht als cool.
>
> (That is a question of culture. Since 1945 we have a very strongly westward oriented culture. We still perceive many things ... that come from there as advanced, as trendsetting. I cannot think of any trend from Bulgaria, from Mongolia or from Siberia that we have integrated here in the last few years. Well, that is strange. And these things are also often regarded as uncool. I mean, we would have had the chance to adopt many terms from the GDR after reunification, which partly were funny too, also with a certain humour in everyday language. Nothing, that simply was not regarded as cool.)

This journalist was even more critical on the matter and mentioned the use of English in German in the context of cultural imperialism.

> Jetzt hast du eher einen Kulturimperialismus. Amerika galt immer als wegweisend und letztlich glaube ich in vielen Dingen ist es auch trotzdem noch so.
>
> (Nowadays what we have is more likely cultural imperialism. America has always been viewed as pioneering, and I believe that in the end in many cases it is still this way.)

However, the extent of American influence throughout the twentieth century was not the only explanation journalists gave for the widespread dissemination of English. A journalist working for Public Service Station 2 stated:

> Na, ich glaube, das hat sich schon seit dem 2. Weltkrieg eingebürgert und wahrscheinlich schon seit der Kolonialzeit. Also es ist halt einfach die Lingua Franca, hö hö.
>
> (Well, I believe that has already been established since the Second World War and probably already since the colonial age. Well, it simply is the lingua franca, ha ha.)

This journalist's slightly cynical remark on the function of English in intercultural communication hints at another explanation for the use of English in German that frequently appeared throughout the interviews. While mostly journalists in their late forties and above explained that anglicisms are used in German as a result of the Allied occupation time after WWII, many journalists in their twenties and thirties held a different opinion. Many younger journalists stated in the interviews that they believe that English is simply 'the' lingua franca. These statements show that journalists almost take it for granted that they do not use any other language besides German to such an extent as English in their wordings on air. MacKenzie states that 'English has become an additional language rather than a foreign language' (2012: 28) for many Europeans, and this increased proficiency in English leads to an even greater diffusion of English across Europe – a phenomenon that can certainly be observed in Germany and many other countries, such as France, Spain and the Netherlands (see Gerritsen et al. 2007; Zenner, Speelman and Geeraerts 2012). In this context, English is associated with the concept of globalization by several journalists and becomes a symbol of interconnectedness for them:

> Heute glaube ich, überwiegt einfach, dass wir in Zeiten der Globalisierung und der weiten Reisen einfach mit Englisch super gut durchkommen überall und deshalb ist es so geläufig geworden.
>
> (I believe that nowadays it prevails that in times of globalization and in times of travelling far we simply can get through with English very well everywhere and therefore it has become so common.)

One of the younger journalists who worked for Private Station 1 even stated:

> Englisch ist erstmal aus einfachen Gesichtspunkten halt nun mal die Weltsprache; das hat sich irgendwie mal so vor Jahren durchgesetzt.
>
> (English is first of all from a simple perspective the world language; this has gained acceptance somehow sometime years ago.)

The topos of *English as a world language* was often linked by journalists to other social and cultural developments, as the following interview statements show. A journalist working for Public Service Station 3, for example, gave a broad range of reasons surrounding the idea of English being the world language:

> Na ja, Englisch ist die Weltsprache. Ich glaube es kommt natürlich viel durch die Popmusik, Rockmusik, die halt eben von da kommt, zustande. Du hörst heute viel mehr diese Künstler. Mehr Menschen sind der englischen Sprache mächtig überhaupt durch die Schule. ... Finde, es ist alles nicht mehr so weit weg, wie das früher mal war.

(Oh well, English is the world language. I think it is a lot due to pop music, rock music, which simply comes from there. One listens far more to these musicians nowadays. More people master English after all because of school. ... I believe, everything is not as distant anymore as it used to be.)

This statement is insightful in many ways as it indicates that cultural products and commodities – in the case of radio in particular pop and rock music – as well as their distribution throughout the world become associated by journalists with the global diffusion of English – a perception that also shapes their language use on air. In this context, we are reminded of Pennycook's work on hip-hop, in which he examines the influence English exerts on other languages through music culture and argues that English is 'bound up with transcultural flows, a language of imagined communities and refashioning identities' (2007: 6).

The above statements made by the interviewees additionally indicate that these journalists view the English language as a separate code to German and assume an omnipresence of English around the world. Moreover, the latter part of the last interviewee's statement connects the *world language* topos to language education. Since people are in greater contact with deterritorialized cultural products due to greater mobility and interconnectedness, they learn more English in school because it becomes increasingly necessary for intercultural communication. Another journalist working for Public Service Station 3 also made a similar remark, connecting the diffusion of English not only to the myth that English was once officially declared a world language – a common folk belief in Germany frequently discussed in public discourse (cf. Gutberlet 2007) – but also to the role of the German education system in this context:

> Wann war diese Entscheidung, was so quasi die Weltsprache ist. Da gibt es so dieses Gerücht, dass es um eine Stimme nicht Deutsch geworden ist. Ich habe es bis jetzt darauf geschoben. ... Also warum es jetzt aktuell so ist, ist in der fünften Klasse beginnt jeder Schüler in Deutschland glaube ich mit Englisch als erster Fremdsprache.

> (When again was the decision made, what so to speak is the world language. There is this rumour that by one vote it wasn't German. So far, I've blamed it on that. ... So, the reason why it is the way it is at present, is that in fifth grade every pupil in Germany starts with English as a first foreign language I think.)

This reveals that state power in relation to language is taken for granted and is consented to by this journalist. The German state actively fosters the usage of English as a lingua franca through the compulsory tuition of English in its education system, which clearly shows that the state on the one hand reacts to global pressures and changes but on the other hand contributes to the asymmetrical hybridization process. The general aim of German foreign language education in schools is to prepare citizens for the communicative challenges posed by European integration and internationalization of markets.[1] Therefore, the state actively shapes the outcomes of globalization processes in relation to language.

Other forces, however, also play a part and shape these outcomes, which especially becomes evident when we apply a view of globalization as 'a more "niched" complex of processes, developing at several different scale-levels, some of them truly global, others regional, national or even sub-national' (Blommaert 2010: 77). The state is a strong normative power which sets language standards by means of applying labels such as English and German, native and foreign to language in formal education systems. On a local level, however, individuals have growing repertoires of truncated and multifaceted resources, and speakers are subject to a complex web of authoritative forces that affect their speech behaviour, consisting of other individuals (such as the editor in the case of radio media), collectives (such as colleagues at the radio station) and abstract ideas (such as the radio format), of which the state is only one part (Blommaert 2010). Therefore, by applying a more nuanced view, we can acknowledge an imbalance of global flows and at the same time a local appropriation and resemiotization of linguistic and cultural resources in the case of Germany, of which anglicisms are an example.

This resemiotization includes, technically speaking, not only the use of inflectional affixes as in the borrowing *rocken* (to rock) but also pre- and suffixation of borrowed bases as in the hybrid anglicism *herumsurfen* (to surf around) and derivations of borrowings such as the verbal anglicism *brunchen* (*to brunch). A further example of resemiotization are pseudo-anglicisms such as *Profi* (professional) and *Beamer* (digital projector), which are, as outlined in Chapter 3, language-inherent creations. These consist of English lexical material that is given a new meaning in German which is unknown in English. The adult contemporary radio corpus contained 491 hybrid types (lexemes) and 21 pseudo-anglicisms (lexemes). This shows both local appropriation and language productivity on German adult contemporary radio. In addition, when one looks at the token frequency of hybrid cases with 1,287 tokens found in the corpus in comparison to borrowings, which occurred 1,764 times, it becomes evident that hybrid anglicisms occur quite frequently on radio, especially as these make up 40.5 per cent of the overall number of anglicisms detected in the corpus. This is slightly higher compared to the frequency of 37 per cent of hybrids in Glahn's

(2002) television corpus. The medium radio and its characteristics, as outlined in Section 1.2.2, call for a concise language that makes it rather easy for the target listener to understand what is broadcast and this is where hybrid anglicisms come in handy. According to Pfitzner (1978), processes of compounding including the formation of hybrid compounds are also prominent in German journalistic speech in print media (see also Knospe 2014; Onysko 2007). In these processes, semantic information that would otherwise be incorporated in a multiword syntactic element in a stretch of discourse is compressed into a single lexical item. This makes hybrid anglicisms ideal for short and precise language use by the media.

Taken together, the interviews highlight that the use of English in German is perceived by radio journalists as the result of an imbalance in cultural flows, either through a perceived US hegemony in post-war times or through the present hegemonial status of English. As previously outlined, what is needed to explain this omnipresence of English is to adopt a position that allows to take a long-term view on processes of globalization. 'What matters, rather than either celebrating or bemoaning hybridity, or bemoaning its passing, is understanding the process and the *longue durée*' (Nederveen Pieterse 2009: 93). The spread of English should not simply be regarded as a symptom of Americanization since this only allows a limited view on linguistic and cultural changes in Germany. While an Anglo-American impact on German language and culture through Allied powers in the immediate years after WWII has certainly been the case, the hybridization position does not ignore such a scenario but places it in the larger frame of continuous hybridization.

> Relations of power and hegemony are inscribed and reproduced *within* hybridity for wherever we look closely enough we find the traces of asymmetry in culture, place, descent. Hence, hybridity raises the question of the *terms* of mixture, the conditions of mixing. At the same time, it's important to note the ways in which hegemony is not merely reproduced but *refigured* in the process of hybridization.
> (Nederveen Pieterse 2009: 80; italics in original)

Despite their awareness of an asymmetry in global cultural flows, many journalists of both sectors believe that societies gradually move closer together and that long distances and closed borders are no obstacles anymore. Some journalists stated that especially through increased mobility and interconnectedness, also because of digitalization, there is a growing tendency towards internationalisms which transcend language boundaries. By and large, most interviewees seem to view the current use of anglicisms in German more as a positive development reflecting cultural and linguistic mixing, rather than as an actual decline of German culture. One journalist working for Public Service Station 2 even elaborated on this by hypothesizing:

> Wäre es nicht geil, wenn alle Leute auf der Welt dieselbe Sprache sprechen würden? Zum Beispiel Englisch.
>
> (Wouldn't it be great if all people on earth would speak the same language? For example, English.)

He explained that this way it would be a lot easier to communicate and to avoid misunderstandings between different cultures. The presenter further added that for him this would also support international communication and exchange, whereas with the situation in the world today, one is still not able to communicate on the same level with everyone around the globe due to linguistic differences proliferated by various national language policies. Although this view is problematic in many ways, as it raises questions in relation to linguistic and cultural diversity, it nevertheless clearly shows the positive attitude towards 'anglophone cultures' and an acceptance of English and its increased use in German.

In contrast to this presenter, however, other journalists who seemed genuinely open-minded towards other cultures nevertheless stated that if English were used too much in German, it would have a strong effect on German culture – an effect they would not necessarily like. One journalist in an editorial position at Public Service Station 2, for example, stated that although he considers using anglicisms in German a rather positive development, he also finds it silly when people solely use English and thereby disown their own culture. What we can take from this is that it seems acceptable for many journalists to make use of English, however, not to push it too far by using it extensively if there is no proper reason since an excessive use would not be appropriate, especially in the context of their radio format. A further but again different argument on the matter was made by a journalist working for Public Service Station 3, who described the relationship between language, culture and tradition as not limited to established cultural habits:

> Mich treibt so ein bisschen dieser Traditionsbegriff um, weil ... ich habe gemerkt, dass eine Tradition ... immer dann funktioniert auf lange Frist, wenn sie sich entwickeln darf. Und wenn da Sachen reinkommen, Einflüsse / und da könnte man die Anglizismen in der Sprache auch dazurechnen. Eine Sprache ist halt dann lebendig, wenn neue Begrifflichkeiten ihren Weg reinfinden, wenn neue Ausdrucksformen ihren Weg reinfinden.

(What troubles me a little is this term tradition, because … I noticed that a tradition … always works in the long run if it is allowed to develop, and when things enter the tradition, influences / and one could add anglicisms in language to this. A language is simply then alive, when new terms enter it, when new expressions find their way into the language.)

Looking at this statement, we can assume that for this journalist the spatial repertoire is enriched by cultural traditions that are not in a wider sense stable but mobile and change, which automatically enriches language rather than endangers it. From the point of view of Blommaert's (2010) paradigm of a sociolinguistics of mobility, the repertoires of language communities are not fixed by tradition and therefore bounded entities but instead comprise the conceptual frames of all the mobile linguistic resources available to their members.

It is worth noting at this point that journalists nevertheless do not deconstruct boundaries between languages and cultures. As the above statement by this public service journalist shows, language is regarded by him as both a process and entity independent of human action. Although the current state of language mobility and asymmetry in global cultural flows is viewed by journalists as a process in which language and culture are in a continuous state of flux, this ongoing change is largely viewed as an enrichment to the German language through another language and culture and is based on notions of otherness and heterogenization. While many journalists see themselves more as European citizens than as German nationals or at least equally as both, the following statement once more highlights that journalists base notions of mixing on separate, geographically bound languages and cultures. A journalist in an editorial position at Public Service Station 2 described the relevance of the English language and British and American culture in their programme as follows:

Das braucht man natürlich in der Branche sowieso. … Sie werden hier kaum jemanden finden, sage ich mal, in so einer Welle, der sagt, „ich mag England, Irland oder die USA nicht", weil wir alle eben diese kulturelle Nähe dazu haben. … Wer hier arbeitet ist da automatisch ja mit infiziert.

(Of course, one needs this in the profession anyways. … You will hardly find anyone around here, I mean in such a station, who says, 'I don't like England, Ireland or the USA', since we all have that cultural affinity to it. … Everybody who works here is automatically infected by that.)

As can also be taken from this statement, journalists who work for adult contemporary formats have an affinity to 'native English-speaking cultures', mainly the United States and Great Britain, since these cultural areas are connected to the music and the people these stations are focusing on. In the next section, I will elaborate on how these language perceptions are realized in the use of English linguistic resources and in semiotic assemblages on air (see also Chapter 8).

5.2 Mobility, mediascapes and radio language

As previously outlined in Chapter 1, adult contemporary radio needs to contain the semiotic resources necessary for journalists to communicate effectively with their target audience on topics of interest to their listeners, which mainly relate to pop music culture. In Blommaert's words, the audience's interests in popular culture set language standards and norms on this scale which journalists need to comply with to satisfy the expectations of the target listener towards the programme broadcast. The use of English resources is a central element of this. What is worth noting in this context, however, is that by using English linguistic resources not everyone's expectations (outside of the targeted listenership) are satisfied and not everyone has access to this scale. This especially concerns those people who are older than the target audience and may not share this affinity to such cultural forms or largely do not understand these English terms. Since these people do not communicate on the same scale level, out-scaling takes place. In the context of adult contemporary radio, this out-scaling is automatically linked to segmentation of the target audience (see Chapter 6). This means that journalists need to be aware of the limits of the scale they communicate on. The format of adult contemporary clearly has a connection to what is frequently termed 'anglophone culture' and therefore, naturally, a certain number of English linguistic resources are part of the language used in this radio format. However, if there is a chance that the target listener does not understand what is meant, English terms or phrases are generally translated, explained, contextually explained, or avoided and a German equivalent or paraphrase is used instead. Examples from host talk in the radio corpus include:

(8) Vielleicht is' ja ein Beamer eine Alternative, also so ein Projektor. Dazu Tipps auch gleich noch bei uns.

(Maybe a *Beamer* is an alternative, that is a digital projector. Tips on this from us here in a minute.)

(Public Service Station 2, 2 June 2016)

(9) Außerdem haben wir gehört heute früh ..., dass wir diese Curved-TVs, diese gebogenen, eigentlich nich' unbedingt brauchen.

(We also heard this morning ... that we don't really need these curved TVs, these curved ones.)
(Public Service Station 2, 2 June 2016)

As the following statement of a host of Public Service Station 1 shows, journalists know that access to linguistic resources is unevenly distributed within the population and therefore care needs to be taken not to exceed the linguistic resources available to their target audience when using anglicisms excessively.

Wir schließen ja keinen aus, wenn wir Hochdeutsch sprechen, aber wir schließen aus, wenn wir Englisch sprechen.

(We don't exclude anybody if we talk in High German, but we do exclude people if we talk in English.)

As the interviews have shown, journalists seem to orient towards what is often referred to as 'High German' in public discourse – a form of spoken German that is regarded as 'correct German', close to written standard German and therefore as having supraregional reach (see Beuge 2019) – which journalists regard as generally intelligible for their listeners. This again highlights the taken-for-grantedness of the monoglot standard amongst radio journalists. For most interviewees 'High German' also includes established anglicisms, which is an example of how mobile linguistic resources can become sedimented as part of local language practices (Canagarajah 2013). While I will come back to a thorough discussion on the use of English linguistic resources in relation to comprehensibility in Chapter 7, I will first focus on codeswitching or, to be more precise, on English multiword units in this context.

Multiword codeswitches performed by journalists and English-language audio clips played on air offer valuable insights into German adult contemporary radio's entanglement in wider flows of popular and pop music culture. Multiword codeswitches appear in the radio corpus as intrasentential switches and intersentential switches, which both represent different practices of linguistic boundary negotiation. Intrasentential codeswitches occur as switches between sets of linguistic resources within the sentence or clause level and as both obligatory and non-obligatory sentential constituents. Especially obligatory codeswitches are an example of how various sets of resources are amalgamated in translingual practice for meaning-making purposes. Intersentential switches, on the other hand, appear as grammatically complete clauses or sentences in a stretch of discourse and therefore constitute cases in which speakers uphold socially constructed language boundaries.

Due to their additional syntactic dimension, especially multiword codeswitches can cause comprehension problems in a society in which access to linguistics resources is unevenly distributed amongst the population and the stations' targeted audiences. Even though English is taught as a first foreign language in German schools, as I previously mentioned, translanguaging in the sense of frequent codeswitching still exceeds the linguistic resources available to most members of the adult contemporary target audience. Short multiword units or individual words of such syntactic units, however, may be understood by the target listener – or at least the overall message of the codeswitch may be understood – through the assemblages created by journalists. This is the case for the use of short multiword switches from the field of pop and rock music on adult contemporary radio (see Examples (10) and (11)), where it is likely that the audience has come across such phrases in music-related talk before.

By using multiword codeswitches on air, journalists pursue communicative aims beyond the purely linguistic level of meaning. This means that multiword codeswitches are also used to achieve communicative success on a wider semiotic and deeper sociocultural level, where English has an emblematic function. On the verbal level, as we can see in Examples (10) and (11), the salience of multiword codeswitches is used to attract attention on radio and to sound funny or cool, which mostly underlies stylistic motivations. On a deeper cultural level, however, the switches in Examples (10) and (11) bear cultural reference to anglophone music cultures.

(10) *We rock the ocean* und gucken hinter'm Horizont was abgeht.

(We rock the ocean and look beyond the horizon to see what's going on.)
(Udo Lindenberg [audio clip], Public Service Station 1, 14 April 2016)

Example (11)

Time (sec.)	Beat of music (x) / Speech								Music
0.0–1.9	x	-	x	-	x	-	x	-	Alle Farben feat. YouNotUs 'Please Tell Rosie' (chorus)
	Host:								
	Put	your	**hands**	up	**in**		the	**air**	
2.0–3.9	x	-	x	-	x	-	x	-	
	Host:								
					Prei-	sel-	**beer'**		

Note: Stressed syllables of radio host's speech in **bold**.

(Public Service Station 3, 17 May 2016)

The two examples are intrasentential switches that show how translocal pop music culture becomes localized and integrated in the radio stations' programmes. The sentence in Example (10) is part of a promotion piece for a cruise and spoken by a famous German rock musician, who hosted the cruise and gave concerts on board. A cruise conveys the stereotypical image of a relaxation trip and not of a rock concert, which indicates the originality of the event. Since the promotion piece already contains other phrases that indicate the type of event promoted, such as 'Lust auf eine rockige Kreuzfahrt?' (Fancy a rockin' cruise?), the codeswitch used as part of the piece does not bear any additional essential information on a purely linguistic level. It has, however, an emblematic function since it refers to the atmosphere the audience can expect on the cruise. By switching into English, it is made clear to the audience that the cruise centres around Anglo-American rock music culture and light entertainment.

The sentence containing the codeswitch in Example (11) was spoken by a host in rhythm with the chorus of the English-language song 'Please Tell Rosie' by Alle Farben feat. YouNotUs. Through the rhyme of English *air* with German *Preiselbeer'* (lingonberry), the codeswitch functioned as an attention-grabber for the following announcement that this new song, which became popular at the time, will be played later on the show. Furthermore, this English phrase is also used at international concerts and in English-language pop songs, which is where the audience may have come across this phrase before. Therefore, even if the multiword switch may not be understood by a listener on a purely lexical level, it has the emblematic function to convey this international atmosphere in relation to pop music culture while at the same time integrating Anglo-American pop music culture into local cultural practice through the rhyme across constructed linguistic boundaries.

The excerpt in Example (12), taken from a report about a David Guetta concert at the European football championship, shows a typical intersentential switch, which was used by a foreign correspondent. Before considering the codeswitch, it is important to look more closely at the transmodal assemblage of this example. The report contains narrations recorded in studio and on-location recordings from the concert. However, since ambient noises from the concert are played throughout the piece, this does not become evident from a difference in acoustic background between narration and on-location reporting. Instead, it is the materiality of the recording environments and recording devices that contributes this part of the overall meaning. Due to the differences in technical equipment (studio microphone vs. portable recorder) and acoustic characteristics of the recording locations (indoors vs. outdoors), the journalists' voice has a fuller, warmer and clearer sound when recorded in studio. The radio audience can therefore infer from the semiotic assemblage that the codeswitch occurred while the reporter was on location. As becomes evident from the multimodal orchestration of different sounds in the piece, the correspondent performed translanguaging with a French concertgoer and drew on English to facilitate communication – a situation which represents the use of English as a lingua franca that many of my interviewees referred to. The codeswitch used in this piece, unlike the other two examples from the radio corpus, was additionally translated by the correspondent due to a change of interlocutor and therefore a change of scale. Through translating the English phrase, the journalist addresses the target audience at home in Germany. This change of scale between situated personal interaction and professional reporting for a remote audience is therefore expressed in the intersentential switch between language resources. Simultaneously, the English codeswitch performed by the correspondent at the concert to communicate with another concertgoer has an emblematic function as it symbolizes the international atmosphere at the concert for the German audience and thereby creates authenticity. The sound of English 'I go crazy' in combination with the soundscape of a pop music concert allows the listener back in Germany to be part of this international event (for a more detailed semiotic analysis of this example see Schaefer 2022). The three examples discussed recall the statements made by journalists in the previous section on

Example (12)

Time (sec.)	Speech	Music	Sounds
43.3–45.9	C (STUDIO): Aber alle haben nur auf ihn hier gewartet. (But everyone has just been waiting for him.)	hip-hop music, live, French lyrics	ambient noises of crowd
46.0–50.0	F: *David Guetta. Sa voix.* (His voice.) David. **Wow!**		
50.1–52.5	C (CONCERT): **I go crazy.** Ich werd' verrückt. (I go crazy.) David Guetta.		
52.6–54.8	F: **David Guetta, the real David Guetta. Uh!**	concert live music played in background	
54.9–63.0	C (STUDIO): David Guettas Heimspiel, der DJ ist ja gebürtiger Pariser, war eine Sensation. Unter dem Eiffelturm auftreten zu dürfen, das machte ihn schwer glücklich. (David Guetta's home match, the DJ is a native Parisian, was a sensation. To be able to perform beneath the Eiffel Tower made him really happy.)		

Note: C correspondent (in STUDIO or at CONCERT); F French concertgoer
German: standard font; English: **bold**; French: *italics*
English translations in parentheses.

(Private Station 1, 10 June 2016)

English as either being connected to Anglo-American culture or having a greater international appeal through its use as a lingua franca.

In addition to multiword codeswitching, English-language audio clips appeared around twenty times throughout the radio corpus. The only spoken clips played on radio besides clips in German were English-language clips, which is a further indicator for an asymmetry in cultural flows. These English-language clips were usually quotes from celebrities such as Barack Obama (Example (13)) or English-speaking musicians (Example (14)).

> (13) 'He has spent years meeting with leaders from around the world. Miss Sweden, Miss Argentina, Miss Azerbaijan.'
> (Barack Obama [audio clip], Public Service Station 3, 2 May 2016)

Example (13) was used in the context of a report on the White House correspondents' dinner and was played to give the listeners a taste of the jokes that former President of the United States Barack Obama made about the then presidential candidate Donald Trump. This clip was translated afterwards by the host since it was not assumed by the journalists that this clip is understandable for the target audience.

> (14) 'Oh, it's fantastic. Oh, she's a talent, she's a huge talent and it was a real / an honour again, you know.'
> (James Bay [audio clip], Private Station 1, 8 April 2016)

In Example (14), a quote was played from an interview with a singer at the ECHO awards, who talks about his experience of singing with another German singer. The quote was not translated but played twice throughout the morning show and commented on by a private host as follows:

> (15) Ja, der schwärmt hier total über Sarah Connor, mit der is' er aufgetreten.
> (Yes, he is raving here about Sarah Connor, with whom he performed.)
> (Private Station 1, 8 April 2016)

Concerning short and rather easily understandable English sentences, this host later explained in the interview that they generally think that the audience can understand such simple clips. However, as can be taken from this example, additional hints were nevertheless given by the host in his broader explanation following the clip. The host's comment, containing the most important message of the clip, functions to guarantee that everyone in the audience understands the message. Therefore, as the practice of this host shows, this station's journalists do not automatically expect their target listeners to understand short English clips. What is relevant to note in this context is that according to a host working for Public Service Station 3 such native English clips are, nevertheless, not dubbed either since

> wenn du einen englischen Künstler abspielst, dann will ich hören, wie der klingt. Also das finde ich unmöglich, da direkt drüber zu reden, also dann sollte wenigstens die Originalsprache etwas frei stehen. Ich meine, du spielst ja auch englische Musik, ja, also von daher finde ich das vollkommen wirr, zu sagen, „dann wollen wir den aber nicht reden hören". … Es ist immer viel schöner / also gerade, wenn jemand ein Sänger ist, den reden zu hören und zu wissen, wie der klingt, wenn der spricht.

> (when you play an English artist, then I want to know what he or she sounds like. Well, I find it impossible to dub it directly, then the original speech should at least stand in parts on its own. I mean, you also play English music, well, therefore, I find it completely confused to say, 'but then we don't want to hear him or her speak'. … It is always way nicer / well, especially when someone is a singer, to hear him or her speak and to know what he or she sounds like when he or she talks.)

In line with this journalist, one of her colleagues stated that they wish for their target audience to get an idea of what a celebrity sounds like. According to some journalists working for both sectors, such clips are an important emotional component in their show. Therefore, it appears that for many stations the cultural authenticity of the original quote and the idea of hearing the actual voice of a celebrity is an effective communicative device on radio. This shows that the cultural connection between English-language songs and the English-speaking musician who sings the song or has produced it shall give the listener a sense of proximity to the global product. The following example further confirms the role of English clips for such purposes.

> (16) 'It should be a big party, it's not my usual crowd but yes we're gonna have fun, that's the point.'
> (David Guetta [audio clip], Public Service Station 3, 10 June 2016)

This example is remarkable for two reasons. First, the statement was made by a French DJ regarding his concert at the opening ceremony of a fan area around the Eiffel Tower in Paris in the context of the French-hosted European football championship. It is therefore an example of a musician giving interviews in English to reach his global audience, although it is not his 'mother tongue'.

Second, it can be assumed that the radio station that played this clip would have also been able to avail of a recording of an interview in French, especially due to the setting of the interview. Considering the statements of journalists above, to reflect the cultural atmosphere of this event – a French musician giving a concert in his hometown Paris beneath the Eiffel Tower – a French-language clip that gives the listener an impression of what this celebrity sounds like in his 'mother tongue' would have been much more effective. The station's use of a clip of a musician speaking English with a French accent therefore demonstrates how much the global music culture is shaped by English and that the station expects their target audience to be more attracted by the sound of an English-language clip than by a clip in the musician's 'mother tongue' French.

In contrast to such clips, longer interviews with English-speaking celebrities are usually dubbed or translated following the original interview since, according to the interviewees, the target audience cannot be expected to understand lengthier English-language interviews. According to a journalist working for Public Service Station 3:

> Anders sieht es jetzt zum Beispiel wieder aus bei englischen Interviews. Wenn Leute sehr lange eine fremde Sprache verfolgen sollen, wird es anstrengend. Also das machen wir zum Beispiel in der Morningshow auch grundsätzlich nicht, englische Interviews, weil das einfach … vom Verfolgen her kompliziert ist.

> (The whole thing looks different with English interviews for example. When people have to follow a foreign language for a very long time it gets stressful. Well, that for example we strictly do not do in the morning show, English interviews, since that is … complicated to follow.)

This explanation furthermore highlights that the German language is regarded as domestic while other languages are perceived as foreign, which again indicates the journalists' orientation towards an ideology of a monoglot standard of language competence. Regarding the use of English-language interviews, a journalist in an editorial position stated that they

> setzen in der Regel nicht voraus, dass jemand Englisch versteht. … Die meisten verstehen irgendwie so ein bisschen was und können ein bisschen Englisch, aber selbst dann ist es, wenn man es nur im Radio hört und es so an einem vorbeirauscht und zum Teil nur leise ist und so, und man nicht Muttersprachler ist oder es regelmäßig auch hört, einfach schwierig.

> (generally do not expect that one understands English. … Most people are able to somehow understand a little and are able to speak a little English, but even then, if you only hear it on the radio and it rushes by and partly is not really loud, and one isn't a native or hears it on a regular basis, it is simply difficult.)

As becomes evident from the three interview statements above, cultural authenticity and a certain proximity to the cultural product are important when English-language clips are played; however, comprehension is clearly prioritized. If comprehension on behalf of the audience is not guaranteed, the cultural message attached to English-language pieces, which is to create a close connection between the listener and the global products of pop music culture, cannot be fully transmitted. This, according to the interviewees, would make the use of such clips ineffective on radio.

One public service journalist further explained that in the past most of these clips were dubbed directly, often also because of time constraints. Nowadays, such clips are usually translated afterwards instead of dubbed to bring out the cultural authenticity of the clip, which indicates a change in radio language and that it has become increasingly important to get greater proximity to the 'foreign' product on a global scale. This reminds us of the concept of transcultural flows (Pennycook 2007) and the relevance that cultural connectivity to the global music market, shaped by a hegemony of English (see Demont-Heinrich 2020), has for adult contemporary radio stations. These changing practices also bring me to the last point I want to make here. When I asked whether they have noticed a significant change in media language over the last few years, the interviewees held different opinions. While it appears that some journalists do not notice a change, a host working at Public Service Station 1 stated:

> Ja, man registriert es, aber ich glaube wir haben nicht mehr den Anspruch / Also früher waren wir Sprachvorbild. Ich glaube, das ist eine andere Rolle. ... Ich glaube heute ist der Anspruch klar, wir wollen so sein wie unsere Hörer, so sprechen wie unsere Hörer, nicht besser, nicht schlechter. Und wenn alle so reden, dann reden wir halt auch so, weil wir Nähe wollen, und Nähe bedeutet Quote letztlich.

> (Yes, one notices it, but I think we do not have the aspiration anymore / In the past we were language role models. I believe that is a different function. ... I think that today the aspiration is clear, we want to be like our listeners, we want to talk like our listeners, not better, not worse. And if everyone talks like that then we talk like that too, because we want to have proximity, and proximity in the end means audience ratings.)

Other journalists additionally mentioned that new technologies such as the internet have changed media language, which makes cultural practices associated with new digital media an example of transcultural flows that leave their traces on German media language. This also recalls the concept of linguascapes and their entanglement with other scapes (Pennycook 2003).

To find out in which domains global cultural flows have the greatest impact on radio media language, I will turn to lexical fields of anglicism lexemes in the following section. Since the mass media and the images they disseminate are themselves part of cultural flows (Appadurai 1996), I will show how adult contemporary radio stations in Germany position themselves within these global cultural currents through the image they wish to present to their target listener via station imaging elements. The following section reveals which cultural domains and therefore lexical fields German adult contemporary radio stations draw on to create their very own station image and how anglicisms used in the overall radio corpus contribute to this.

5.3 Investigating lexical fields

The analysis of lexical fields of catachrestic and non-catachrestic anglicisms in the overall radio corpus shows that nearly one-fifth of all lexemes containing lexical elements of English origin are used in the lexical field of *General Language* and hence could not be placed in an individual lexical field (see Figure 2). A substantial number of types of anglicism lexemes were, however, found in the lexical fields *Lifestyle/Fashion/Leisure*, *Media/Communication/Entertainment* and *Music/Dance*. The rather large number of types in the lexical field *Music/Dance* is due to the specific context of adult contemporary radio language, where many anglicisms such as *Pop*, *Hit*, *Song* and *Mix* are disseminated alongside American and British pop music culture (see appendix Table A.1 for a list of anglicism lexemes found in the radio corpus and their respective lexical fields). In addition, all anglicisms detected in the lexical fields *Lifestyle/Fashion/Leisure* and *Media/Communication/Entertainment* fit well into the adult contemporary radio format, which due to its American role model is open to many words accompanying asymmetrical cultural flows of the mediascape.

Other lexical fields that show a rather large number of anglicisms, as depicted in Figure 2, are the lexical fields of *Technology*, *Sport* and *Journalism*. In particular, the relatively large number of anglicism types found in *Technology* highlights the influences of transcultural flows that accompany modern technology or, in Appadurai's (1996) words, the technoscape. Examples of such anglicisms include *Smartphone*, *WhatsApp* and *Mail*. The large number of anglicisms in the lexical field *Sport* again fits well into the radio format of adult contemporary since many topics are in fact related to sport due to its popularity amongst the radio format's target audience. Parts of the radio programme in which anglicisms

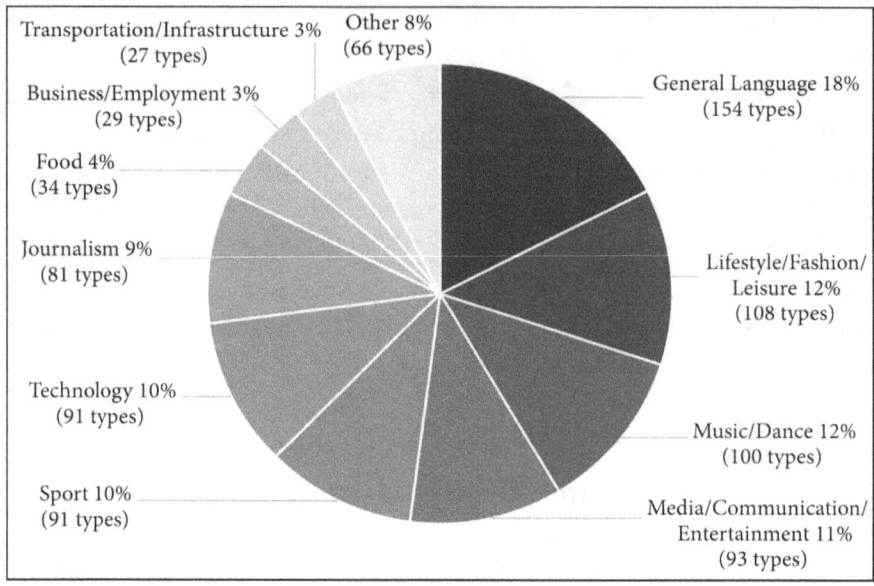

Figure 2 Lexical fields of anglicism lexemes (types) in the overall corpus.

related to sport were found include not only sports news but also promotions of events related to sport and sports betting. What is also worth noting in this context is that, in addition to the usual number of sports-related topics as part of the morning show, two weeks were taped at the time of the European football championship in 2016, which may have additionally affected this result. Examples from the lexical field of sport found in the corpus include the anglicisms *Trainer* (trainer) and *Coach* (coach), *Downhill* (downhill), *Derby* (derby), *Foul* (foul), *Fitness* (fitness) and the hybrid compound *Surfbrett* (surfboard).

In her study on anglicisms in Austrian public service television and radio news, Sagmeister-Brandner (2008) concludes that many anglicisms enter journalistic speech due to opinion leaders such as politicians. The case study presented in this book does not confirm this since only a small number of anglicisms were found in the lexical field *Politics* in the radio corpus (1.3 per cent, included in *Other*). In addition to the very small portion of anglicism types coming from the field of *Politics*, none of the interview sources mentioned politicians or other opinion leaders as having an effect on their language choice on air.

The station imaging corpus contained anglicisms from thirteen out of a total of nineteen lexical fields. As the results have shown, the lexical fields *Music/Dance*, *General Language*, *Lifestyle/Fashion/Leisure*, *Media/Communication/Entertainment* and *Journalism* have the highest number of catachrestic and non-catachrestic anglicism types. The content of station imaging materials mainly consists of words that function to promote the station's image. Some lexical fields in station imaging are therefore predetermined mainly due to the product that is advertised, in this case the station itself, its music, programme, and a station's hosts or events. Hence, the high frequency of anglicisms in the two lexical fields of *Music/Dance* and *Media/Communication/Entertainment* is not surprising. Anglicism occurrences such as *Song* and *Beat* come from pop music culture and therefore function to promote the music genre the station plays. The high number of anglicism types in *General Language* benefits the comprehension of such lexical items in the context of radio language since those words in general language usage are in most cases easier for the listener to follow.

For promotional purposes of events organized by the station, the non-catachrestic anglicisms *Party* and *Event* from the lexical field *Lifestyle/Fashion/Leisure* were frequently used. In the same vein, anglicisms such as *Show*, *live* and *Tickethotline* occurred frequently to promote off-air events organized by the stations. As can be taken from these results, pragmatic markedness of non-catachrestic anglicisms seems to be beneficial for the promotion of events organized by the stations and contributes to the overall presentation of the radio stations' image (see Section 6.4 for a further discussion on pragmatic markedness of anglicisms).

The frequent use of anglicisms in *Journalism* seems to be attributable to two reasons. First, German journalism culture has for a long time been shaped by the cultural influences emerging from journalism in the United States and the UK. Many journalism-related terms are borrowed from English and serve as productive bases in German. Examples include *Update* (update), *Reporter* (reporter), *Interview* (interview) and *Service* (service). Some of the borrowed terms, such as *Reporter* and *Interview*, have even lost their pragmatic markedness for speakers of German and hence function as standard terms. According to the *AWB*, *Reporter* was first documented in a German dictionary in 1880 and *Interview*, in 1887. Second, anglicisms in the lexical field of *Journalism* that have additional pragmatic meaning are used by journalists to attract the listeners' attention to certain parts of the morning show. Examples of such salient names for programmes or programme parts include *Markencheck* (brand check), *Wettertrend* (weather development) and *Verkehrsservice* (traffic news).

During the analysis of lexical fields in the station imaging part of the radio corpus, one repeatedly played imaging element, however, showed linguistic features that did not coincide with the general trend observed in other station imaging elements. With this particular station imaging element, Private

Station 3 promoted its image of being a regional broadcaster, and it contained no non-catachrestic anglicisms at all since the private station used German terms from general language use instead. Examples include occurrences such as *schönsten, glücklich, Familie* and *in Ordnung*, for which they could have used *coolsten, happy, Family* and *okay* instead since these English lexical items also appeared in several other parts of the overall corpus including in Private Station 3's morning show content. It becomes evident that for this private station, non-catachrestic anglicisms, besides for the purpose of promoting a service, event or music, are not regarded as suitable for all areas of self-promotion. This shows that, in cases where non-catachrestic anglicisms are used, the rather frequent usage of such anglicisms from a certain domain may be dependent on the communicative intent of the message. In addition, this different choice of linguistic resources also helps journalists to adopt a voice that highlights their strong connection to their *Heimat*. This again shows the dichotomy of portraying a global versus local identity and how specific language resources appear as tied to places and cultural practices: English is global; German is local.

The qualitative interviews have further confirmed that the communicative intent of a message is generally relevant for word choice on radio. A host from Public Service Station 2 stated that he personally would only use the anglicism *Special* instead of its German equivalent *Sonderausgabe* when referring to a soft news story[2] on the internet and this host added:

> Aber ich würde niemals sagen, „zu dem schweren Eisenbahnunglück mit dreißig Toten haben wir im Netz ein Special". Das würde ich niemals sagen, sondern dann würde ich immer sagen, „dazu finden sich auch alle Informationen bei uns im Netz".

> (However, I would never say, 'we have an online special on the fatal train accident causing the deaths of thirty people'. That I would never say, but rather I would always say, 'all related information can additionally be found on our website'.)

In this example the communicative intent is evidently one of informing about a hard news topic rather than about a soft news story, and the use of the non-catachrestic anglicism *Special* therefore appears less suitable. Furthermore, through this choice, the presenter adopts a serious, trustworthy voice as opposed to a more laid-back entertaining style and thereby constructs his on-air identity, also shaped by the communicative intent of the message and the genre conventions on radio.

Another example that confirms this finding is the use of the non-catachrestic anglicism *Mix* in the radio corpus. As the quantitative analysis of the corpus revealed, *Mix* occurs 175 times either as an independent lexical item or as part of compounds throughout the corpus, while its near-equivalent *Mischung* amounts to only four tokens. The analysis of the two terms shows that in the context of weather announcements *Mix* (ten tokens) as well as *Mischung* (three tokens) are used to describe a mix of sunny spells and scattered clouds. However, for the promotion of a station's music selection, *Mix* is used exclusively by journalists. This shows that in the context of weather announcements the German equivalent *Mischung* as well as the anglicism *Mix* seem appropriate to use for radio journalists. Both words serve the communicative intent of informing about the weather and are used interchangeably for variation purposes. In contrast, *Mix* appears as the only appropriate term in relation to music on adult contemporary radio since the communicative intent here is to promote the music selection a station plays, which adds to the station's image and identity.

5.4 English linguistic resources and asymmetrical hybridization in Germany

I pointed out in this chapter how German radio journalists think about the use of anglicisms in the light of the global/cultural environment and how this larger context shapes their language worlds and language perceptions. The interviewees were asked about their viewpoints on why English is used in contemporary German and why in the present context no other language has the same impact on German instead. To sum up my discussion in this context, it remains to be noted that overall the results from the interviews show that there is no uniform answer to these questions. There seems to be, however, a tendency towards generational viewpoints. Journalists who are around 40 years of age and above mainly mentioned the impact of the United States after 1945 on the Western world including Germany as a reason for the current presence of English. As another explanation for the dissemination of English in Germany, younger journalists pointed towards the use of English as a modern world language. English, according to these journalists, is necessary for international communications and therefore taught early in German schools, which was also given as a reason for why it is ultimately used in German. Therefore, younger journalists see the usage of English in German more as a consequence of its omnipresence in a globalized world today than caused by an American cultural influence having emerged in post-war times.

This viewpoint shared by the younger generation of journalists reminds us of Tomlinson's (1991) thoughts on cultural imperialism and that, according to him, such a concept should in the contemporary world be replaced by globalization. In line with Tomlinson, it also recalls Becker's (2006) claim that globalization in the present German context is the more appropriate term in contrast to Americanization. Even though a perception of being subject to Americanization for most journalists is not part of their lifeworlds, the term 'globalization', as proposed by Tomlinson and Becker as an alternative to designate the reasons for cultural change, is nevertheless not appropriate in this context. As we have seen, it is a rather vague term that blurs the imbalance of cultural flows and the power these flows exert in the locality of Germany. When we combine the viewpoints of both generations of journalists, bearing in mind both the historical and the current context of language and cultural developments in Germany, we are reminded of the notion of asymmetrical hybridization.

The analysis of the radio corpus and the examination of the interview statements have revealed that the global/cultural environment shapes adult contemporary radio formats and at the same time is an intrinsic part of social practices on radio. The format of adult contemporary radio in Germany is itself an example of asymmetrical hybridization since, as I outlined in this chapter, the format is traversed by popular culture originating from the United States and Great Britain. This focus on pop culture is to a large extent expressed through the music mix of adult contemporary stations in Germany (see also Section 1.2.1). The music mix is the primary reason why people decide to turn on the radio and listen to a station. Additionally, the structure and style of the adult contemporary radio format, mainly adopted from American role models, contribute to the popularity of the morning programmes.

As can be taken from the analysis of the corpus and from the interviews with journalists, processes of asymmetrical hybridization become especially evident in radio content through the use of exclusively English-language clips. This matches with the music playlists of the stations examined in this study, which contain predominantly English-language titles. I will come back to this in Section 7.3. Especially the fact that most clips of English-speaking celebrities and musicians are played without direct dubbing – to give the audience a feeling of proximity and cultural authenticity – is indicative of the acceptance of English but also illustrates the cultural connectedness towards English-speaking countries.

Multiword codeswitching in the radio corpus confined itself to short multiword switches which were used for emblematic purposes on a deeper cultural level, to sound funny or cool, and to attract attention on a linguistic level. Especially the use of multiword codeswitching to evoke deeper cultural meanings relating to Anglo-American popular culture and pop music, and to create an international atmosphere for the listener, is in line with journalists' perceptions of English as an international language closely tied to popular culture.

While the interviews have revealed that the separateness of languages is largely taken for granted amongst journalists, most journalists regard anglicisms as a rather positive language development. Some journalists also mentioned that language is in a continuous state of flux, which does not necessarily mean that tradition or culture is lost. Other journalists, however, also disagree on the matter and treat anglicisms with greater caution by means of trying not to use these excessively. An intense usage of anglicisms to many interviewees would not be effective on radio since it would seem unnatural and therefore artificial to the target listener.

In this chapter, I also looked at lexical fields of anglicisms and in which lexical fields transcultural flows are most influential. Besides appearing frequently in the lexical field of *General Language*, anglicisms are also frequently used by radio journalist in the lexical fields of *Lifestyle/Fashion/Leisure*, *Music/Dance* and *Media/Communication/Entertainment*. The large number of anglicisms in these three lexical fields can mainly be attributed to the format of adult contemporary based on its American role model, which is susceptive to asymmetrical cultural flows from the mediascape. The analysis of lexical fields in station imaging has revealed that a high quantity of anglicism tokens was additionally used in the lexical field of *Journalism*, which in the overall corpus was not amongst the lexical fields with the highest number of anglicism tokens. Since station imaging functions to promote the station and its image amongst the target audience, many anglicisms were part of wordings created by the stations to designate parts of their programme, such as their music selection. In such wordings anglicisms such as *Hit*, *Mix* and *Song* were frequently used. Hence, the high quantity of anglicisms in the lexical field of *Music/Dance* in station imaging materials is not surprising. Overall, against the background of asymmetrical hybridization, the analysis of lexical fields turned out to be a useful method to shed light on how global cultural flows become part of the language worlds of radio journalists.

6

Competition and Segmentation

The German dual broadcasting system, divided into a public service and private sector, and the two different kinds of competition – economic and editorial (see Gundlach 2010; Hoffmann-Riem 1991; Weischenberg 2004) – are spatiotemporally situated within the grouping of influences of the media system but also connected to the larger network of factors of all four groupings of influences in the Media Language Model. The German broadcasting system is an example of asymmetrical hybridization, where traditional European public service broadcasting, modelled after the BBC, is combined with a commercial sector shaped by an American role model. In this chapter, I will show that this duality of the German broadcasting system is a factor that shapes language choice on radio. In the analysis of the quantitative corpus data and the qualitative interviews, two points turned out to be particularly relevant in this context: first, the audience each station targets and the segmentation processes behind this, and second, how the image a station wishes to present to its listener shapes the language used by journalists working for competing stations and sectors. This also includes acknowledging the role of the imagined audience, which, as mentioned in Section 4.2.3, has been found to shape journalistic content (Bauer 1958; Pool and Shulman 1959; Ross 2014). In relation to language choice, findings by Bauer (1958) and Pool and Shulman (1959) are consistent with Blommaert's (2010) concept of polycentricity, according to which different imagined audiences act as authority centres. These authority centres simultaneously shape the language produced by journalists. In addition to competition, I will look at how German broadcasting regulation based on the *Rundfunkstaatsvertrag* (Interstate Broadcasting Treaty) shapes the use of English linguistic resources by German radio media.

6.1 The role of the target audience

According to Hesmondhalgh, a 'significant and much discussed change since 1980 has been that more and more texts are produced for particular segments of the audience rather than a "mass", undifferentiated audience' (2019: 444). Even though adult contemporary stations generally aim for the same listenership in terms of age, their target audiences in this age group vary. As a presenter of a public service station explained:

> Ich glaube schon, dass es auch wichtig ist, dass jeder [Sender] so ein bisschen auch seine Nische hat, und dass es auch unterschiedliche Angebote gibt, wo jeder [Hörer] sich ein Stück weit aufgehoben und angesprochen fühlt.

> (I think that it is also important that everyone [station] somewhat has their own niche and that there is an availability of different offers, where everyone [listener] feels in a way to be in good hands and addressed.)

These different audiences that broadcasters target may depend on the geographic reach of the broadcaster, the broadcasting landscape a station is situated in, the particular focus a station places on its music selection and the organizational form of the station. One journalist of Private Station 1 stated that aiming for a local audience is of benefit when competing with their public service opponent. Concerning the private sector, the broadcasting law regulating this broadcasting landscape prioritizes the establishment of local radio stations, and in 2016 the private sector was organized as a network of local stations. Another journalist of the same private station stated that especially their focus on locality allows them to go deeper into local issues in their reporting, which would not be feasible for their public service competitor.

In addition, target audiences vary in terms of education. Journalists working for Public Service Station 2 in a different broadcasting area stated that in their programme they put more emphasis on information since their actual audience contains the highest proportion of higher-educated listeners of all stations on the adult contemporary market. The focus of stations regarding their target audience can therefore also be placed on different social strata, which, according to one of the journalists working for this station, also affects their language use on air. A journalist in an editorial position of Private Station 2 explained that their programme mainly targets a female listenership since their actual audience consists of approximately 60 per cent female listeners, which turned out to be their particular market segment. Two hosts of Public Service Station 1 further described the social groups targeted by their station as people who according to marketing studies are success-oriented, work-oriented or take a great interest in their family life. This means that not only demographic criteria are relevant for defining a station's target audience, but personal characteristics of the listeners are also central. The aim is therefore not only to target certain social groups but also, more specifically, each station has a model listener they wish to address. A journalist from Private Station 1, for example, explained that the core listener they have in mind when writing content is a middle-aged, settled family man with two children. During one of the interviews at Public Service Station 3, a journalist working in an editorial position directed me to a poster which represented the core listener whom all their staff producing content should always have in mind. The poster depicted a woman in her thirties and included a list of her personal characteristics and interests. This so-called model listener represented the imagined audience for this station. Therefore, the imagined audience is also a centre of authority shaping journalists' choices of topics and the coverage they produce (see Bauer 1958; Pool and Shulman 1959; Ross 2014). In this particular case, the imagined audience has even become part of the material ecology of the radio station through its material representation on a poster that is visible to all staff in the newsroom.

Furthermore, many of the interviewees working for both sectors stated that they wish to adapt to their target audience not only in relation to topic choice but also in relation to the audience's preferences when it comes to language use. A journalist working in an editorial position for Private Station 2 stated:

> Also wir wollen so reden, wie die Menschen reden, für die wir senden und da überlegen wir schon genau auch, benutzen wir zum Beispiel Fremdwörter; das ist auch so ein Riesenthema bei uns.

> (We want to speak in the same way as those people for whom we broadcast and for that we think carefully about, for example, do we use foreign words; that is also a huge topic at our station.)

In this context, two hosts working for Public Service Station 1 mentioned the audience's reactions regarding particular wordings on radio for which the hosts avoided catachrestic anglicisms and used uncommon literal translations of these English lexical items instead. One of the two hosts explained that his creative German translation *heiße Leitung* (*hot wire), instead of using the anglicism *Hotline*, led to a lot of positive audience feedback since his idea of highlighting the taken-for-grantedness of English linguistic resources in everyday German by deliberately avoiding such words was acknowledged and appreciated by their listenership.

> Ich habe mir einen Spaß daraus gemacht, den Begriff Hotline nicht zu benutzen und gesagt „unsere heiße Leitung ist jetzt geschaltet." Das klingt natürlich für viele total bescheuert, aber es sollte eigentlich nur den Sinn haben, dass wir uns ab und zu wieder klar werden … warum sollen wir nicht wo es geht auch deutsche Begriffe benutzen. … Da gibt es Hörerbriefe und Anrufe und so, „ey das finde ich klasse, dass Sie da heiße Leitung gesagt haben, nicht Hotline". Gibt es eben auch sofort Reaktionen auf sowas, weil es auffällt.

> (I made a joke out of not using the term *Hotline* and said, 'our hot wire is now open'. Of course, this sounds completely ridiculous to many, but it was only meant to remind us every once in a while … why not use German terms whenever possible. … We get letters from listeners and calls and they go 'ey I think it is great that you said hot wire instead of *Hotline*'. You get immediate reactions for that because it stands out.)

The second host explained her use of the rather uncommon German loan translation *Heimseite* instead of the anglicism *Homepage* on radio. This journalist, too, explained that their listeners love exceptional word choices and generally like such wordings

> weil sie originell sind und auf originelle Formulierungen stehen unsere Hörer immer, wenn sie hochdeutsch sind.

> (because they are original and original phrasings are what our listeners always go for, if these are in High German.)

These examples show that language boundaries bear social meaning in the language worlds of these two journalists and that they at times also engage in practices of boundary maintenance to receive appreciation from their listeners. In this sense, socially constructed language boundaries do not impair radio journalists in their language use but instead can be used by them for their own purposes. In addition, this host stated that when their wording does not appeal to their audience, for example when they use anglicisms perceived as unnecessary, listeners immediately write to them in studio, asking why they do not use a German equivalent instead. Therefore, according to the findings of the interviews, word choice stands in relation to the image journalists create of their target audiences' language preferences and whether a journalist wishes to appeal to his or her audience. The latter is crucial in the morning show situation, where the likeability of the personalities of hosts and presenters impacts rating figures and therefore is essential for a station to remain competitive in the market (Buchholz 2017). This is again consistent with findings by Pool and Shulman (1959), who conclude that some journalists wish to get appraisal by the target audience for the content they produce and therefore base their communicative behaviour on the reactions they expect to get from their audience.

Furthermore, the interviews have revealed that journalists sometimes even make use of anglicisms that do not match their own language preferences and thereby try to adapt to the language of their model listener. Regarding his use of the phrase *live performen* instead of its German near-equivalent *auftreten* (to perform live) when promoting a musician who was to perform at a concert organized by his station, a host of Public Service Station 3 explained:

> Also wenn ich zu Hause am Kaffeetisch sitze, sage ich live auftreten. Aber wenn es um Musik geht, unsere Hörer musikaffin sind ... also da glaube ich, hat es sich durchgesetzt ja, „geil performt, ey hat der geil performt". Der Begriff, dass der zielgruppenaffin ist, dann bin ich ja Dienstleister meinem Hörer gegenüber. Also, ich will Auftritte auch nicht ausschließen, das findet sicher auch statt. Aber da [performen] weiß ich, dass sich die Zielgruppe damit wohl fühlt, die die wir anpeilen.

> (Well, when I'm at home sitting at the coffee table, I say *live auftreten*. But concerning music, our listeners are attracted by music ... well there I think it has established itself, 'awesome performance, ey he gave an awesome performance'. The term, that it is target audience specific, then I am service provider for my listener. Well, I don't want to preclude *Auftritte*, this of course will occur too. But here [*performen*] I know that the target audience feels comfortable with this, the one that we aim at.)

The above statements made by the interviewees show that the discourse around anglicisms and their necessity in German and on radio is very much part of the language worlds of journalists and their audience. In addition, these statements show the complex role of the target audience, which both as an imagined and actual audience functions as a centre of authority that shapes the linguistic resources used on air and sets orders of indexicality. This is in line with observations made by Weischenberg, Löffelholz and Scholl (1998), who state that the target audience is the major source of influence external to the media organization that shapes journalistic work in Germany.

When I asked whether competition also has an impact on their language choice on air, a journalist working for Public Service Station 1 stated:

> Ja, auf jeden Fall ... wir sind voll in dieser Kommerzialisierung, auch als Öffentlich-Rechtliche, sind den Regeln des Verkaufes komplett unterworfen und insofern wird man eine Sprache wählen, mit der man meint, dass man dieses Publikum kriegt auf eine Art und Weise.

(Yes, of course … as public service broadcasters we too are completely involved in this commercialization, are subjugated to the rules of marketing, and insofar one will choose a language by which one believes that one can get this audience in a certain way.)

In contrast to this statement, a journalist from Private Station 2 stated that competition has no effect on their language choice whatsoever. Even though most journalists did not specifically name competition in relation to word choice on air, what can be taken from the overall results of the interviews is that most journalists wish to adapt to the language of their target audience. This strategic language use, however, is ultimately linked to segmentation and therefore is the result of competition. Thus, through segmentation, adapting language to how it is used by the target audience leads to competitive advantages for a station on the radio market. The following two sections will deepen the discussion on competition and segmentation starting with an overview of the quantitative results of the use of anglicisms by different broadcasting sectors and stations.

6.2 Anglicism frequency

While the results of the quantitative analysis of anglicisms in the radio corpus were generally used to inform the qualitative analysis and the interview part of the case study, I have included the results of the frequency counts in this chapter since there is a close connection between anglicism frequency, competition and segmentation, the target audience, and a station's image. My intention with this section is to mainly give an idea of the use of anglicisms between the two broadcasting sectors and amongst the individual radio stations, which will support the discussions of the following sections and chapters. As I previously outlined, the quantitative part of the case study mainly involved determining the frequency of anglicisms in relation to the time recorded (anglicisms per minute). In addition, I determined the frequency of anglicisms in relation to the total word count of the overall corpus (anglicisms per 100 words). Both types of counts additionally give an idea of the scope of anglicism use on German adult contemporary radio in comparison with previous studies on anglicisms in broadcast and print media. While I compare my findings from 2016 with mostly older studies, these studies are in terms of their spatiotemporal scope nevertheless most relatable to the present study as they allow for an overview of the quantitative dimension of anglicisms used in larger traditional mass media corpora in the German-speaking area.

Figure 3 depicts the results for anglicism unit occurrences for each of the broadcasting sectors per minute. These show a higher token frequency for the private sector by 13.3 per cent, which indicates that the differences between the sectors have an effect on the quantity of anglicisms. This calls for further investigation in Chapters 6 and 7. The overall results for both broadcasting sectors show an average of 2.57 anglicisms per minute in the adult contemporary radio corpus (or 1.57 anglicisms per 100 words). In comparison to Glahn's (2002) analysis of a television corpus, whose results have shown that an anglicism was used every 56.5 seconds, the analysis of this radio corpus has revealed that an anglicism is used every 23.4 seconds. This means that compared to Glahn's quantitative results twice as many anglicisms are used in German adult contemporary radio content. Furthermore, Glahn (2002) follows Betz's (1959) typology and therefore, unlike the present study on radio language, he includes conceptual transmissions in his anglicism count. Therefore, if conceptual transmissions were included in the count of anglicisms in the present study, the frequency of anglicisms per minute would be even higher. Onysko (2007) found 1.11 anglicism occurrences per 100 words in his study on a print corpus of the German news magazine *Der Spiegel*. Furthermore, Knospe (2014) found a total of 1.27 anglicisms per 100 words in *Der Spiegel* issues of 2006 and 2007. Again, if Onysko's (2007) and Knospe's (2014) method to count anglicisms word by word and not as units of meaning were applied to the radio corpus, the

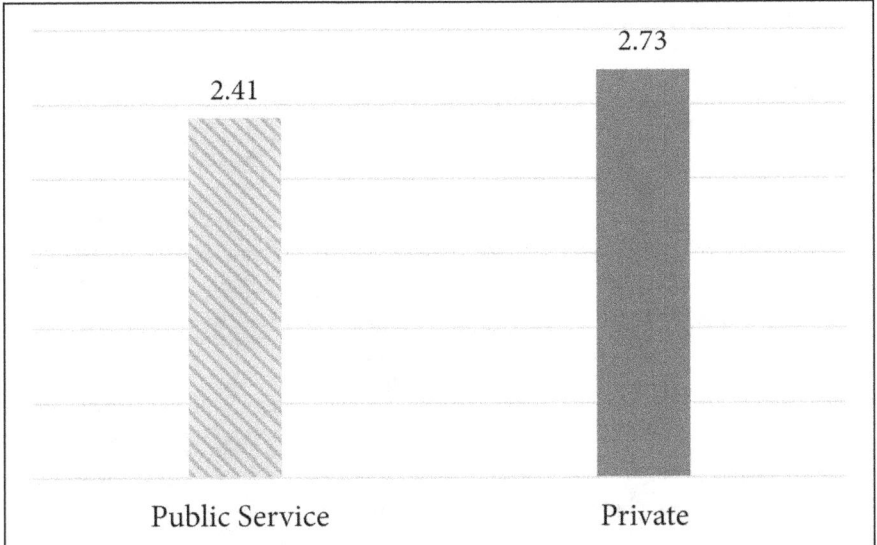

Figure 3 Token frequency of anglicisms per minute for each sector.

frequency of anglicisms would be even higher (1.60 anglicisms per 100 words). In her study from 2004, Adler found an average of 1.14 anglicisms per minute in a German public service radio corpus of four different stations compiled in 2001. While Adler's definition of what constitutes an anglicism is similar to the one applied in this study, none of the four stations examined in her study belongs to the format of adult contemporary. The large difference in anglicism frequency compared to the results of anglicisms per minute for the public service sector of the present study may therefore be attributable not only to the temporal difference between the datasets of the two studies but also to the characteristics and the sociocultural context of the format of adult contemporary.

When broken down into each of the six stations, as shown in Figure 4, it becomes evident that Public Service Station 3 uses most anglicisms per minute and Public Service Station 1 uses the least anglicisms per minute of any station. This is rather striking when we compare these results to the private sector, in which each station uses anglicisms nearly equally as frequent. The results indicate that each of the public service stations follows a different strategy when it comes to reaching their target audience. The private sector on the other hand seems to follow a more standard success model for reaching its individual target audience, which may be due to their market-driven orientation. I will elaborate on these findings in Section 6.3, where the interview results will shed further light on the matter.

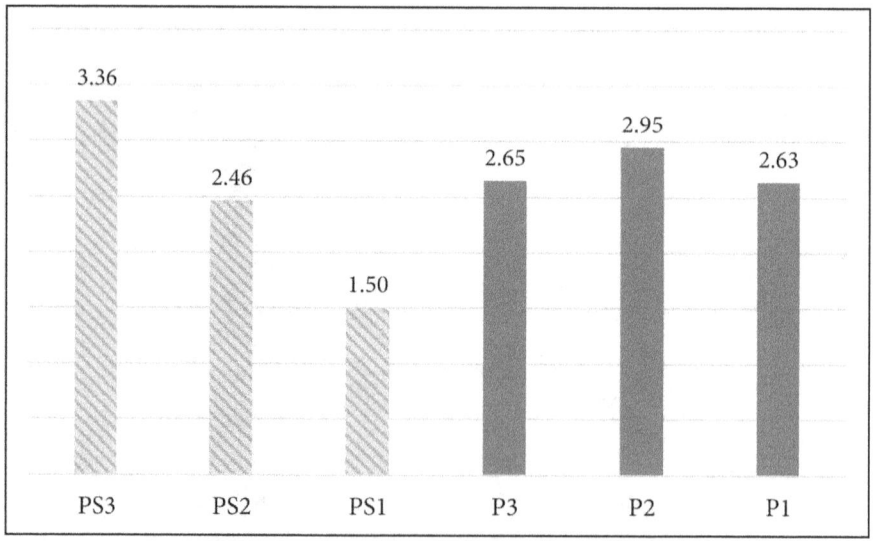

Figure 4 Token frequency of anglicisms per minute for each station.

When we split the results shown in Figure 3 further into station imaging, news and the rest of the spoken content, it becomes evident that most anglicisms are used in station imaging (see Figure 5). This can be mainly attributed to the function of station imaging in a competitive radio market, which is to attract the listener to the radio station, its hosts, services and music. In the case of adult contemporary programmes, mostly the service and the music of the station are promoted (see Chapter 1). Furthermore, several studies such as by Piller (2003), Gerritsen et al. (2007) and Díaz (2019) on advertisements in print media have shown that anglicisms are used to promote an image of modernity for the consumer. I will come back to this claim in Chapter 8.

In contrast to station imaging, the analysis of news content shows the lowest frequency of anglicism occurrences. However, like for station imaging, there is no significant difference between the two broadcasting sectors. The use of verbal resources in news bulletins differs significantly from station imaging. News bulletins require a rather conservative language with precise and easily understandable sentences (see also characteristics of radio language in Section 1.2.2). In comparison to the results of Sagmeister-Brandner (2008), which indicate an average of 0.74 anglicisms per minute in Austrian public service radio news, the frequency of anglicisms in news content of both the German public service and the private sector is nevertheless more than twice as high (PS: 1.51 anglicisms per minute; P: 1.56 anglicisms per minute). This

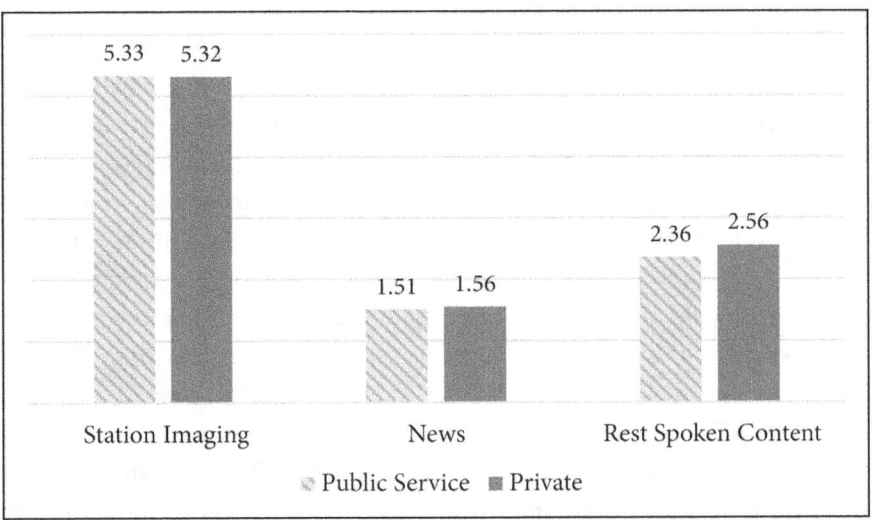

Figure 5 Token frequency of anglicisms per minute in station imaging, news and the rest of the spoken content.

difference is striking since Sagmeister-Brandner's study not only applies a similar definition of anglicisms[1] but also analyses adult contemporary radio content. It should be noted here, however, that she only examines one public service station, which may have also affected her results. Furthermore, additionally to her study being older, Austria provides a different sociocultural environment for radio production than Germany.

For the rest of the spoken content, including the genres of service, comedy and host talk, slightly more anglicisms were used in comparison to news. This is most likely because journalists can talk more freely and therefore use more colloquial language in these other genres. In line with the anglicism frequency of the overall corpus, the private sector uses more anglicisms than the public service sector in the rest of the spoken content – to be exact 8.5 per cent more anglicisms per minute than the public service sector. Against the background of a socially grounded spatial approach to language, the following sections of this chapter and of Chapter 7 combine the quantitative results of the case study with the qualitative results of the corpus analysis and qualitative interviews to get a deeper insight into journalists' language worlds.

6.3 The station's image: Language use and competition

All public service stations have different editorial concepts when it comes to reaching their target audiences and creating their station image. One journalist working for Public Service Station 1 stated that they see themselves as communicators and mediators between people and that mood management on air becomes increasingly important. Another journalist working for the same station stated that they are an information broadcaster that provides its listeners with background information but has also fun on air. The findings from the interviews with journalists working for this station are in line with the quantitative results, which have shown that this station in comparison to the other two public service stations uses more time on air for news coverage.

In contrast to this broadcaster, journalists working for Public Service Station 3 stated that their objective is mainly to entertain alongside providing reliable information. Therefore, according to a journalist working in an editorial position for this station, their morning programme 'hat diesen Showcharakter' (has this show-like character). As became evident from the interviews, the journalistic team of this station has a specific way of interpreting the noun *Unterhaltung* (entertainment). One journalist stated about their morning show:

> Auf jeden Fall ist es eine unterhaltungsorientierte Morningshow, wobei auch ein ernstes Thema unterhaltend sein kann, im Sinne von Unterhaltung ist das, worüber sich die Menschen unterhalten. ... Ist aber nicht Entertainment, sondern das ist journalistische Unterhaltung.
>
> (Definitely it is an entertainment-oriented morning show, whereby a serious topic can be entertaining too, in the sense of the word entertainment meaning what people talk about. ... This, however, is not entertainment [as amusement] but journalistic entertainment.)

Despite an interpretation of entertainment in the more formal sense of journalistic entertainment, which goes more along the lines of information wrapped with an entertainment coating, this station uses most anglicisms of all six stations in the overall content as well as in their station imaging and news content. This is mainly due to the image this station wishes to present to its audience. As one journalist working in the production of station imaging stated:

> Meine persönliche Aufgabe ist zu gucken, wie kriege ich jemanden in den Arm genommen, aber trotzdem ihm gesagt, „hey, wir sind die coolsten hier".
>
> (My personal task is to work out, how can I give someone a hug but still tell someone 'hey, we are the coolest around here'.)

Similar to the journalists working for this public service station, journalists working for Public Service Station 2 named entertainment as an important component in their morning show concept. However, they added that it is also key for them to provide reliable background information and not only breaking news. According to the quantitative data gained from the overall content analysis of the radio corpus and the frequency of anglicisms found in station imaging, this station lies somewhat between the other two public service stations in its use of anglicisms, which is also reflected in the interview statements of journalists working for this station.

Moving to the private sector, private radio stations, as I explained in Section 4.2.1, are mainly focused on economic competition due to their organizational form (see Gundlach 2010; Hoffmann-Riem 1991; Weischenberg 2004). This is in line with statements made by interviewees working for the private sector, who explained that private stations focus mainly on entertainment to attract the largest audience possible. Private adult contemporary stations in particular orient along the lines of American commercial radio models through their easy listening programme (e.g. strict time limits for spoken pieces, avoiding controversial or stirring topics, and a strong focus on entertainment), while the public service stations are eager to find a compromise between the popularity of the format radio concept and the obligations imposed upon them by regulations. One journalist working for Private Station 2 stated that it depends on the day whether entertainment becomes more important than information for them; however, the goal remains to keep a balanced mix. This journalist also stated that he would rather make a distinction between information and emotion than between information and entertainment and added that for him emotion is more important than broadcasting dry news. He furthermore stated that, in contrast to public service stations, their aim is to present information as compactly and concisely as possible, and this journalist continued that their public service competitor

> sich auch schon mal Zeit nimmt, den ein oder anderen Rand noch zu beleuchten, der für den Hörer immer noch interessant ist, wo wir aber schon sagen würden, „lieber noch einen Titel mehr".

> (occasionally takes the time to shed light on the edges which are still of interest to the listener, where we, however, would already say, 'let's rather play another song'.)

Another journalist working for the same station called this mix 'infotainment' with a clear prioritization of entertainment. In addition, the quantitative results for this station further show that in comparison to the other two private stations, journalists working for this station use about 67 per cent more anglicisms in their news content. In terms of the overall anglicism frequency, this private station additionally uses the highest number of anglicisms in its sector. This gives first indications towards a higher use of anglicisms in cases where an entertainment-driven morning show content is prioritized.

Interviewees from Private Station 1 stated that they wish to be the voice of their local area; also, they want to entertain and inform the audience, however, with a clear focus on entertainment. According to one journalist:

> Man kann ja auch Sachen gut verpacken und trotzdem so hinten rum Sachen aufklären, wo Menschen gar nicht merken, „ich werde gerade informiert". Die fühlen sich nur unterhalten. Wenn sie dann noch was mitnehmen, ja umso besser.

> (One can of course wrap things nicely and still get to the bottom of things unobtrusively, where people do not notice at all, 'I am being informed'. They just feel entertained. If they then additionally have learned something, well even better.)

For Private Station 3, the corpus analysis also shows a very entertainment-driven radio morning programme. The station's morning show incorporates a lot of self-promotional elements related to on-air prize games and events organized by the station throughout its broadcasting area. Therefore, entertainment seems to play a key role in creating this station's image. In terms of anglicism frequency, this station's use of English linguistic resources in its overall content is comparable to the other two private stations (see Figure 4).

In sum, the qualitative and quantitative results for stations of both sectors indicate an increased use of English linguistic resources in cases where more emphasis is put on entertainment in the morning programme. The public service sector, despite Public Service Station 3's emphasis on entertainment, nevertheless clearly prioritizes information in contrast to stations of the private sector. Public Service Station 3, like the other two public service broadcasters, must keep a certain standard, which means, as outlined by a journalist working for this station, that entertainment to them is more to be understood along the lines of entertainment with a high journalistic standard. The language used on air and therefore the presentation of content may be more entertainment driven and rich in anglicisms; the content itself, however, still has a higher information standard. In line with observations made by Peiser (2000) and Schneider, Schönbach and Stürzebecher (1993), these results therefore confirm differences between the public service and the private broadcasting sector. The quantitative data for the three private stations show that the frequency of anglicisms in the overall corpus is fairly equal amongst the stations. Overall, stations of the private sector share a similar economically driven editorial concept, which shows that there is a common strategy for success for private stations that is determined by the market and therefore mainly shaped by economic competition. One journalist of Private Station 2 stated regarding their strategy:

> Ich weiß zumindest von der Strategie her, dass es bei uns im Haus ein großer Punkt ist, dass man die Menschen versucht zu erreichen, die von dort [Öffentlich-Rechtliche] gewillt sind auch mal woanders hinzuwechseln, auch mal was anderes zu hören. Also man guckt bewusst, wie kann ich eine Alternative bieten für einen öffentlich-rechtlichen Hörer, der auch gerne mal zu wechseln bereit ist.
>
> (I know that at least strategy-wise at our station it is an issue of great importance to try to reach people who are willing to occasionally switch from there [public service] to somewhere else, to listen to something different every once in a while. Therefore, one looks purposely, how can I offer an alternative for a public service listener, who is once in a while gladly willing to switch.)

And this journalist explained that if a public service listener is willing to switch, he or she will be rewarded with getting a predominantly lockereres und leichter hörbares Programm. ... Leichtere Kost einfach.

(unconstrained and easier to listen to programme. ... Simply lighter fare.)

In contrast, the difference in anglicism frequency amongst the three public service stations (see Figure 4) seems to be related to the different editorial strategies these three stations pursue. The public service stations have greater freedom in establishing their editorial concept, and regarding their content, one host of a public service broadcaster stated:

> Wir werden ja nicht nach Quote bezahlt und so weiter. Und das ist dann natürlich gut, weil man da dem Hörer nicht so nach dem Mund reden muss. ... Also wir können auch nicht alle Quote verlieren; ja, aber wir können da uns wesentlich mehr trauen als private Kollegen.
>
> (We are not paid according to ratings and so on. And that of course is good since one does not have to say only what the listener wants to hear. ... Well, we cannot lose all ratings either; however, we can be substantially more daring than our colleagues from the private sector.)

This is also in line with a statement made by a journalist of Private Station 2 concerning the matter.

> In Seminaren kriegt man immer die Regel aufgedrückt „mean what you say". Und da finde ich die Öffentlich-Rechtlichen zum Beispiel gegenüber den Privaten immer noch ein großes Stück mehr im Vorteil, weil sie oft die Freiheit haben, sich aufgrund dieser Reglementarien was die Länge angeht und die Präsentation angeht mehr aus dem Fenster lehnen zu dürfen.
>
> (In seminars one usually gets told the rule 'mean what you say'. Regarding this, I believe that public service stations, for example, in comparison to the private stations, are still to a large extent at an advantage since they often have the freedom, due to these rules concerning length and presentation, to go further out on a limb.)

Therefore, not only is the continued existence of public service stations far less dependent on their audience shares, but they also belong to a group of stations run by a respective public service broadcaster that in its totality provides a programme for a broad audience. The differences in the programmes of the three public service stations clearly highlight the public service sector's focus on editorial competition. In addition, this notion of being able to be more daring than the private sector also further explains the differences in anglicism frequency amongst the three public service stations. As we have seen, by looking at the quantitative data and journalists' statements in combination, it becomes evident that those stations which follow a more entertainment-oriented approach use more English linguistic resources than those stations that focus more on the factual presentation of information. While the qualitative results, as discussed in Section 6.1, have revealed that most journalists of both sectors do not mention competition as affecting their language choice, competition nevertheless sets the overarching structures that shape their language use. Furthermore, although the quantitative findings show that in the overall result for each of the two sectors the private sector uses more anglicisms, when one takes a closer look, language use additionally seems to stand in relation to the individual market situation between the two competing stations from different sectors in their overlapping broadcasting areas. It also appears that competition between two stations has more effect on anglicism use than the larger broadcasting sector these stations belong to. In all three broadcasting areas, the three stations initially selected as the biggest adult contemporary stations used anglicisms less frequently than their direct competitors in the overall result of anglicisms. If one compares the anglicism frequencies of competing stations not only on the level of the overall results, but if one also splits the overall content into news, station imaging and the rest of the spoken content, in all but one case the results are consistent with the overall result. To interpret these findings, it is necessary to consider the individual cases of competition between the three biggest stations and their competitors, which in each case are different due to the diverse broadcasting landscapes in each *Bundesland* and their differing broadcasting laws.

In the case of the first of the three pairs, the stronger adult contemporary station is Public Service Station 1, which in 2016, as discussed in Section 6.1, enjoyed the benefit of being situated in a broadcasting landscape in which the competing private broadcasting sector consisted of a network of local stations. Therefore, due to their advantage in size as a public service station but also because of their by far bigger broadcasting area, journalists working for this station perceived competition with the private stations in their broadcasting area not as intense as they claimed other public service stations in radio markets of other *Länder* do (see especially the case of Public Service Station 3 and Private Station 3 below). As one of the journalists working for this public service station stated in relation to anglicism use on radio:

Vielleicht ist es ... noch ein anderer Radiomarkt, wo das nicht so nötig ist, so marktschreierisch zu sein.

(Maybe it is ... still a different radio market, where it is not as necessary to be so blatant.)

This shows that the use of English linguistic resources also stands in direct connection with competition. On the contrary, journalists working for this station's strongest local private competitor perceived this public service station as a strong opponent and therefore stated that their station tries to focus on specifically that niche which the transregional public service station is not able to cover. This niche is Private Station 1's focus on producing radio coverage on local topics and issues. Hence, this private station seems eager to make its own programme distinguishable from its competitor, which affects journalists' linguistic choices on air.

In the case of Public Service Station 2 and Private Station 2, the station that occupies the more comfortable market position is again the public service broadcaster. The main opponents for Public Service Station 2 are a few regional private stations that, when taken together, cover the same broadcasting area. While journalists working for this public service station claimed that their station is the leading one on their market and that others tend to compare themselves with their programme, they were nevertheless well aware of the competitive situation they find themselves in, with mainly larger regional private stations operating in their broadcasting area. Some of the journalists working for this public service station stressed that to stay at the top it is necessary to keep an eye on the private competitors as well as on the overall market situation in Germany, which includes other public service stations. According to journalists working for the strongest private competitor of this public service station, the journalistic team of Private Station 2 listens to four other stations each day including to their public service opponent. Some journalists of this private radio station additionally stressed the importance of providing an alternative to the public service programme.

In the third competition case, in contrast to the other two examples already mentioned, the broadcasting law in this *Land* gives room for a head-to-head competition for listeners between two adult contemporary stations sharing the same broadcasting area. Over time, Private Station 3 managed to take the lead in this race for audience shares and at the time when the data were collected had an advance of approximately 50 per cent more listeners compared to their public service competitor. While some journalists of this public service station did not engage in questions about competition and programme strategies in the interviews, a journalist in an editorial position revealed that journalists working for Public Service Station 3 watch other stations in the area that are in direct competition closely and focus on the competitors' wordings, which means to look out for how the other stations sell themselves.

In sum, this unique competition situation seems to affect the quantitative results of Public Service Station 3, which uses more English linguistic resources than any other station in the case study. This was somewhat unexpected since, due to their obligations and duties, public service broadcasters in general can be expected to use a more conservative language than the private sector. According to statements made by interviewees of Public Service Station 3 and when we take a closer look at this station's morning show concept, it appears that the difference in language use is due to an entertainment-oriented presentation of information and may additionally result from a strong focus on the hosts' personalities. By means of using colloquial, cool and airy talk on air, the atmosphere amongst the hosts gives the audience the impression that the hosts are ordinary everyday blokes from around the corner. For this purpose, anglicisms seem to be useful in keeping up and strengthening this image. In line with these observations, the results have also revealed that this station's morning show journalists use the highest number of English discourse markers in their content (e.g. *yes*, *hi* and *hello*).

Let us now once more compare the other two public service stations in terms of their frequency of anglicism occurrences in their morning programmes and comments made by journalists working for these stations with Public Service Station 3. One journalist working in the production of station imaging materials for Public Service Station 1 commented on anglicism use in their content as follows:

> Mich wundert daran ein bisschen, dass die Leute das seit dreißig Jahren cool und modern finden. Deswegen glaube ich, dass es nicht mehr so ist, oder jedenfalls nicht automatisch so funktioniert und deswegen versuchen wir das zu vermeiden, weil wir glauben, dass das eher was Anbiederndes und ja fast eher schon Uncooles hat, jedenfalls für uns. Und weil gerade viele Radiosender das ja machen, gerade mit Anglizismen arbeiten und wir uns dadurch auch ein bisschen absetzen wollen.

> (I'm a little amazed that people have been finding that cool and modern for the past thirty years. That is why I think that this is not the case anymore, or at least it does not automatically work that way, and this is why we are trying to avoid this since we believe that it is rather chumming up and rather uncool, at least for us. And because many radio stations do exactly that, working with anglicisms, and we additionally wish to stand out from that a little.)

This again contrasts with the statements made by a journalist working for Public Service Station 2, which in terms of anglicism frequency lies in between the other two public service stations. Even though their station plays the same music format, this journalist working in an editorial position stated regarding their use of anglicisms and why they do not avoid these that:

> Das passt auch nicht in eine Pop-Welle, weil es ist auch völlig unlogisch. Achtzig Prozent dieses Programms wird englisch gesprochen, hauptsächlich gesungen, insofern wäre es ein bisschen affig dazwischen zu sagen, „wir verzichten komplett auf Anglizismen".
>
> (That does not fit into a pop music station, because it is completely illogical. Eighty per cent of this programme is spoken in English, mainly sung, insofar it would be a little silly to say in between 'we completely refrain from using anglicisms'.)

This once more highlights the different editorial strategies within the public service broadcasting sector but also that the concept of anglicisms is perceived by journalists as meaningful for their everyday practice. Even though in all three examples of the competing station pairs the effects of competition appear to shape language usage on air in the same way, it is striking to see that the broadcasting landscape including broadcasting laws applicable for each area, the audience targeted and the organizational form of a station all shape language usage differently on air. Overall, the results of the qualitative interview stage confirm that the specific broadcasting sector journalists work for and the competitive situation of each of the stations in their individual broadcasting areas shape a journalist's language use on radio. For the overall quantitative results, it therefore seems that the direct competitors to each of the largest stations use more anglicisms to attract their target audiences. All three direct competitors follow an entertainment-oriented programme strategy, presentation-wise or both presentation and content-wise, and it seems that the use of anglicisms additionally aids to strengthen this image and the position of a station on the market.

In a competitive market, the promotion of a station's programme and the programme's hosts via station imaging is essential for survival and audience shares. We have already seen in the quantitative results that the highest frequency of anglicisms in the spoken content of each of the stations' morning shows was found in station imaging. In addition, the proportion of non-catachrestic anglicism tokens as opposed to catachrestic anglicisms was higher in station imaging (91 per cent) than in the rest of the spoken content (78 per cent). To deepen the analysis of segmentation and competition and their effects on radio language, I will examine in the following section whether the fact that non-catachrestic anglicisms have experienced diachronic development or not impacts their use in station imaging materials, and I will compare these results with the results for the rest of the spoken content.

6.4 Pragmatic markedness of anglicisms

As the previous section has shown, radio stations of both broadcasting sectors compete for audience attention. I therefore examined whether the fact that an anglicism has experienced diachronic development or not plays a role for an anglicism's use in station imaging materials. To provide the broader context for this analysis, let me first give a brief overview of the frequency of non-catachrestic anglicisms in the radio corpus. The overall corpus contained 402 different anglicism base types of which 239 were identified as non-catachrestic types and 158 anglicisms were identified as catachrestic types amounting to 2,585 non-catachrestic tokens in comparison to only 609 catachrestic tokens (see appendix Table A.2 for a list of anglicism bases found in the radio corpus). Overall, the radio corpus showed a high number of non-catachrestic types amongst the most frequently used anglicisms. The top twenty anglicism bases contained no catachrestic anglicisms at all and merely two anglicisms that showed both catachrestic and non-catachrestic tokens. In comparison, Onysko and Winter-Froemel's (2011) analysis of a news magazine corpus resulted in six catachrestic types in their top twenty of anglicism bases. The total of catachrestic and non-catachrestic anglicisms found in station imaging elements amounted to 102 anglicism types of which sixty-eight occurrences were non-catachrestic types and thirty-two anglicisms catachrestic types. Two of the anglicisms showed both catachrestic and non-catachrestic tokens. Overall, this resulted in 738 non-catachrestic tokens in the station imaging corpus.

Despite the fact that many non-catachrestic anglicisms in station imaging stem from the lexical field of *General Language*, most non-catachrestic types found in imaging materials show no diachronic development from M- to I-implicatures (see Figure 6). When one further looks at the token frequency of non-catachrestic occurrences found in the station imaging corpus (Figure 7), it becomes evident that those English linguistic resources with no diachronic development are also repeated more often. The use of non-catachrestic anglicisms with no diachronic development seems to provide an advantage for the self-promotion of adult contemporary radio stations. This becomes apparent in the most repetitive non-catachrestic occurrences found in station imaging materials of both the public service and private radio stations. These are the anglicisms *Hit* (PS 53; P 142), *Mix* (PS 63; P 64) and *Service* (PS 20; P 50). With the recurring usage of these three terms, the characteristics of adult contemporary formats are clearly highlighted. These include playing modern, successful music in a well-chosen mix, together with the services radio is expected to provide. Therefore,

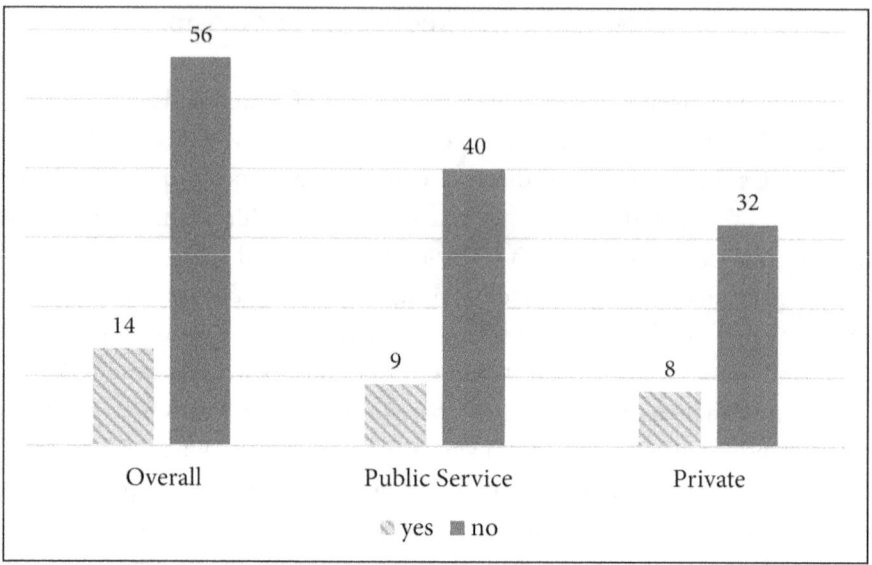

Figure 6 Number of types of non-catachrestic occurrences in station imaging that show diachronic development (adapted from Schaefer 2019, with permission from Elsevier).

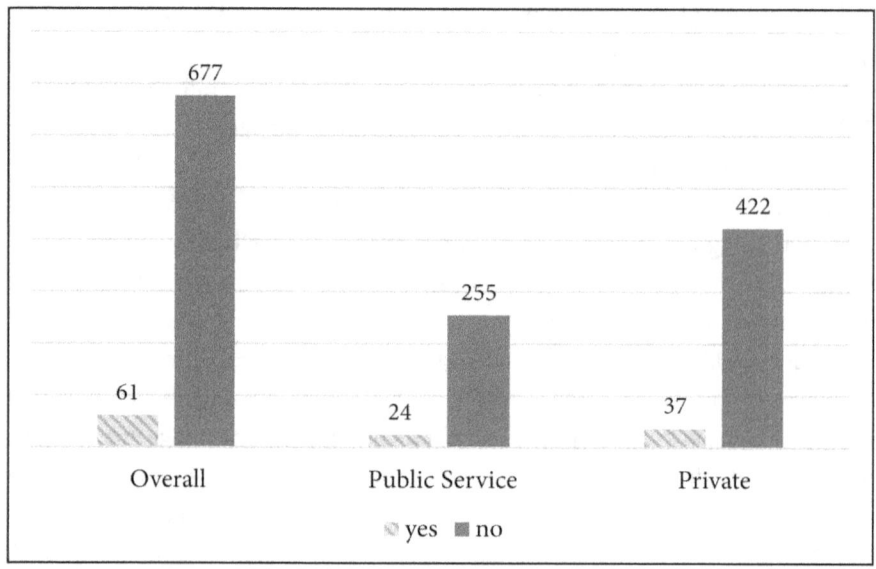

Figure 7 Number of tokens of non-catachrestic occurrences in station imaging that show diachronic development (adapted from Schaefer 2019, with permission from Elsevier).

the results show that non-catachrestic anglicisms which bear pragmatic markedness are favoured in station imaging materials on adult contemporary radio over non-catachrestic occurrences that show diachronic development and hence are pragmatically unmarked. Examples of non-catachrestic anglicisms in station imaging that have experienced diachronic development and therefore sedimentation and 'naturalization' include the phrase *made in Germany*, the noun *Trainer* (coach) and the pseudo-anglicism *Handy* (mobile phone).

The catachrestic/non-catachrestic analysis of the rest of the spoken content has additionally confirmed that adult contemporary radio stations make greater use of those non-catachrestic anglicisms that have pragmatic markedness in station imaging materials since for the remainder of the spoken content anglicisms that have experienced diachronic development are more frequently used. From this we can take that even though all content is fitted to the target audience's language preferences, the genre of station imaging, due to its primary function as self-advertisement of radio stations, requires a particularly catchy language that draws the listeners' attention to the product the station is selling. I will come back to pragmatically marked anglicisms in relation to journalists' perceptions of modernity in Chapter 8.

6.5 Language choice and segmentation

I pointed out in this chapter how competition and segmentation shape journalists' language choices on air and their use of English linguistic resources. While the quantitative results have shown that overall the private sector uses more anglicisms than the public service sector, a closer analysis revealed that the use of anglicisms is not necessarily dependent on mere competition between sectors but more on competition between each of the stations and their strongest direct competitors. Despite producing content for the same radio format, each station aims at a specific target audience that has different demands when it comes to language use. These demands also function as a centre of authority in the journalists' language worlds that indirectly shapes the language they choose to attract listeners. Processes of segmentation underlying their word choice on radio primarily concern demographic features of the listenership but also personal characteristics of the target audience.

As both the quantitative and qualitative findings have revealed, the frequency of anglicisms stands in direct connection with the construction of a station's image. The image a station wishes to present to its listener, therefore, additionally functions as a centre of authority which sets certain language standards. Public Service Station 3, of which a journalist stated that they wish to be the coolest on air, uses most anglicisms in their station imaging materials. The use of English resources therefore is related to both the hosts' and station's identity constructions as part of the station's image. This at first reminds us of the claim that anglicism use stands in direct connection with expressing modernity (see amongst others Díaz 2019; Gerritsen et al. 2007; Piller 2003), the idea being that when one uses anglicisms one automatically sounds cool and polyglot. However, this proves to be not generally the case. For some journalists working for Public Service Station 1, which uses the least anglicisms, the use of such English linguistic resources does not automatically create a cool and modern image of a station but rather the opposite. According to these journalists, an extensive use of anglicisms would be perceived by their audience as rather uncool and even as an ingratiation (for a further discussion on anglicisms and perceptions of modernity see Section 8.2).

A higher token frequency of anglicisms was found in the content of those stations which put more emphasis on entertainment than information. This discovery holds for mainly the private sector but is not confined to it, as the results for the public service sector have shown. The results of the quantitative analysis of the public service sector were rather striking due to the large differences in anglicism frequency of the three public service stations. As gathered from the interviews with journalists working for both sectors, because public service stations are not as dependent on audience shares in the competitive German broadcasting market, these stations enjoy greater autonomy in establishing their editorial concept as opposed to stations belonging to the private sector.

The analysis of non-catachrestic anglicisms in station imaging materials and the rest of the spoken content in relation to whether an anglicism has experienced diachronic development from a pragmatically marked to an unmarked lexical choice or not has shed further light on what effects competition has on anglicism use in the morning shows of adult contemporary stations. The analysis has revealed that diachronic development is not a facilitating factor for the frequent use of anglicisms in station imaging materials since non-catachrestic innovations that show no diachronic development and are less sedimented are more frequently used in this radio genre. This is mainly due to the characteristics of non-catachrestic anglicisms, which without having undergone a diachronic development have pragmatic markedness and additional pragmatic meanings. These additional meanings are an important component of the language used in station imaging materials. Furthermore, the results of the analysis of diachronic development of anglicisms in the rest of the spoken content confirm that non-catachrestic anglicisms without diachronic development are purposefully used in station imaging materials since these occurred more frequently in the stations' self-advertisements than in the rest of the spoken content.

7
The Workplace

The workplace as the immediate surrounding of radio journalists during content production at the radio station comprises of various centres of authority. In this chapter, I will show how the workplace surrounding shapes media language by examining different centres of authority spatiotemporally situated within the grouping of influences of the media organization and connected to the larger network of factors in the Media Language Model. These centres of authority include the station's routine practices, editorial procedures and the radio format. I will particularly focus on investigating whether language policies are implemented by the stations regarding the use of English linguistic resources and, if so, whether such policies are overtly implemented (see Breed 1955; Weischenberg 2004). Additionally, I will shed light on the role and power of the chief editor and other journalists in editorial positions in relation to anglicism use (see Weischenberg 2004). The language used on radio is also adapted to the radio format and its various genres. In Section 7.2, I will therefore give examples from different radio genres focusing in particular on the use of novel anglicisms by radio journalists and how these novel items are made comprehensible in line with genre conventions. By bringing these aspects together, I will discuss the complexities of the journalists' workplace and how this complexity shapes language use on radio.

7.1 The workplace, content production and the role of the editor

There are several factors that can shape radio language, which may arise during different stages of content production. One of these factors is how information is gathered. Since public service stations in Germany are part of the ARD, they share correspondents and news coverage, which also affects the language used in reports by these stations. An example for this from the radio corpus is the use of the anglicism *Singer-Songwriter* in connection with the German musician Joris. The anglicism was exclusively used by the three public service stations on the same day in the context of the ECHO awards. In the case of *Singer-Songwriter*, it is therefore likely that this wording stemmed from a single source within the ARD's network of correspondents.

In terms of other production processes, the range of authors involved, such as journalists who draft content for hosts, and how much a host then changes content for his or her individual needs are shaping factors on radio language. It appears that the main body of content, which includes pieces for radio on various topics, is chosen by a team of journalists on the day before the next morning. Each host then can decide to accept presentation suggestions for lead-ins and rephrase them in his or her own words or to write his or her own script based on the main facts provided by colleagues. As a host of Public Service Station 1 stated:

> Also es gibt teilweise Vorschläge. Am liebsten habe ich nur Stichworte, weil ich mir die immer mundgerecht für mich formuliere, und ich schreibe alles auf, damit ich es einmal klar im Kopf habe. In der Präsentation bin ich dann frei, da gucke ich mit einem Auge drauf. Aber es geht darum, selbstgeschriebene Texte halt so zu präsentieren, dass sie einfach so sind, wie sie sind, dass sie erzählt sind.
>
> (In parts there are suggestions. I prefer bullet points only because I can then put them into my own words, and I put everything to paper, so that I have everything clear in my head once. I'm free while presenting; I only peek at it with one eye. However, it is all about presenting self-scripted texts in a way that they simply are the way they are, that they are told.)

In contrast to this host working at a public service station who prefers to speak more freely than others on air to make the morning show more authentic, a journalist working for Private Station 1 explained:

> Ich sag mal 95 Prozent der Sachen, die in der Sendung laufen, sind dann wirklich auch vorbereitet vor der Sendung. Da sind wir also, wenn wir um sechs [Uhr] in die Sendung gehen, damit fertig und dann geht es da ums Präsentieren. Und dann natürlich darum, dass man guckt, dass es halt nicht abgelesen klingt, sondern dass es für die Hörer klingt wie in einem Gespräch, was wir gerade dann haben. Das ist dann so ein bisschen die Kunst dabei.
>
> (Let's say, 95 per cent of the content that appears on the show really is prepared in advance of the show. When we open the show at six [o'clock] we have completed that and then it's about presenting. And of course, it's about paying attention

that it doesn't sound like read off but that it sounds to the listeners like in a conversation we are then just having. This is a bit of the trick of it.)

The interviews have further revealed that there are several levels of editorial quality assurance during content production that can have an impact on language use. According to a news presenter working at Public Service Station 2, news scripts are read by at least two journalists before being broadcast. The editor does not give an official debriefing specifically on news but listens to the news after it is broadcast to give feedback if necessary. For instance, feedback is given by the editor when parts of the text are not appropriate according to the editor's judgement in terms of content or wording. In contrast to news, comedy-related content that is not produced directly by the team of the morning show of this public service station undergoes additional checks before it is broadcast. Depending on the size of the station, besides the chief editor, editorial duties are assigned to journalists working in different positions. While preproduced pieces for radio are checked by the responsible duty editor for general errors and wording, the rest of the spoken content presented by hosts including lead-ins is their own responsibility. According to a journalist in an editorial position at Public Service Station 2:

> Und es ist bei uns grundsätzlich so, dass Moderationen nicht kontrolliert werden im Vorhinein, sondern es gibt nur im Nachhinein ein Debriefing.

> (Generally speaking, at our station the hosts' talk is not checked beforehand; instead, there is merely a debriefing afterwards.)

In addition, as has become evident from the interview with this journalist, journalists in higher positions responsible for editorial supervision of content, for example the chief editor, discuss the show after it is broadcast in a conference with the team of hosts and journalists. Journalists in editorial positions therefore have only indirect influence on the content and wording by making suggestions and providing advice or critique.

This contrasts with the procedures regarding content production at Private Station 2, where a journalist working in an editorial position clarified that before something goes on air the editor is the last approving authority. Despite these editorial means of control, according to most interviewees, no specific language policies are implemented by both public service and private stations regarding the use of anglicisms in their broadcasts.

> Also das ist so. Wir sitzen täglich zusammen und besprechen diese Dinge und wenn mir auffällt, in einem Beitrag ist irgendwo ein Wort drin, wo ich denken könnte „oh, das verstehen die Leute vielleicht nicht", dann spreche ich es an.

Und dann reden wir am nächsten Tag nochmal drüber. Aber es ist nie so, dass es jetzt mal ein Briefing gab, „ihr dürft niemals englische Wörter verwenden". Das gab es nicht, aber es ist immer eine Einzelentscheidung.

(Well, the thing is this. We meet daily and discuss these things, and if I notice that there is a word somewhere in a piece of which I think 'oh, people may not be able to understand that', then I address it. And then we talk about it again the next day. But it never is the case that there has ever been a briefing like 'you shall never use English words'. That has never happened, but it is always an individual decision.)

This means that journalists in chief editorial positions may shape content directly; however, it is not the general procedure for all stations. Nevertheless, the editor functions as a centre of authority and reminds hosts and journalists of possible comprehension problems for the listeners and of the importance of avoiding these on air. This is in line with Weischenberg (2004), who states in his description of organizational structures of newsrooms that the chief editors' power to make definite decisions, even if not exerted directly in all processes of production, still influences the decisions made by journalists regarding their coverage.

Further factors that shape the language used on radio are colleagues at the workplace and the differences in the workplace environments of public service and private stations. When I asked one of the journalists about her unique use of different verbal derivations of the catachrestic noun *WhatsApp* in the corpus, such as *whatsappen* (to whatsapp), *gewhatsappt* (to whatsapp, past participle) and *zurückwhatsappende* (*back-whatsapping; a participial construction describing a person who replies to a WhatsApp message), this host stated:

Das erstaunt mich, weil das höre ich eigentlich nur so. Also auch meine ganzen Kollegen sagen das so.

(That astounds me because I only hear it that way. Well, all my colleagues say it like that too.)

The fact that the direct workplace surrounding and the people a journalist is in contact with throughout the day at work shape their language on air and therefore the language worlds of journalists is also in line with observations made by Breed (1955) and Weaver and Wilhoit (1991). According to these studies, the social surroundings at work and therefore the workplace environment shapes a journalist's attitudes and tendencies, which also, when viewed from a language-as-social-practice perspective, incorporates decisions on appropriateness in language choice.

Regarding the differences in the workplace environments of public service and private stations, the interviews further show that the workplace environment at private stations is more stressful and constrained. According to a journalist who worked at a private station before working at a public service broadcaster:

> Aber den Unterschied habe ich ganz extrem gemerkt. Also das ist wirklich beim Privatrundfunk / da ist die Stimmung komplett anders in der Morgenshow. Es gibt auch supergute Phasen, aber es ist alles sehr stressig / und wenn was Aktuelles passiert, wie Fukushima oder was damals war, sofort unter der heißen Nadel und jetzt schnell rein und in 30 Sekunden gehen wir on air.

> (However, I have noticed this difference extremely. Well, at private stations it is really / the atmosphere there is completely different in the morning show. There are really great times too, but everything is very stressful / and when something current happens, such as Fukushima or whatever happened at the time, immediately write it up and now quickly add it and in 30 seconds we go on air.)

And this journalist continued, comparing experiences made at the private broadcaster with the current position at the public service station:

> Sie [Öffentlich-Rechtliche] lassen dich mehr machen. Also die vertrauen dir einfach und dadurch kannst du dich auch gut entfalten. Beim Privatfunk ist es so streng, weil alle so Angst vor den Zahlen haben. Es geht alles um die Zahlen, da fieberst du so auf diese zwei Tage im Jahr hin, wo diese Zahlen rauskommen und dann ist die Stimmung entweder ganz unten oder sie ist Sekt, Schampusflaschen.

> (They [public service stations] let you do more. Well, they simply trust you and therefore you can develop. At private stations it is so strict because everyone is so afraid of the ratings. Everything is about ratings, so you feverishly await those two days in the year, when these ratings are published and then the mood is either down or it is champagne and bubbly bottles.)

Therefore, having worked for two different sectors, this journalist concludes that one enjoys greater freedom to produce pieces for radio at public service stations due to lesser constraints when compared to private stations, which is an aspect of the public service workplace environment that also shapes journalists' language use on radio. This is in line with Shoemaker and Reese (2014), who state that the degree of power and autonomy journalists enjoy within their workplace environment influences content production. The more journalists must adhere to policy and routines, the more they stick to the professional roles they have adopted. Journalists who are given more freedom to express themselves, however, tend to be more influenced by their personal attitudes and beliefs. I will come back to this in Chapter 8.

7.2 Novel anglicisms and comprehensibility

Instead of specific language policies, there is mutual understanding amongst journalists writing content for radio not to use terms that may cause comprehension problems or else, if it is unavoidable to use such terms, to explain or translate these (Schaefer 2019). The corpus analysis has confirmed that this also applies to novel anglicisms, which contrasts with previous findings by Pfitzner (1978) on German print media and by Baum (2016) on German adult contemporary radio. Baum (2016), for example, states in his dissertation that the general strategy of adult contemporary radio formats is to neither translate nor explain anglicisms to the audience. As all the journalists I interviewed – including those in editorial positions responsible for content and wording – stated, it is of primary importance that the audience understands what the hosts and presenters want to get across.

> Die größte Gefahr beim Radio ist für uns tatsächlich, dass die Leute uns nicht verstehen und dann hast du sie verloren. Und deshalb wollen wir es ihnen so leicht wie möglich machen.
>
> (The greatest danger for us in the radio business is indeed that people don't understand us, and then you have lost them. And that's why we want to make it as easy as possible for them.)

However, according to my interviewees, some anglicisms cannot simply be avoided. Against the background of asymmetrical cultural flows and adult contemporary's focus on pop music culture, journalists of adult contemporary stations at times make use of novel anglicisms to inform and entertain the listeners by introducing new concepts and words to them that they may come across more often in the future. Examples from the radio corpus include the incipient borrowings *Organic Cotton* and *Curved-TV*. In addition, creative novel anglicisms such as *Sun-Blogger* and *Hand-Entertainment*, often coined by journalists themselves, keep their programme attractive and innovative. Novel anglicisms, therefore, are effective communicative devices which contribute to achieving the communicative aims of the station and to show that they are always up to the minute in relation to new trends and concepts of popular culture. When using novel anglicisms on radio, journalists have to nevertheless carefully consider and balance aspects of comprehensibility, currency of their programme, and their target audience's interests and language use to create an appealing programme for their audience. This clearly shows the complexity of normative forces that impact the use of novel anglicisms on radio. Novel anglicisms need to be at all times translated, explained or contextually explained by the journalists to ensure their comprehensibility for the listener, which requires additional communicative effort. In the following, I will show how journalists invest additional communicative effort in different genres of the morning show to avoid possible comprehension issues that are associated with the use of novel anglicisms and therefore with mobile linguistic resources that blur the boundaries between socially defined languages.

Let me first give some examples of novel anglicisms that occurred in the genre of service journalism (for further examples see Schaefer 2021b). Service pieces provide solutions and information to consumer-related problems or, as Eide and Knight state, the task of service journalism is 'responding to and offering commentary and advice on the everyday concerns of [the] audiences' (1999: 526). This advice is often given in the form of detailed information on new products, trends and concepts. In line with the communicative aim of this genre, novel anglicisms used in service pieces were elaborated on in greater detail by means of translating or explaining these to the listenership.

In the following example taken from a service piece, the journalists call on their listeners to change their consumer behaviour and thereby to help mitigate the risk of bee death. In the excerpt, the concept of clothes, and therefore consumer products, labelled *Organic Cotton* is presented and explained as an opportunity for the individual to take part in the solution of the problem.

(17) Erstens natürlich Bio einkaufen und das Bio bezieht sich nicht nur auf Lebensmittel, auch auf Baumwolle. Denn gerade beim Baumwollanbau wird oft ohne Rücksicht auf Verluste gespritzt. Schon deshalb macht es Sinn Klamotten zu kaufen auf denen Organic Cotton, Bio-Baumwolle steht.

(First of all, buy organic and that does not only relate to groceries but also to cotton. In particular when cotton is grown, pesticides are often applied regardless of the consequences. Hence it makes sense to buy clothes labelled as *Organic Cotton*, organic cotton.)

(Public Service Station 2, 20 April 2016)

Another example of how incipient borrowings are used in service pieces on radio is the English lexical item *Cornrows*. The listeners were informed by the journalists about the risks they take when riding a bicycle without wearing a helmet due to vanity regarding their hairstyle. The novel anglicism *Cornrows* was presented as a possible solution that the journalists deemed to be unknown to their listeners.

(18) Tipp drei. Wenn wehende Haare stören, diese zu einem tiefliegenden Zopf zusammenbinden. Auch ein Dutt kann helfen. Bei Frauen sind locker geflochtene Cornrows wieder in, also kleine, an den Kopf angeflochtene Zöpfe.

(Tip three. If waving hair is a bother, simply tie it to a low hanging plait. Additionally, a bun can help. For women, loosely braided cornrows are back in fashion, which means small braids plaited close to the head.)

(Public Service Station 2, 26 April 2016)

As can be taken from this service piece excerpt, the English lexical item *Cornrows* was explained and functioned as an innovative suggestion for a hairstyle that is not ruined by wearing a bicycle helmet and therefore solves the apparent problem. Additionally, by describing the hairstyle as 'in fashion', the concept is linked to current fashion and popular culture, which signals that the possible gains of the service piece's advice go beyond personal safety and that the station is abreast of time.

Journalists at times also deliberately exceed their imagined audience's repertoire and cross constructed language boundaries to achieve particular stylistic effects in different genres of the morning show. Novel anglicisms and especially new creations often sound witty and thereby catch the listeners' attention, which makes them particularly suitable to use in comedy pieces. Since adult contemporary radio stations have a strong focus on entertainment, the genre of comedy is a fundamental part of the radio morning show. In contrast to other radio genres, the audience expects that a higher cognitive effort may be necessary to infer the humorous meaning of a message as part of comedy for the benefit of being amused, which shifts the effort–effect balance in such a way that more complex and ambiguous linguistic forms such as word coinages, wordplays or metaphors can be used by journalists without the message losing relevance for the audience (see Grundy 2020). The novel pseudo-anglicism *Sunblogger* was used in the following way in this genre.

(19) Wie nennt man Fachautoren zum Thema Sonnenbrand? Sunblogger.

(What do you call specialist authors on sunburns? *Sunblogger.*)

(Public Service Station 3, 9 May 2016)

This example is incorporated in a series of short jokes concerning sunburns, where *Sunblogger* functions as the pay-off of the joke. This pay-off is made in the form of a pun based on English lexical items, where *Sunblogger* is created by analogy to the anglicism *Sunblocker* (sunblock). As the phonological assimilation of *Blogger* in German shows, the wordplay between *Blogger* [ˈblɔgər] and *Blocker* [ˈblɔkər] is based on the phonetic similarity between the two terms. In the case of *Sunblogger*, the actual context in which the novel anglicism was used including little hints the journalist left in his comedy piece, such as the reference to 'Fachautoren zum Thema Sonnenbrand' (specialist authors on sunburns) in the preceding question, aided the listener to infer the humorous meaning of the message. In addition, the particular format of such joke questions (What do you call …?) encourages the listener to actively think for herself or himself what the possible answer to the question might be. The journalist's intonation and a preceding break put additional emphasis on the newly created anglicism *Sunblogger*. The analogy of *Sunblogger* to the established anglicism *Sunblocker* additionally aided the comprehension of the novel anglicism.

The novel hybrid compound creation *Hand-Entertainment* was used by a journalist in the same comedy piece. In this example, the borrowing *Entertainment* was not used in its established meaning according to the *Duden online*, 'berufsmäßig gebotene, leichte Unterhaltung' (professionally offered light entertainment) but in the sense of an act of keeping one's hands busy, which created the humorous effect. The journalists again made sure in this piece that the meaning of the message can be inferred by the audience from the contextual usage of the novel word:

> (20) Und wenn man sich im Achselbereich die Haut verbrennt, dann hoch die Hand, Sonnenbrand. Muss eingeschmiert werden, das ist dann Hand-Entertainment.
>
> (And when one burns one's skin in the armpit area, then lift your hand, sunburn. [The skin] has to be rubbed in [with lotion], that is *Hand-Entertainment*.)
>
> (Public Service Station 3, 9 May 2016)

All novel anglicisms found in this genre were made comprehensible via the context in which these were used. This is in line with the stylistic conventions of the genre of comedy, which is based on humorous language and jokes. As Grundy states, humour can be defined as 'the occurrence of an unusually enhanced positive cognitive effect resulting from an unusually greater processing effort' (2020: 109). Therefore, a direct explanation of novel words would impair the humorous effects intended.

When constructing the station image in station imaging materials, journalists carefully choose their wording and especially consider the connotations that the words used to describe the station and its programme entail. Due to the stations' pop music focus, for most journalists anglicisms are an important element in station imaging (Schaefer 2019). This becomes evident from the high overall number of anglicisms found in station imaging of adult contemporary radio stations. While station imaging only makes up 12.2 per cent (approx. 2 hours 31 minutes) of the morning show content analysed, this genre contains 25.4 per cent (805 tokens) of all anglicisms found in the radio corpus. Most adult contemporary journalists make use of semantic and pragmatic meanings and connotations of established anglicisms to promote their station since the radio station's audience is familiar with these anglicisms and their meanings. However, as I previously mentioned, all interviewees agree that if an anglicism is not deemed comprehensible for the target audience or cannot easily be made comprehensible it is not used. Similar to the genre of news, station imaging does not allow for clarification by means of inserting additional explanations or translations of terms that might cause comprehension problems since this would violate the short and catchy commercial-like style of station imaging messages. Additionally, in contrast to print or audio-visual advertisements, radio station imaging does not offer the recipient visual clues that can help to infer the denotative and connotative meaning of unknown terms. The constraints of the genre in combination with the materiality of the medium radio therefore limit the usage of novel anglicisms in station imaging to those cases that journalists deem not overly complex and therefore comprehensible from the limited context provided in station imaging elements. The two novel anglicisms used in the station imaging part of the corpus are examples of such cases. Both are based on wordplay, which results in novel, salient expressions that, however, are easily made comprehensible due to their morphological structures and the contextual clues provided for the listener. With the novel anglicism *app-solut*, a station promoted its official smartphone application.

(21) Das ist app-solut genial, auch für die Pfingstferien, die Radio-X-App für Smartphone und Tablet.

(This is *app-solutely brilliant, also for the Whitsun holidays, the Radio X app for smartphone and tablet.)

(Private Station 3, 17 May 2016)

App-solut is a near-homophonous wordplay based on the phonetic similarity between the established borrowing *App* [ɛp] and the first syllable *ab* [ap] of the German adverb *absolut* (absolutely). This kind of pun is based on embedding an existing lexical item 'into a context which creates an element of surprise' (Braun 2018: 180). In this excerpt, the journalist's intention to create a play on words becomes obvious through the context ('die Radio-X-App für Smartphone und Tablet') as well as through the function of the creation *app-solut* as a degree adverb that is used like the near-homophonous German degree adverb *absolut*.

The creatively formed anglicism *Private Viewing* was used to promote a prize game organized by Public Service Station 1 in the following way:

> (22) Ihr Private Viewing zum nächsten EM-Spiel der deutschen Nationalmannschaft. Sie laden bis zu zwanzig Fußballfreunde ein und wir kümmern uns um den Rest. Catering mit dem Grillbike und Getränke vom Fass. Jetzt bewerben.
>
> (Your *Private Viewing* for the upcoming European championships match of the German national team. You invite up to twenty football friends and we take care of the rest. Catering by grill bike and drinks on tap. Apply now.)
>
> (Public Service Station 1, 10 June 2016)

Private Viewing is used in analogy to the by now well-established pseudo-anglicism *Public Viewing*, which stands for an activity where large groups of people meet to watch mainly football and other sport events on a large screen in public. In this station imaging excerpt, the first part of the original pseudo-anglicism *Public* is substituted by its antonym *Private*, which creates salience by referencing the rather uncommon reverse concept of the popular *Public Viewing* activity. Comprehension of this novel anglicism by the audience is aided by the close relationship of the two modifiers and by its usage in the context of a sporting event. Furthermore, *Private Viewing* is a creation that, although rare in usage, is not completely unknown in German, as can be seen by its recurring appearance in the *ZDL-Regionalkorpus* in the years of the soccer world cups and European championships (i.e. the years of 2010, 2012, 2014, 2016 and 2018). This is why journalists possibly also considered the term as unproblematic to use as part of station imaging.

As we have seen, achieving the communicative goals that are associated with the use of novel anglicisms in different genres involves specific communicative practices, such as translating, explaining or contextually explaining these. In the following, I will look at some further examples of journalists' communicative practices which, in contrast to the discussion above, involve more sedimented English resources used as part of daily working routines by radio journalists.

7.3 Routine practices

As I discussed in Chapter 2, the post-war period in West Germany transformed German journalism styles and practices. Many of these were adopted from British and American examples, including news values and professional journalistic terminology as well as American radio formats like adult contemporary. As a result, mainly English-language terminology is used nowadays at the workplace of radio journalists in Germany. Terms such as *Wording, over-voiced, Jingles* and *Cliff-Hanger* are used daily and have become standard vocabulary in journalistic language.

> Also die Begriffe mit denen was beschrieben wird sind alle sehr englisch. Wir reden eigentlich nie von Wortwahl, wir reden immer von Wording. Die ganzen Soundelemente, die wir haben im Programm, heißen Bumper, Stinger und so weiter. Diese Dinge sind eigentlich alle aus dem amerikanischen Radio übernommen.
>
> (Well, the terms describing things are all very English. We actually never talk about *Wortwahl* (word choice), we always talk about *Wording*. All the sound elements we have in the programme are called *Bumper, Stinger* and so on. Actually, these terms are all adopted from American radio.)

According to the interviewees, this professional journalistic terminology used off air at their workplace is avoided in content produced for the morning show. Journalists therefore draw a boundary between on- and off-air language and consider themselves as a community of practice with their own specific jargon.

> Es macht keinen Sinn / Wir haben interne Unterlagen, da würden wir auch von Wording sprechen; aber nach draußen im Radio würde niemand von Wording sprechen. Das ist, das bleibt ein Fachbegriff, auch wenn *word* vielleicht da draußen der eine oder andere versteht. Aber das sind für uns Fachbegriffe, die haben da nichts verloren.
>
> (It makes no sense / We have internal documents, in which we would also talk of wording; however, directed to the public on radio nobody would speak of wording. That is, that remains jargon, even though 'word' may be understood by one or two people out there. However, these are terminological phrasings to us which have no place there.)

However, as Example (23) from a private station's morning show content shows, the use of English terminology at a journalist's workplace still impacts the way journalists talk on air. In the example, *weggefadet* relates to *fade out*, an expression from journalistic terminology which means to gradually decrease the volume of a music piece or sound effect, also in the context of mixing music or sound effects with speech. The journalist evokes this meaning by, so to speak, glossing the potentially unknown expression *weggefadet* as *weggeblendet* (faded out). Furthermore, the song played prior to the journalist's use of the anglicism *weggefadet* contained the English word 'faded'. By using *weggefadet*, the host therefore also picks up the topic and the word choice of the preceding song and creates a thematic complex of several elements. These elements include the meaning of 'faded' in the sense of 'fade away' as used in the pop song. The song is set in minor key and the negative connotation of 'faded' is additionally highlighted because 'faded' as part of the song's chorus is repeatedly sung in a melancholic manner. Since the German *weggeblendet* does not bear a negative connotation, this only becomes clear to listeners who do not understand the English term through the music. The German term *Frühling* (spring) then evokes connotations of this season such as blooming and blossom time. Together these meanings symbolize a premature fading of spring due to cold weather. The meaning of *weggefadet* in its journalistic sense, as discussed above, provides an additional metaphoric description of the inconsistency of spring weather. This clearly shows how both the use of English terminology off air and the English-language music played on air shape the use of anglicisms. Furthermore, the example illustrates how the material ecology of the radio studio is part of the assemblage of radio language. The act of 'fading something out' is a routine, embodied practice for radio journalists in which they interact with their studio equipment (i.e. moving a fader on the mixing desk).

Example (23)

Time (sec.)	Speech	Music
		preceding song: **Alan Walker** 'Faded' (instrumental outro, piano, minor key)
0.0–1.3	**Host:** Elf Minuten nach sieben, (Eleven minutes past seven,)	
1.4–10.7	guten Morgen mit Alan Walker und „Faded" hier bei Radio X. Tja, faded. Ist der Frühling vielleicht schon weggefadet, weggeblendet? Momentan sieht es nämlich eher nach Winter aus. (good morning with Alan Walker and 'Faded' here at Radio X. Well, faded. Has spring already faded away, faded out? Because currently it rather looks like winter.)	instrumental background music (rhythm guitar; major key)

Note: English translations in parentheses.

(Private Station 2, 26 April 2016)

Journalistic terminology used at adult contemporary radio stations, however, is not the only way of how journalists get in contact with mobile English resources in their daily working routine. As previously mentioned in Chapter 6, a journalist in an editorial position working for Public Service Station 2 also stated that up to 80 per cent of the songs they play on adult contemporary radio are English-language songs. This was confirmed by the quantitative results of the case study, which show that 87 per cent of all songs played in the recorded content of the morning shows were English-language songs (see Schaefer 2021a). Furthermore, this journalist stated that most celebrities interviewed by journalists of their station either are native English speakers or use English as the main language for communication. Therefore, according to this interviewee, it would not make any sense for a radio station playing contemporary pop music to avoid anglicisms in spoken radio content since a large part of the content played on air including music and interviews contains English (see also Section 5.2). Radio stations aim at creating a continuous flow in programming and therefore, according to my interviewees, at creating a harmonious acoustic pattern. This means that journalists focus on the overall message of a programme, which needs to be as attractive as possible for the listener. According to a journalist, their station even has advisors with whom they discuss topics such as tone of voice, how to play with music, how to convey the mood of a ballad and how to make a bridge to a rocky song; and that also concerns word choice. The rhythm and mood of the preceding song often affect the opening of the host's talk thereafter (see Example (23)). One of the journalists described his station as offering a pop programme, in which the modes of music and speech blend so well that the so-called flow is maintained, and he added that it is important to always keep the audio-aesthetic aspects of the show in mind. This clearly shows that transmodal meaning-making practices of adult contemporary radio journalists are shaped by the radio format, which functions as a centre of authority for their daily routines at the workplace.

In addition, as we have seen in the previous section on novel anglicisms and comprehensibility of these in different genres, genre conventions within the radio format of adult contemporary also shape journalists' daily translingual practices as part of their working routines. Adult contemporary morning shows are personality-driven programmes, and, concerning routines practices, one of adult contemporary radio journalists' greatest aims is to create proximity to the listener especially through their host talk. The genre of host talk (see Example (23)) functions as the basic framework that connects all programme parts such as news, comedy and music to form the overall message of the programme. Host talk is characterized by a mix of different communicative practices, such as conversations between hosts and/or their sidekicks, short interviews with listeners and radio guests, as well as fillers and transitions between music and other genres (for the latter see Example (23)). Therefore, host talk can be considered as a genre colony grouping together sub-genres that all share the communicative goal of providing infotainment (see Bhatia 2014). Due to the above-mentioned morning show's focus on the hosts' personalities, host talk is also more colloquial than the language used in other genres not only to generate a sense of closeness to the listener but also to create a friendly atmosphere (Fitzgerald 2006; Tolson 2006). This means that journalists get more freedom to give a personal touch to the topics discussed, which includes the use of discourse markers, such as *tja* (well) and *guten Morgen* (good morning) in Example (23). Public Service Station 3, as previously mentioned, tries to reach its target audience by putting together a unique morning show team of hosts that represents typical members of their target audience. As a host of this morning show stated, their aim is to create a casual atmosphere that generates proximity to the listener where different voices from the general population are present and have a say about issues and topics that currently concern people. Creating this casual atmosphere in host talk as part of their routine practices is also expressed by the frequent use of English discourse markers such as *yes*, *hi* and *hello* in this station's morning show content.

As we can see from this discussion, several centres of authority shape journalists' working routines: the adult contemporary radio format including its music focus and programme flow, genre conventions, and journalistic jargon used off air at the workplace. What is also often discussed in editorial conferences amongst journalists concerning further routine practices is how to make language generally more precise and suitable for radio. One of the rules of writing which applies to the wording of all content produced for radio is defined by the acronym KISS (keep it short and simple). In his analysis on anglicism use in German newspapers, Pfitzner (1978) states that a tendency towards shortness is a general phenomenon in German language development, and he continues that using anglicisms is handy for print journalists since anglicisms are usually shorter than their German equivalents. Anglicisms, according to him, are therefore a simple way of avoiding writing too many long words to save space in a paper, which benefits the production costs of the newspaper. This is in line with observations made by Sagmeister-Brandner (2008), who states that radio journalists in Austria are under extensive pressure to make their pieces for radio fit the demand of producing mainly short pieces due to time constraints on air. According to her, this ultimately benefits anglicism use on radio. In the following section, I will explore whether brevity is also a factor that shapes the use of anglicisms on German adult contemporary radio.

7.4 Brevity of anglicisms

As the results of the analysis of non-catachrestic anglicisms in relation to brevity show, in most cases non-catachrestic innovations used in the overall radio corpus are shorter than their suitable German near-equivalents (see Figure 8). This is also in line with findings by Winter-Froemel, Onysko and Calude (2014). Examples from the corpus include the anglicisms *Event* and its German near-equivalent *Veranstaltung*, *Special* and *Sonderausgabe*, as well as the English lexical item *News* and its German near-equivalent *Nachrichten*. As shown in Figure 9, the proportion of non-catachrestic anglicism tokens that are shorter than their possible German near-equivalents is even higher in station imaging materials than in the average of the overall corpus. Especially for station imaging, shortness of non-catachrestic anglicisms is relevant since for self-promotion purposes it is especially useful to choose a language that is short and brings it straight to the point. An example for this is the anglicism *Hit*, which is shorter in comparison to its German equivalents *Schlager* or *Gassenhauer*.

The quantitative results of the analysis of non-catachrestic anglicisms in relation to brevity are also in line with statements made by an interviewee (Private Station 2), who explained that when one writes for radio, one tries to generally phrase sentences as short and concise as possible. Anglicisms therefore sometimes can

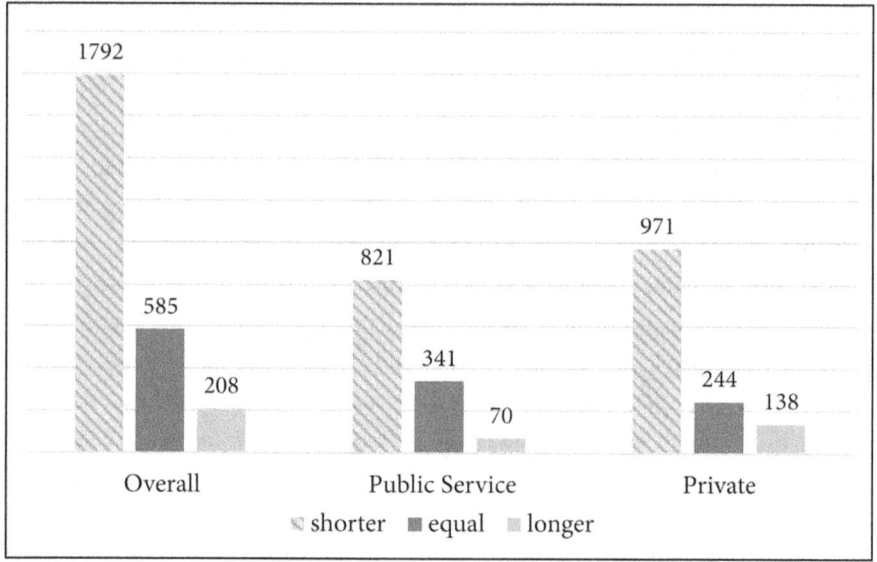

Figure 8 Word length of non-catachrestic innovations in number of tokens in the overall content.

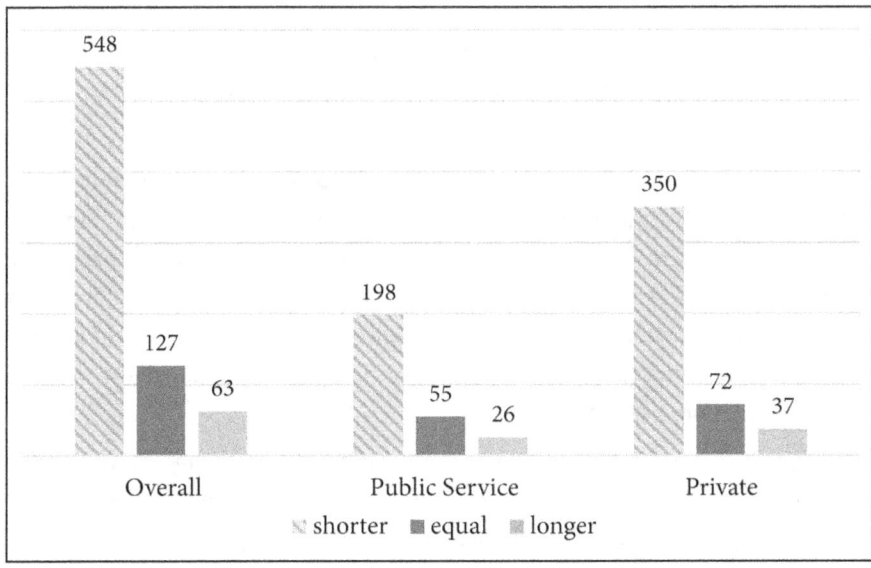

Figure 9 Word length of non-catachrestic innovations in number of tokens in station imaging (adapted from Schaefer 2019, with permission from Elsevier).

be handy to use for this purpose on radio. Despite this, however, this journalist and other journalists from both sectors also indicated that shortness of some English lexical items is not necessarily a decisive factor, and in addition, some journalists even claimed that shortness is not a factor at all. This contrasts with findings by Pfitzner (1978) and Sagmeister-Brandner (2008) since, according to my interviewees, if an anglicism is used because it is shorter but the word is not known to the target audience and thereby exceeds their standard repertoire, they would have to translate the anglicism, which in turn would lengthen their phrasing. This shows that the acronym KISS is understood by journalists as 'keep it short *and* simple'. For the case of anglicism use on radio, according to my interviewees, this means that comprehension is prioritized over brevity of expression.

A journalist working for Private Station 2 explained their procedure in the morning show to minimize the likelihood that the target audience does not understand an anglicism as follows:

> Das ist auch so, dass wir uns morgens im Studio ganz oft darüber unterhalten haben. „Du weißt, was das ist, ne? Gut, okay, alles klar." Oder [ich frage meinen Co-Moderator]: „Hast du das schon mal gehört?" Also da spricht man schon drüber. Oder es wird einfach offen in den Raum die Frage gestellt: „Surfbrett ist klar, ne?"

(The way we do it here is that we often spoke about this in the morning in studio. 'You know what that means, right? Great, okay, all clear.' Or [I asked my co-host]: 'Have you heard of this before?' So one definitely talks about that. Or one simply asks everybody around: '*Surfbrett* is clear, right?')

This reminds us of Weischenberg's (2004) interpretation of organizational structures of a newsroom, where routine decisions are often made jointly in the journalistic team (whereby the hierarchical order within the editorial team must be observed). In addition, to meaningfully discuss the comprehensibility of an anglicism for the listenership, it is beneficial that journalists themselves constitute part of the targeted audience in terms of age. One journalist working for Private Station 1 stated:

> Wir haben jetzt wenig ganz junge Leute. ... Beziehungsweise eher so im Alter der Zielgruppe, was glaube ich ganz gut ist, weil man dann auch ziemlich genau weiß, was geht und was nicht geht moderativ.

> (We have only few very young colleagues. ... More specifically rather in the age of the target audience, which is quite good I think, since one therefore knows quite accurately what is appropriate and what is not appropriate in terms of presenting.)

A public service journalist who previously worked for a private station stated about how they handled the question of comprehensibility of anglicisms at this private station:

> Es gab schon immer wieder Diskussionen, ob ein bestimmter englischer Begriff wirklich universell verstanden wird und ob auch alle das Gleiche drunter verstehen, was ja auch wichtig ist. ... Es wird dann auch vielleicht mal getestet. Habe ich jetzt hier [bei dem öffentlich-rechtlichen Sender] noch nicht erlebt, dass so ein Begriff getestet wurde, aber bei [dem privaten Sender] schon / dass ein englischer Begriff mal getestet wurde, ob genügend Leute verstehen was das heißt.

> (There were repeatedly discussions about whether a certain English expression really is universally understood and whether everyone has the same understanding of the term, which is also important. ... It perhaps is also tested from time to time. I have not seen that happen around here [at the public service station] yet, that such a term was tested; however, at [the private station] I have / that an English expression was tested whether enough people understand what it means.)

These three statements are examples of the social practices of boundary negotiation between colleagues at radio stations. Journalists collectively decide what is part of their shared repertoire and what exceeds it. Using anglicisms for achieving brevity in their wordings on air is therefore subject to a complex assemblage of various centres of authority, such as the materiality of the medium and the repertoire of linguistic resources that is shared amongst the target audience.

7.5 The workplace environment

As becomes evident from the analysis of the workplace in this chapter, the process of radio content production can involve several supervising authorities depending on the type of content. The journalists in editorial positions, such as the editor-in-chief, function as centres of authority – at times directly by checking the work of journalists before it is broadcast and at times indirectly through editorial conferences or daily debriefings. No official language policies are implemented regarding the use of anglicisms, and journalists therefore must decide themselves whether to use an anglicism or not. However, regarding such decisions there is mutual understanding amongst journalists that no anglicism should be used on air that causes comprehension problems with the target audience, which also applies for anglicisms that are shorter than their German semantic near-equivalents and therefore, against the background of time constraints on air, would offer a more efficient way of expression. This shows how journalists align available linguistic resources in their meaning-making practices under the spatial constraints of the medium radio (i.e. its auditory-only channel of communication and its ephemerality) for successful communication with the target audience. When in doubt about the use of an anglicism, journalists often consult their colleagues, and the decisions are made collectively since their aim is to generally make language on air as easily understandable as possible. In contrast to single-word codeswitching and established borrowings, novel anglicisms are therefore at all times translated, explained or indirectly explained via the context in which these are used by hosts or presenters. This is because novel anglicisms function to inform and entertain the listener and to show that the radio station is always up to the minute in relation to new trends and concepts of popular culture, which forms the basis of the adult contemporary radio format (see also Schaefer 2021b). Therefore, additional communicative effort on behalf of the journalists is invested to make these novel words comprehensible for the listener.

At the workplace of a journalist, many English words and journalistic terminology are used off air amongst members of staff. As I have shown, it is possible that such professional terminology is used on air. Even though orders of indexicality change as a journalist moves from the scale of off-air language amongst journalistic staff to the scale of on-air radio language addressed to the target listener, the indexical orders that are regarded as appropriate on each of the two scales may get mixed in the process of switching between these. This indicates that the language used at the workplace of journalists off air also impacts the language used on air.

In addition, one of many factors shaping the routine practices of journalists are the conventions of each individual radio genre, which require a distinctive language use that matches with the communicative aims of a genre (for a detailed analysis on genres see also Schaefer 2021b). In the genre of host talk, a station aims to evoke closeness to the target audience, usually achieved through the hosts and their likeable personalities on air. The editorial concept behind a radio show as a shaping factor and a journalist's personality, therefore, go hand in hand. Although the personalities of the presenting team are the voice of a radio programme, with most radio pieces it is not easy to identify who has written what or who has proofread radio content before it is broadcast, as the output is the product of a form of corporate authorship. This is due to complex production processes that allow for only limited transparency (see Burger and Luginbühl 2014) and additionally influence language use on air and the journalists' language worlds.

The adult contemporary radio format also shapes transmodal practices of journalists at their workplace, such as through its focus on predominantly English-language music and through journalists' contact with English-speaking musicians and celebrities whom the station invites. In addition, I pointed out that the kind of workplace environment a journalist has worked in before getting their present position – shaped by the individual broadcasting sectors – also affects their language use on air. Since the success of stations of the private sector very much depends on getting as much audience shares as possible, the organization of the newsroom is more constrained to not take any risks regarding the content broadcast. Therefore, this environment allows less freedom than one would have at a public service station. The greater freedom in content creation at public service stations subsequently shapes the language used by radio journalists of this sector.

Besides the fact that most professional journalists working for radio are trained to write broadcasts and speak on air, there are a number of personal factors that impact the professional language of journalists and therefore ultimately the content they produce. Therefore, a journalist's attitudes, beliefs and personal style, as I will further elaborate on in the following chapter, are additional factors that shape the use of English linguistic resources on German adult contemporary radio.

8

The Journalist

In this chapter, I will move to influencing factors on radio language that can be attributed to the individual journalist and will specifically focus on journalists' attitudes towards anglicism use on radio. This allows further insights into their language repertoires and their linguistic choices, which will help us to understand semantic and pragmatic functions of these resources in journalistic texts. The individual journalist's language perceptions are therefore investigated as an additional centre of authority shaping the content journalists produce. For this, I will also look at how the perception of modernity in a journalist's language world influences their speech behaviour.

According to Weaver et al. (2007), Fjaestad and Holmlov (1976) and Plaisance and Skewes (2003), journalists see themselves in different roles, such as the informer, interpreter or educator. I will investigate how this professional self-understanding pointed out in previous studies shapes a journalist's language use on air. Findings by Weaver et al. (2007) on journalists' role perceptions also support the interdependence of influences in the Media Language Model and remind us of the rhizomatic linkages between different influencing factors. By analysing, for example, how organizational factors can shape the formation of a journalist's role perception, the authors conclude that 'the journalist's work environment has a powerful impact on how he or she perceives the roles that the news media perform in today's society' (2007: 147). Furthermore, Shoemaker and Reese (2014) state that influencing factors attributable to the individual journalist are shaped by the personal and professional background of each journalist. In line with the concept of the rhizome, this means that influencing factors that emerge from each journalist are connected with other influencing factors within the network of authority centres on the scale of adult contemporary radio. I will start by exploring to what extent personal and professional backgrounds exert an influence on journalists' values, attitudes and beliefs and therefore on their language practices.

It is important to note here that a journalist's language attitudes as an influencing factor on radio language must not be understood as leading to an individualist language use on radio exclusively based on the journalists' agency as speech producers. Journalists align transmodal resources with spatial ecologies for successful communication with their target audience but do so under spatial constraints imposed by, for example, the materiality of the medium, sedimented practices in the newsroom or audience expectations. Therefore, journalists should not be considered as fully agentive but rather as strategic in aligning and mediating complexities of spatial repertoires, diverse assemblages of semiotic and material resources, and scalar influences in media messages (see Canagarajah and Minakova 2022).

8.1 Language worlds and attitudes

Journalists' language choices are shaped by their personal background and career but also by their age and circle of friends. As I mentioned in Chapter 7, especially hosts are selected for their unique personality in the team of hosts. This personality also needs to match with the station's image, and journalists are therefore employed according to how much they appeal to the target audience and how much the target audience can identify with the journalist (see Buchholz 2017). In this way, a host's or presenter's personal language preferences get incorporated into his or her on-air language. The following two statements provide further clarity on the matter. Regarding his use of the anglicism *Family* instead of the German equivalent *Familie* on radio, a journalist working at Private Station 1 explained:

> Das ist nicht bewusst, muss ich sagen. Das ist so / weil ich das auch privat benutze irgendwie das Wort Family.
>
> (That happens unconsciously, I have to say. That is / because I also use the word *Family* in my private life.)

He added that especially when he tells someone that he drives home to visit his relatives he would in fact often use the anglicism *Family*. Another journalist working for Public Service Station 1 said about his use of the anglicism *Lady*:

> Das tue ich tatsächlich in meiner freien Rede auch gelegentlich. Also ich war jetzt in einem Seminar wieder für mehrere Wochen und ab und zu habe ich meine Teilnehmer zusammengerufen mit „Ladies and Gentleman, es geht weiter".

(That I actually occasionally do use in my free speech as well. I just had been giving a seminar again for a few weeks and from time to time I called my participants together with 'ladies and gentlemen, let's continue'.)

In line with these two statements, many journalists of both sectors explained that, despite the specific language used on radio, they try to stay as authentic and natural as possible on air, which means that they try to speak on radio like they would with their friends after work (see also Sagmeister-Brandner 2008). When asked the question what influences their word choice, a host replied:

> Mein Gefühl in dem Moment. Wie viele Wörter ich gerade in mir habe und welche Wörter oben liegen. Man hat ja auch Lieblingswörterphasen, ne. Und auch Formulierungs-Lieblingswörterphasen einfach und das ändert sich immer so quartalsweise. Merke ich auch. Also ich habe auch pubertierende Kinder und ich merke, was ich von denen echt auch / Ja, manchmal hat man halt solche Sachen im Kopf, und ich habe einen sehr gewachsenen Freundeskreis, in dem wir auch reden / da gibt es schon mal Formulierungen, da lache ich mich kaputt und die nehme ich einfach auch mit.

(My feeling in a particular moment. How many words I currently have in my head and which ones lie on top. One also has favourite wording phases, right? And also favourite word phrasing phases and that changes quarterly. I notice that. Well, I also have children in their puberty and I notice what I also from them / Yes, sometimes one has such things inside one's head, and I have a very much grown circle of friends in which we also talk / sometimes there are phrasings where I'm in fits of laughter and these I simply take with me.)

In this context, a public service journalist of Station 3 stated:

> Also, ich finde nichts alberner als Leute, die anfangen Begrifflichkeiten zu verwenden, weil sie glauben, dass sie damit jugendlich klingen. Dann kommt man ganz schnell in dieses berufsjugendliche Ding rein. Also ich würde zum Beispiel niemals anfangen zu sagen „Mum and Dad", was meine Kinder auch tun, ja. ... Also Sachen, die mir nicht natürlich über die Lippen gehen, die verwende ich auch nicht.

(Well, I find nothing sillier than people who start using terms because they think it makes them sound juvenile. Then one quickly enters this professionally juvenile thing. I would, for example, never start to say 'mum and dad', which my children do too, yeah. ... So, things that don't go naturally off my lips, I do not use.)

When I asked her why she uses anglicisms, she explained:

> Ich verwende die nicht, um damit was zu erreichen, sondern ich verwende die, weil die in meinem Sprachgebrauch sind.

(I do not use them in order to get something out of it, but I use them because they are in my language use.)

As these statements show, the use of English linguistic resources is largely perceived as part of everyday speech practice, which indicates that anglicisms are an established part of journalists' language worlds including their private lives. It also shows that journalists try to be as authentic as possible to perform a certain peer-group identity which is part of the product that is sold by the broadcasters. Therefore, although journalists seem to be aware that anglicisms offer special communicative affordances, they do not always exploit these to avoid jeopardizing their authenticity. In addition, the different goals each journalist sets himself or herself and each journalist's function in the journalistic team shape language choice on air. Therefore, journalists can set themselves different centres of authority in daily routine practices and thereby different language standards, which also includes that journalists see themselves as having different duties to fulfil towards their listener as part of the journalistic team. This is largely dependent on their function in the radio show but also on what genre (e.g. news, comedy, station imaging) they are producing content for. In line with observations made by Weaver et al. (2007), some of my interviewees see themselves as informers, investigators or advisors; others, however, as we have seen in previous chapters, more as entertainers – the latter mainly applying to those journalists working for the private sector. The interviews have further revealed that journalists who participate in the morning show are chosen because there is a cool way about them and not because they are fond of using English. As explained in Chapter 7, as a recruitment criterion it is important for a broadcaster that journalists can represent the target audience. Therefore, as some journalists claimed, the language they use on air shall sound young but not adolescent since there is a difference between the two terms. Young means staying young in the heart; however, trying to be adolescent on air may appear unnatural and artificial to the listener.

Furthermore, according to my interviewees, the personal background, also including how and why people became journalists, shapes their linguistic choices in the radio programme (see also Shoemaker and Reese 2014). Some of the interviewees stated that they have always been interested in how journalists talk on air and therefore in journalists' linguistic choices even before they became journalists themselves. According to a public service journalist working for Station 3:

> Ich kann eine Geschichte aus der Kindheit erzählen. Ich wollte schon immer Radio machen oder Nachrichtensprecher werden. Und ich erinnere mich tatsächlich noch an einen Nachrichtensprecher bei der Tagesschau, der hieß Werner Veigel, der ist schon lange tot, und der hat gesagt, „wegen Mordes

und zweifachen <u>versuchten</u> Mordes ist XY zu lebenslanger Freiheitsstrafe verurteilt worden". Ich weiß diesen Satz wie heute noch, weil ich total fasziniert war von der Betonung und habe mir überlegt, warum sagt der jetzt dieses „<u>versuchten</u> Mordes". Wegen Mordes und zweifachen <u>versuchten</u> Mordes, das ist eigentlich eine unnatürliche Sprache. Er hat das wichtige durch die Art der Sprache und Betonung herausgehoben; nicht nur weil er Mord gemacht hat, sondern weil er es auch nochmal versucht hat, wird er weggeschlossen plus Sicherungsverwahrung. ... Das sind so Erlebnisse von Nachrichtensprechern aus meiner Kindheit, über die ich nachgedacht habe und wo ich gemerkt habe, mich fasziniert Sprache und wie man sich damit ausdrücken kann.

(I can tell a story from my childhood. I always wanted to do radio or become a news anchor. And I actually remember a news anchor from the *Tagesschau*, his name was Werner Veigel, he died long time ago, and he said, 'for murder and twice <u>attempted</u> murder XY is sentenced to livelong imprisonment'. I still remember this sentence today, because I was completely fascinated by the word stress, and I started thinking, why does he say this '<u>attempted</u> murder.' For murder and twice <u>attempted</u> murder, that is actually an unnatural language usage. He highlighted what is important with his language use and word stress; not only because he committed murder but also because he tried it again, he is locked away plus preventive detention. ... These are such news anchor experiences from my childhood that made me think and where I noticed, I am fascinated by language and how one can express oneself with it.)

With this anecdote, in which I have underlined those words that the host particularly emphasised, the journalist shows awareness of the fact that the professional language used by journalists differs from everyday language use in society. This perception in turn ultimately also shapes this journalist's language choices when writing broadcasts.

Furthermore, how journalists grew up especially in the light of their connection to British and American culture is of relevance in relation to anglicism use. One journalist working for a private station stated about his childhood:

Ich glaube, dass besonders in meiner Kindheit amerikanische Produkte, amerikanische Menschen und amerikanische Lebensgewohnheiten sehr stark an uns herangetragen wurden. Dass also man amerikanische Fernsehserien gesehen hat, dass man amerikanische Produkte zum Essen bekam, dass man teilweise auch amerikanische Freunde in der Bekanntschaft hat.

(I believe that especially in my childhood American products, American people and the American lifestyle were very much brought near to us. That one watched American television series, that one got American products to eat, that one also partially has American friends in the circle of acquaintances.)

This clearly shows that this journalist has a positive attitude towards the American way of life because he has been in contact with American culture since his childhood. In our conversation, he described this culture as easy-going, relaxed and laid-back, which he believes is also reflected in the way Americans speak. In the language world of this journalist, English is connected to this particular identity, and since he likes American culture, he feels somewhat connected to it. Additionally, as he claims, this specific way of speaking and the American attitude to life are also part of his character traits, which he regards as beneficial for his work as part of the morning show team.

> Gerade für eine Morningshow, zum Beispiel, ist das sehr interessant, weil sind wir mal ehrlich, wer von uns will jeden Morgen jemanden hören, der einem die Ohren vollheult, wie schlimm das doch da draußen ist und was in der Welt wieder gerade alles Böses passiert ist. Wir wollen doch eher immer den Blick auf das optimistische, schöne, neue am Tag richten und da ist es doch besser, wenn man jemanden hat, der einem auf die Schulter klopft.

> (In particular for a morning show, for example, this is very interesting, because let's be honest, who of us would like to listen to a person every morning who moans about how bad things are out there and what evil things have just happened in the world again. We would rather like to always cast an eye on the optimistic, nice, new things of the day, and therefore it is better to have someone who pats one on the shoulder.)

Furthermore, he added that in his opinion the American way of life generally appeals to Germans and that Germans are eager to adopt certain elements of this culture, which he also regards as a reason for the use of anglicisms by the German society. This reminds us once more of the role that asymmetrical hybridization and resemiotization of cultural resources play in journalists' language worlds. In the next section, I will engage more closely with the functions of English linguistic resources in radio broadcasts in relation to journalists' language perceptions.

8.2 Language perceptions and the functions of anglicisms in journalistic texts

Concerning the functions of anglicisms in journalistic texts, I will start with some examples that further clarify what I said regarding the use of non-catachrestic anglicisms in relation to modernity in previous chapters. Looking at examples of how anglicisms were used by radio journalists together with journalists' comments on this use allows us to further engage with this topic from the perspective of the journalists' perceptions of anglicisms. Anglicisms, according to some of my interviewees, sometimes have additional meanings in comparison to their German counterparts, which makes them an interesting choice for communication on radio. It became evident throughout the interviews that what is interesting about these anglicisms for journalists stands in direct connection with radio's lack of a visual component and therefore with the affordances these words offer for evoking certain images with their listeners. Many interviewees stated that anglicisms can, for example, connote modernity, progress, multiculturality and polyglotism (see Piller 2001, 2003) and are therefore sometimes used instead of a German term. Regarding their use of the phrasal anglicism *to go* as part of a creative compound in one of the stations' imaging materials, a journalist stated:

> Alle haben Coffee-to-go und hier noch ein Irgendwas-to-go und das ist gerade ein superpopulärer Begriff.
>
> (Everyone has coffee to go and here another something to go and that currently is a very popular term.)

And this journalist added:

> To go beinhaltet natürlich auch diese Schnelligkeit, das ist ganz kurz, weil was to go bedeutet, ich verliere damit keine Zeit.
>
> (*To go* connotes of course this sense of quickness, something that is very short, because something to go means that I do not lose any time with it.)

The anglicism *to go* is used here as it connotes an image of a modern, mobile lifestyle, which the German equivalent *zum Mitnehmen* does not bear. Regarding his use of the non-catachrestic anglicism *Song* instead of the German noun *Lied*, a host stated:

> Lied sagt niemand mehr. Lied würde ich wirklich nur noch ironisch sagen. Ich glaube mit Lied verbindet man ein Lied von Maria und Margot Hellwig, oder noch ein Chanson. ... Ich finde Lied ein schönes Wort, aber ich finde im Zusammenhang mit unserer Musik, würde eine Lücke klaffen. ... Ein Song ist was anderes als ein Lied. Ein Lied ist auch ein Kinderlied.
>
> (Nobody says *Lied* anymore. I would actually only use *Lied* ironically now. I believe with *Lied* one thinks of a song by Maria and Margot Hellwig or perhaps a chanson. ... I think that *Lied* is a beautiful word; however, I think in relation to our music, it would leave a gap. ... A *Song* differs from a *Lied*. A *Lied* is also a children's song.)

It is rather striking to note here that while this public service journalist and fellow colleagues working for the same station (Station 2) really did not use *Lied* in their coverage, other stations, including the public service station that uses most anglicisms and wishes to have a rather cool image, used *Lied* in combination with *Hit* or *Song*.

Example (24)

Time (sec.)	Speech	Music
4.5–10.7	**Station voice:** Und ab 9 bei der Arbeit, immer extra viel Musik. Extra gut gemischt. (And from 9 am onwards at work, always a lot of extra music. Particularly well mixed.)	light pop music (rhythm guitar and synthesizer; major key)
10.8–13.6	**Vox pop 1:** Echt supercoole Musik. Lieder wo ma' einfach gerne mitsingt. (Really super cool music. Songs where one likes to sing along.)	light pop music intro (building up tension; synthesizer, piano and percussions; major key)
13.7–18.3	**Vox pop 2:** So'n perfekter Mix aus alten und neuen Hits, und es gibt einfach nichts Besseres. (A perfect mix of old and new hits, and there is simply nothing better.)	
Note: English translations in parentheses.		

(Private Station 3, 2 June 2016)

(25) In einer Minute von „müde" zu „ich liebe dieses Lied". In einem Beat von der Bar auf die Tanzfläche. In einem Herzschlag von neu entdeckt zu „genau mein Ding". Diese Stelle, diese Stimme, dieser Song. Radio X.

(In one minute from 'tired' to 'I love this song'. In one beat from the bar to the dancefloor. In one heartbeat from newly discovered to 'this is my type of thing'. This part, this voice, this song. Radio X)

(Public Service Station 3, 20 April 2016)

As can be taken from these two examples, the pragmatically unmarked term *Lied* can be applied in relation to the music played on adult contemporary radio if the additional pragmatic meaning which the anglicism *Song* bears – modern, international pop and rock music – is represented through the wider semiotic assemblage. This is the case in Example (24), an excerpt from station imaging where not only the non-catachrestic anglicisms *supercoole* (super cool) and *Hits* clearly determine the kind of music the term *Lied* refers to but also the music bed in the style of contemporary pop music played throughout the station imaging element creates an image of the station's pop music orientation and thereby prevents a misinterpretation of the term *Lied*. Similarly, the non-catachrestic anglicism *Beat* and the additional use of *Song* in the station imaging excerpt in

Example (25) prevent a possible interpretation of *Lied* as connoting a type of music which does not fit into an adult contemporary playlist. This shows that if *Lied* is used as part of assemblages that unambiguously connote modernity, it does not necessarily seem to be perceived by all journalists as incompatible with the music played on adult contemporary radio.

Besides the relevance of the affordances that anglicisms offer for evoking certain images with the listener, such as in relation to modernity, it also generally matters how a word sounds on radio, where anglicisms are sometimes the means of choice. According to a journalist in an editorial position at Private Station 2:

> Wir haben ja jetzt auch noch den Begriff Hit-Tipp. Das klingt halt einfach besser, zu sagen unser Hit-Tipp, als unser Song-Tipp oder unser Lied-Tipp. Unsere Lied-Empfehlung. Also Radio ist ja auch immer so ein bisschen / ja das ist irgendwie auch immer so ein bisschen cool und Englisch gehört tatsächlich so ein bisschen auch zum cool sein dazu. Deshalb machen viele Firmen ja auch in ihren Slogans irgendwie was Englisches rein, obwohl es eigentlich totaler Bullshit ist, dass sie das machen. Und ich benutze auch viele Anglizismen, wie ich gerade merke.

> (We now additionally have the term *Hit-Tipp* (hit recommendation). That simply sounds better to say, our *Hit-Tipp* than our *Song-Tipp* or our *Lied-Tipp*. Our *Lied-Empfehlung*. Well, radio is always a little / yes, that is somehow also always a little cool, and English indeed is also somewhat part of being cool. That is why many companies somehow insert some English in their slogans, even though it is actually complete bullshit that they do that. And I also use many anglicisms, as I've just noticed.)

In addition, a journalist from Public Service Station 3 thinks that English is generally used on radio

> weil es einfach gut klingt. Also manche Begrifflichkeiten sind auf Englisch einfacher auszudrücken, unkomplizierter finde ich. Ich finde es klingt besser und es klingt cooler. Also ich kann nachvollziehen, dass man, wenn man einen coolen Klang erzeugen will / Wobei ich ehrlich gesagt nicht das Gefühl habe, dass wir es da übertreiben. Also da gibt es ja ganz andere Möglichkeiten. Also den Eindruck habe ich nicht. Also ich finde das alles im Rahmen.

> (because it simply sounds good. Well, some concepts are easier to express in English, less complicated, I think. I think it sounds better and it sounds cooler. I can understand that one, when one wishes to create a cool sound / Whereby I honestly do not have the impression that we overdo it here. Well, there are completely different ways of doing this. I do not have this impression. I think everything is within the scope.)

As we saw in Section 6.3, in contrast to many journalists perceiving the use of anglicisms as connected to modernity, journalists working for Public Service Station 1 try to largely avoid anglicisms in their content because they do not find them cool at all and use the smallest number of anglicisms in the overall corpus as well as the smallest number of anglicisms in their station imaging content. One journalist working in the production of station imaging materials at Public Service Station 1 explained why the non-catachrestic anglicism *Talk* was nevertheless used in one of their station imaging elements:

> Talk würde ich jetzt auch nicht unter die Begriffe zählen, die so fürchterlich cool wirken, aber das Wort kommuniziert halt auch in Deutschland sofort eine bestimmte Form von Sendung. Und ich finde, wenn das so ein kommunikatives Ziel erreicht, dass man einfach sofort versteht worum es geht, dann kann man das machen.

> (*Talk* I would not count as one of the terms that appear so terribly cool; however, in Germany the word immediately communicates a certain type of programme. And I find that if it reaches a communicative goal that one immediately understands what is meant by it, then one can use it.)

The anglicism *Talk* therefore is used by this station since it directly evokes the specific image of a talk show, unlike its German equivalent *Gespräch*, which refers to a conversation amongst people more generally. In line with this journalist's argumentation, anglicisms that do not directly reach a communicative goal are often not perceived as appropriate for use on radio. In this context, I will briefly discuss a well-known and often-quoted example, the borrowing *Kids* and its equivalent *Kinder* (cf. Busse 2008; Onysko 2007; Onysko and Winter-Froemel 2011), which also occurred in the radio corpus. As stated by a journalist working for Private Station 1:

> Kids finde ich klingt tatsächlich knackiger, also das ist so ein bisschen / [schnippt mit den Fingern] in dem Fall jünger so ein bisschen und was aber auch jeder versteht.

> (*Kids* I find sounds actually snazzier, well that is somewhat / [snaps his fingers] in this case a little younger and a word that however everyone understands.)

Despite this journalist's perception of modernity in relation to the anglicism *Kids* and Busse's (2008) personal observations that journalists exaggerate with using *Kids*, the anglicism occurred only nineteen times in the radio corpus including once as a hybrid compound – *Einlauf-Kids* (mascot children), used in the context of football. The German noun *Kinder* on the other hand appeared eighty-six times in the radio corpus. *Kids* therefore does not generally seem to be the preferred choice over *Kinder* to achieve the communicative goals of the stations despite it being perceived as the more modern term by some journalists. It rather shows that *Kids* has a restricted use in the radio corpus and has not reached a broader sedimentation in journalistic speech. In addition, it indicates that an extensive use of *Kids* would most probably be perceived as unauthentic by the broad adult contemporary audience.

One host working at Public Service Station 2 also gave his opinion on the use of the anglicism *Party* instead of *Fete*, a noun originally derived from French in the eighteenth century but established in German:

> Fete ist ein Achtziger-Jahre-Begriff. Ich würde nie mehr sagen, „das ist eine tolle Fete", da würden die alle sagen: „Oh Gott, wie ist der denn stehen geblieben?"
>
> (*Fete* is an eighties expression. I would never say 'that's a great *Fete*' again. Everyone would say then: 'Oh my god, how outdated is he?')

Two other journalists working for Public Service Station 3 made similar remarks about the term *Fete*. One of these journalists stated that *Fete* in contrast to *Party* does not constitute part of their target audience's language preferences and therefore, if used, it would give their station the appearance of an old man's station. The second journalist made a somewhat different remark regarding the use of *Fete*. On the one hand, in line with the explanation given by his fellow colleague, this journalist also explained that *Fete* is an old-fashioned expression that one relates to the kind of parties his parents went to and therefore *Fete* is not compatible with their target audience's language use. On the other hand, he stated that stations aiming at younger, more urban audiences than his station would especially make use of *Fete* and similar 'überdeutsche' (hyper-German) expressions again since for their audiences *Party* would appear as dated, and hence they want to distinguish themselves from adult contemporary stations. Since language resources are mobile, their indexical functions are constantly up for refashioning and appropriation in different sociocultural contexts. We also see here the cyclical nature of pop culture, where what was once old-fashioned can become cool again, not only temporally but also in terms of cultural origin (i.e. French instead of English).

Although these two journalists claimed that *Fete* would be incompatible with their target audience's language use, their station nevertheless made use of the term in a station imaging element promoting an event organized by the station. It therefore seems that reasons other than the journalists' language perceptions can also have an influence on their word choice in cases where a decision between two semantic near-equivalents has to be made.

Even though modernity seems to be relevant for the use of some non-catachrestic anglicisms by journalists in station imaging materials, other factors appear to be overriding. With the use of the German noun *Fete* instead of *Party* in the promotion piece, it seems that the public service broadcaster aimed at additionally reaching this younger generation who would use the term *Fete* again. Therefore, *Fete* contributes to reaching the communicative goal of promoting the event to the younger generation who is soon to become part of their target audience.

A further reason for the use of *Fete* instead of *Party* in the promotion piece is that the near-equivalent *Fete* provides a welcome variation since the non-catachrestic anglicism *Party* was already used five times in the station imaging element of only 47 seconds in length. Other journalists of both public service and private stations also stated that non-catachrestic anglicisms can serve variation purposes – a stylistic motivation for the use of anglicisms that has additionally been identified by previous research (Galinsky 1963; Onysko 2004; Pfitzner 1978). A journalist working for Private Station 1, for example, explained that he occasionally says *Stop-and-go* (stop-and-go traffic) instead of *stockender Verkehr*, or *City* (city centre) instead of *Innenstadt*. The following examples from the corpus additionally highlight that the use of anglicisms for the purpose of variation in radio content seems to be a welcome stylistic feature amongst radio journalists.

(26) Natürlich wollen Motorradfahrer das nicht alles so auf sich sitzen lassen, die haben auch mitdiskutiert. [Hörer X] … findet, alle im Straßenverkehr die müssen aufeinander Rücksicht nehmen, nicht nur Biker; und überhaupt, nicht alle Motorradfahrer sind auch laut.

(Of course, motorcyclists won't take all of this just like that, they also participated in the discussion. [Listener X] … believes that all people on the road they have to be considerate of one another, not only bikers; and after all not all motorcyclists are noisy.)

(Public Service Station 1, 8 April 2016)

(27) Die Streiks treffen morgen auch den Frankfurter Flughafen. Hier sind vor allem die innerdeutschen Verbindungen betroffen. Die Passagiere können ihr Ticket aber als Fahrkarte für die Deutsche Bahn nutzen.

(Tomorrow, the strikes will also hit Frankfurt Airport. Mainly the domestic German connections are affected here. Passengers can however use their boarding pass as a train ticket for the German railway.)

(Private Station 2, 26 April 2016)

According to the *AWB*, the anglicism *Biker* connotes motorcyclists who ride their bikes as a leisure activity. The German semantic near-equivalents *Motorradfahrer*, *Kradfahrer*[1] or *Mopedfahrer* do not bear this connotation. Example (26), however, illustrates that the additional pragmatic meaning of *Biker* instead of its German semantic near-equivalents was not decisive in this context since the term *Biker* was used together with *Motorradfahrer* for variation purposes and different terms for motorbike (*Motorrad* and *Moped*) were additionally used throughout the discussion of the topic by the host.

As shown in Example (27), using the English linguistic resource *Ticket* as opposed to using the German equivalents *Bordkarte* or *Flugkarte* (boarding pass) helps to avoid the repetition of *Karte* in the news broadcast. Furthermore, the anglicism *Ticket* was only used for variation purposes to replace *Bordkarte* or *Flugkarte*, instead of replacing *Fahrkarte* in the context of a ticket for the train. In contrast to the previous example of *Biker*, where the connotation of the anglicism was not relevant for variation purposes, it can be assumed that *Ticket* was used only in the context of air travel here because a plane represents the more modern means of transportation in contrast to a train. This becomes also evident in the use of the non-catachrestic anglicism *jetten* (to jet) in the context of travelling by plane in the corpus. The borrowing *jetten* bears the connotation of a modern, travel-oriented lifestyle. In contrast, there is no alternative anglicism for *Zug fahren* (to go by train) in German which would connote this sense of a modern way of travelling.

In addition to the relevance of anglicisms' connotations in relation to modernity for some journalists and their potential usefulness for reaching a communicative goal, it is also relevant whether a non-catachrestic occurrence is more precise in signifying a certain concept than its German near-equivalent. According to a journalist of Public Service Station 2:

> Wenn ein Begriff, der es hundertprozentig trifft, aus dem angelsächsischen kommt, dann würde ich den auf jeden Fall verwenden. Und vor allen Dingen auch, wenn er längst im allgemeinen Sprachgebrauch ist, dann würde ich nicht in einer deutschtümelnden Weise versuchen da zwanghaft ein deutsches Wort zu verwenden, was im Grunde 90 Prozent der Menschen nicht mehr benutzen. Das ist ja Quatsch, das würde ich auch nicht tun.

> (If a term which puts it right on the spot is Anglo-Saxon, I would definitely use it. And above all when it is already in general language use for some time, then I would not in a German-chauvinistic fashion try to compulsively use a German word, which in principle 90 per cent of the population does not use anymore. That is nonsense, that I would not do.)

This is in line with findings by Galinsky (1963) and Pfitzner (1978), who also found that anglicisms are used for the purpose of precision in journalistic texts. Examples from the corpus include the non-catachrestic anglicisms *Show* and its equivalent *Sendung*, *Newcomer* and *Neuling*, and *Lady* and *Dame*. Even though these English lexical items can be considered to have similar semantic meanings to their German counterparts, these linguistic resources are either semantically more precise than their German equivalents or are the emotionally stronger term. A presenter working for Public Service Station 2 stated, for example, that the non-catachrestic innovation *Show* is used because it connotes an entertainment programme – a semantic specification that the German near-equivalent *Sendung*, which functions as a hypernym in the sense of English 'programme', does not bear. This confirms Onysko and Winter-Froemel's (2011) observation that some non-catachrestic anglicisms adopt specific meanings in contrast to their semantic near-equivalents.

Another example from the corpus which illustrates that English linguistic resources can adopt more specific meanings as compared to their German counterparts is the anglicism *Newcomer* used in host talk instead of the German semantic near-equivalent *Neuling*.

> (28) Barbara Schöneberger hat das ganze wieder richtig gut gemacht. … War wieder sehr selbstironisch, richtig tolle Gags und hat das gesagt, was andere denken. Zum Beispiel über die lustige Frisur von Newcomer und Grammy-Gewinner The Weekend.
>
> (Barbara Schöneberger did the whole thing very well again. … She again was very self-ironical, really nice gags and said what others think. For example, about the funny haircut of newcomer and Grammy winner The Weekend.)
> (Public Service Station 3, 8 April 2016)

The word *Newcomer*, which appeared five times in the corpus on different stations in the context of the ECHO awards, bears an additional specific meaning of a person being successful, which is not conveyed by the more general term *Neuling*. This is also considered in the reference entry for *Newcomer* in the *Duden Fremdwörterbuch* (2015):

> **New|co|mer** [ˈnjuːkamɐ], der; -s, -:
> jemand, der noch nicht lange bekannt, etwas, was noch neu ist [aber schon einen gewissen Erfolg hat]; Neuling
>
> (someone who became popular only recently, something that is still new [however, already has a certain success]; beginner)

According to a public service journalist working for Station 1, who used the anglicism *Lady* to describe a female elephant instead of using the German equivalent *Dame*:

> Ich finde Lady klingt schöner als Dame. Dame klingt so nach Dutt und alt und faltig und goldener Brille. Lady klingt nach elegant und anziehend.
>
> (I think that *Lady* sounds nicer than *Dame*. *Dame* sounds like topknot and old and wrinkly and with golden glasses. *Lady* sounds like elegant and attractive.)

Therefore, for this host, *Lady* clearly has a different connotation than *Dame* and, depending on the context, *Lady* is more precise and emotionally complex in its use as it evokes a different stereotypical image of the subject it refers to. In addition, *Hit* was mentioned by a producer as a further example of an English linguistic resource that is the emotionally stronger word in contrast to the German word *Musik* (music):

> Musik ist quasi ohne Wertung. Hit ist Musik bewertet.
>
> (*Musik* is so to speak without judging. *Hit* is music valued.)

Moreover, *Hit* according to this producer stands for a successful song, whereas the possible equivalent *Schlager* bears a different connotation. The innovation *Hit* brings it straight to the point in terms of connoting a popular song of the genre of rock/pop music, in contrast to *Schlager*, which also stands for a popular song but connotes a different music genre, namely that of German Schlager music. A journalist working for the same public service station stated that they have a hit parade on radio for over 35 years in which the most popular current hits are played. For the name of the show, they used to use *Schlager* instead of *Hit* or *Song*, which they had to change since people were confused about what kind of music they should expect. According to him, their target audience today relates *Schlager* to a different kind of music, namely German Schlager music, than their audience did at the time when the show was launched.

In addition, as became evident from the interviews, journalists also perceive anglicisms as sometimes easier to sing than their German counterparts, which especially applies to their use in station imaging materials. *Lieblingsmix* (favourite music mix), according to a producer, is an example for this, where *Mix* is much easier to sing in a jingle than the German word *Mischung*.

Furthermore, anglicisms are particularly suitable for various other stylistic purposes besides variation due to their salience on air. A station imaging producer explained that anglicisms are also often used along with their German equivalent to emphasize once more what is already said. Hence, for intensification purposes, an English lexical item may be used followed by its German semantic near-equivalent and vice versa (see Pfitzner 1978). The following excerpts taken from station imaging pieces show anglicisms used for intensification purposes in claims together with their German near-equivalents.

(29) Immer up to date mit den aktuellen Hits.

(Always up to date with the current hits.)

(Private Station 2, 8 April 2016)

(30) Die beste Comedy, der meiste Spaß.

(The best comedy, the most fun.)

(Private Station 1, 8 April 2016)

The use of the non-catachrestic occurrence *up to date* together with its German near-equivalent *aktuell* in the same sentence additionally emphasizes the currentness of the music played by the station. By using both, the German noun *Spaß* and the anglicism *Comedy*, a station once more highlights how funny their comedy programme is.

Different types of anglicisms including pseudo-loans and single-word codeswitches were also used in the corpus in a stylistic fashion as part of rhymes formed with German words. Some examples from the radio corpus include the following:

(31) *Goodbye*, Ü-Ei, sag' ich nur. Es is' so weit, die Überraschungseier verabschieden sich heute in die Sommerpause.

(Goodbye, Ü-egg, I say. It is time, the surprise eggs say goodbye today for their summer break.)

(Private Station 3, 17 May 2016)

(32) Einen hervorragenden Merksatz hamm wir grad noch bekommen hier von [Hörer X] ... Er schreibt, „also ich sag' das meinem Kurzen immer so: ‚Mit Helm fahren die Profis, ohne nur die Doofis.'"

(We just got a brilliant take-home message there from [Listener X] ... He writes, 'well, I always say to my little one: "Professionals ride with helmets, only dummies go without."')

(Public Service Station 2, 26 April 2016)

In Example (31), the single-word codeswitch *goodbye* rhymes with *Ü-Ei*. Here, a catchy phrase is created that works well on radio to attract the listener's attention. The consumer information that underlies this phrase, given by a host of Private

Station 3, was linked to the idea that the host would open the last available Kinder surprise egg to give a song as a gift to the listeners.

At one time in the morning show of Public Service Station 2 (Example (32)), as part of a discussion on the importance of wearing helmets when riding a bicycle, styling tips were given to the listeners on how to keep one's hair in shape under the helmet. To support the use of bicycle helmets when cycling, one host read out a message the morning show team received in studio from a listener. As we can see from this example, by using the take-home message from this listener the morning show team found a clever way to provide the audience with a catchy phrase including the rhyme of the pseudo-anglicism *Profis* (professionals) with German *Doofis* (dummies). The intention here is that the take-home message will hopefully stay in the minds of the audience to remind them in an easy way to wear helmets when riding bicycles. Anglicisms that are deployed for rhyming purposes as a stylistic feature were also described by Pfitzner (1978) in relation to print media. Pfitzner gives several examples of rhyming, such as of an anglicism and a name (*Quiz* and *Chris*) or of two anglicisms (*Beat* and *Sweet*), but does not specifically give an example that reflects the use of an anglicism along with a German term where both words are used semantically independently from one another. This could indicate that language creativity in journalistic speech today involves more cross-over and mixing than four decades ago and that journalists' practices around language boundaries have shifted since Pfitzner's study.

Furthermore, the stylistic device of alliteration was used in the radio corpus to create wordings that sound attractive to the listeners. Examples from the radio corpus that illustrate the use of anglicisms to create a catchy sound through alliteration are the hybrid compound nouns **Kult-Comedy** (iconic comedy) and *Topthemen* (top topics). According to Onysko (2007), the alliteration between compound elements of hybrid anglicisms gives these words an additional harmonic quality. This of course is particularly relevant for radio since due to its characteristics – and especially its lack of a visual component – radio lives from various semiotic resources creating a catchy, vivid language.

For stylistic purposes, polysemy of some anglicisms was also used in the corpus. The anglicism *rauskicken* (to kick out), for example, appeared as part of a comedy song piece by Private Station 2 in the context of the opening of the European football championship not only in the sense of 'to throw something or somebody out'. By singing 'Frankreich, euch rauszukicken, *oui* das reicht' (France, to kick you out *oui* that will do), the anglicism *rauskicken* was simultaneously used by a journalist in its second more specific meaning of 'to kick a ball' in the sense of to kick the ball in a football match and by doing so to throw a team out of the competition by winning the match.

A further reason for the use of anglicisms in radio coverage, according to some journalists, is that some established anglicisms are not perceived as really foreign anymore due to their frequent use on air. Concerning the often-used anglicisms *Service*, *Party*, *Trend* and *Gag* in their radio content, a journalist in an editorial position at Public Service Station 3 explained:

> Also das sind alles Begriffe, die im deutschen Duden stehen. Deutsche Wörter, die natürlich einen englischen Ursprung haben.
>
> (These are all terms that are in the German Duden. German words that of course have an English origin.)

Regarding her use of the anglicisms *Date* (romantic meeting) instead of German *Treffen* as well as *dissen* (to diss) instead of the German near-equivalent *beschimpfen*, which are both established anglicisms listed in the *Duden*, a journalist stated:

> Date finde ich absolut eingedeutscht. Also die Sachen, die ich verwende, sind in meiner Welt eingedeutscht. Also auch dissen / meine Kinder ... sagen gedisst und deswegen habe ich das auch verwendet. Ja, aber da stehe ich auch dazu, also das finde ich auch nicht schlimm.
>
> (*Date* I find absolutely established in German. Therefore, things that I use on radio are established in German in my world. Therefore, also *dissen* / my children ... say *gedisst* and this is why I also used that term. Yes, and I adhere to that, I don't think that is a bad thing.)

These statements show that for most journalists certain established anglicisms that have become part of standard German and are used frequently in their lifeworlds on and off air are perceived as of English origin but not necessarily as foreign. This perception of anglicisms that are more frequently used in journalists' lifeworlds is an example of how mobile linguistic resources are appropriated and can become sedimented as part of language practices (see Canagarajah 2013). While socially constructed language boundaries and materializations of structuralist language ideologies (e.g. in the form of standard language dictionaries, see Blommaert, Leppänen and Spotti 2012) are important features and normative forces in journalists' language worlds, such language boundaries are open to negotiation and subject to constant change.

8.3 The journalist as an influencing factor

To summarize the main points made in this chapter, a journalist's language attitudes and beliefs and how the sociocultural environment affects these on a both personal and professional level shape the use of English on air. As previously mentioned, all influencing factors are interrelated and in aligning resources on radio, journalists are also affected by centres of authority stemming from their personal backgrounds and experiences. How journalists came to their profession, their personal motivations and interests in journalism, and their personal role models in this profession all shape anglicism use on radio. In addition, how journalists grew up; how much they are in contact with American culture through American friends in the neighbourhood, American products or movies; and how much a journalist therefore feels attracted to this particular lifestyle are relevant factors that impact their very own language repertoire and language world. Especially a journalist's personal language preferences get incorporated into radio content, which includes linguistic resources used in conversations with family, friends and other acquaintances.

What we can take from the interviewees' statements is that it is of utmost importance for an adult contemporary radio journalist to be as natural as possible on air for the purpose of authenticity and therefore to achieve target audience appeal. Anglicisms are hence not used to sound adolescent in the radio corpus; however, to sound younger is not necessarily a bad thing. While some journalists see anglicisms in connection to polyglotism and being modern and cool, others are not so convinced and perceive anglicisms as not necessarily related to such notions of modernity but rather as a phenomenon from the 1990s, which according to these interviewees is definitely no sign of modernity any longer. These are expressions of journalists' individual language worlds and the value journalists associate with English in this context, which also shapes their use of English linguistic resources on air. Hence, some journalists believe that they sound cooler when using English as part of their wordings on air, while others find it pseudo-cool and therefore not appropriate to use too many English words. This also stands in correlation with the duties each journalist sees himself or herself having to fulfil towards the target listenership of their station. I have pointed out that from a journalist's perspective seeing oneself as an entertainer – which applies mainly to journalists working for the private sector – has a different impact on one's professional language preferences than when one views oneself in the role of an investigator or informer.

Based on their language perceptions and attitudes, journalists use anglicisms instead of a German equivalent or in addition to a German equivalent to achieve specific communicative goals in a non-visual medium and for various stylistic purposes. These include to form a catchy alliteration, to bring variation into a radio piece, for rhyming purposes, and to place greater emphasis on a topic by using an additional anglicism besides its German equivalent. Furthermore, anglicisms are used for precision purposes in the radio corpus since non-catachrestic anglicisms often have additional meanings a German equivalent does not bear. In addition, some established anglicisms that are quite frequently used in journalists' lifeworlds and especially by their radio station are perceived as of English origin but not necessarily as foreign anymore, which is an example of language sedimentation and shows that constructed language boundaries are open to negotiation.

In sum, as previously outlined, all journalists agree that comprehensibility of anglicisms is overriding to their stylistic functions and connotations on radio and a prerequisite for achieving the intended communicative goals.

9

Conclusion

The paradigmatic parallelism that has evolved in the study around language over the last two decades has led to a wide range of differing interpretations of language phenomena in our globalized world and likewise to frequent mutual criticism amongst researchers in (socio)linguistics concerning ontological and epistemological considerations around the concept of language. This book set out to illustrate what a new holistic perspective on language mobility in complex times of fluidity and fixity can look like – a perspective that combines the best of both paradigms and thereby makes use of the value each perspective offers for a socially grounded spatial approach to language. I hope to have shown what such an approach can offer and how it allows us to better engage with the language worlds of speakers. While a sociolinguistics of mobility and therefore viewing language as a social practice provides a vital foundation for this new perspective, analytical concepts and tools from contact linguistic theory are useful when applied to explore how boundaries are maintained, negotiated and reshaped in everyday linguistic practice of actual language users.

In times of accelerated globalization, the study around language is closely tied to the worldwide diffusion of Englishes, mediatization of societies and cultural mixing across the globe. To find a possible way of bridging the paradigmatic gap in (socio)linguistics, I argue that we need to focus on how these processes affect language users especially in more stable sociolinguistic environments, which has so far not received sufficient attention in studies supporting the mobility paradigm. The use of English linguistic resources in mass media language in localities of Kachru's expanding circle of World Englishes provides us with an excellent example of how fluidity meets fixity and of how mobile language resources become embedded in language produced in highly normative sociocultural environments. By the example of a case study of the use of English linguistic resources in the morning shows of German adult contemporary radio, the book has explored the complexities of sociocultural factors that shape this communicative event and has thereby exemplarily applied the proposed holistic approach in the context of the sociolinguistics of mass media. For a critical sociolinguistics of mass media, methodological pluralism means not only looking behind the scenes at the complex content production processes of mass media messages that shape journalists' language use and acknowledging the channel of communication, its materiality and characteristics but also considering journalists' lifeworlds, their perceptions and attitudes to language use, and the structures and conventions that shape how language is produced in this context.

Grounded on a flat ontology, the book has also introduced the Media Language Model, which combines both notions of mobility and stability and allows for an in-depth investigation of mass media language. While a model per se can only offer a simplified depiction of the multitude of influencing factors that shape journalists' language use, my intention, as I outlined before, is not to make this complexity less chaotic but to provide a guideline for future research that gives possible impulses, ideas and suggestions for more complex interpretations of mass media language that better account for the complexities of meaning-making practices in times of accelerated globalization.

The field of media studies provides a variety of models for the analysis of influences on media content (see Chapter 4); however, these models are not sufficient in themselves to establish the crucial link between factors exerting an influence on the medium radio and language usage on radio. In the same vein, previous studies on traditional mass media language in (socio)linguistics have focused more on the text than on the complex, spatiotemporally entangled meaning-making practices of journalists. By viewing journalists' meaning-making practices as spatially entangled in a rhizomatic network of influencing factors, the proposed Media Language Model functions as a theoretical framework which explains how influences originating from various sources affect the use of transmodal resources by journalists. This theoretical framework, as described in Chapter 4, combines the perspectives of models of influencing factors on media content from media studies with a sociolinguistics of mobile language resources – which also includes notions of linguistic and cultural hybridization – governed by authority centres setting language standards. As demonstrated by the results gained in the case study, the Media Language Model has proven to be a valuable tool for exploring the shaping factors of discursive media practices including the use of English linguistic resources in German adult contemporary radio. The model therefore provides an important guideline and theoretical backbone for future research aiming to examine the spatial repertoires of mass media language.

In the results presented in Chapters 5 to 8, I have described how viewing media language as an assemblage reveals the complexity of the manifold, multifaceted and polycentric factors shaping the use of English resources on radio. The case study presented in this book has thereby illustrated that it is vital for future research in (socio)linguistics investigating mass media language to acknowledge these multiple influencing factors and has revealed the opportunities this approach offers in the context of global Englishes. The combination of quantitative and qualitative contact linguistic methods allowed for a thorough investigation of the use of English linguistic resources on German radio. While corpus linguistic methods provided an important basis for the detection of anglicisms as an example of the structures in journalists' language worlds, semi-structured interviews with the actual language users allowed for an emic perspective and an in-depth investigation of the structures and conventions that govern the language worlds of journalists and how these are at times renegotiated.

In Chapter 5, I showed why language cannot be examined only in terms of linguistic structures set apart from the social and cultural context in which language is practised as often done by traditional contact linguistic research. We need to overcome the binary distinction between text and context, and I hope that this necessity has also become evident throughout the book. The analysis of the cultural and social environment in which language resources are mobile has opened up new perspectives on the use of anglicisms by German adult contemporary radio media by going beyond previous research on anglicisms where this context has mostly been neglected. In the case of Germany, asymmetrical hybridization of culture following WWII – additionally strengthened by accelerated globalization and the global diffusion of English – is mirrored in the use of anglicisms, which are a clear indicator for this asymmetrical mixing. German journalism has likewise been shaped by the asymmetry of hybridizing flows, which also affects the language used by radio journalists. An example for this can be taken from the results of the analysis of lexical field (see Section 5.3). As we have seen, these show that many anglicisms used in the radio corpus are related to the lexical fields of *Lifestyle/ Fashion/Leisure*, *Music/Dance* and *Media/Communication/Entertainment*. The quantity of anglicisms found in these lexical fields is closely related to the format of adult contemporary radio, which is traversed by American and British popular culture, and its thematic priorities such as pop music and entertainment. The frequent usage of anglicisms in the above-named lexical fields in the language of adult contemporary radio stations is therefore a result of the scale within which such stations place their communication and is necessary to relay their messages effectively to their target audiences. The entanglement of media language in social structures and conventions on this scale ultimately demonstrates the importance of stepping away from the monolithic concept of language in the study of global Englishes in times of accelerated globalization. However, it also highlights how normative forces, which can also include standard varieties of a language, still affect language behaviour.

Chapter 6 focused on themes of the media system, which are competition and segmentation of the German radio market. An analysis of these two concepts has revealed how structures of social systems affect journalists' speech behaviour. The results for competition point towards a connection between the communicative aim of a station's programme and its anglicism frequency. The more the editorial concept of a morning show is focused on entertainment, the higher the quantity of anglicisms used by its journalists. The overall frequency of anglicisms resulted in 2.57 anglicisms per minute of spoken radio content, which equals 1.57 anglicisms per 100 words. While the overall results for the two broadcasting sectors indicate a higher frequency of anglicisms on behalf of the private sector, a closer look at the results of each station individually reveals that the public service sector contained both extremes of the spectrum of anglicism frequency, while the private stations showed a fairly similar anglicism use. When it comes to editorial concepts in terms of language and anglicism usage, at first glance, the private sector follows a standard success model where the focus is on entertainment, whereas stations of the public service sector have differing editorial strategies. The private stations also used more time on air for self-promotional purposes in station imaging (16.0 per cent of their overall spoken content in contrast to 8.7 per cent for the public service sector), which has shown the highest frequency of anglicisms of all genres in the corpus. It is interesting to note, however, that Public Service Station 3, which has the strongest private competitor in its broadcasting area, also spent significantly more time for station imaging than the other two public service stations. When one takes a closer look at each of the stations and their direct competitors, it becomes further evident that the use of anglicisms is more related to the individual situation of competition between stations in their respective broadcasting areas than being predetermined by a station's belonging to one of the two broadcasting sectors. The results point towards an increased anglicism usage by those stations that are the weaker competitors in a broadcasting area since these seem to try to strengthen their market position by promoting their image of being an entertainment provider and therefore make use of the indexical value of anglicisms. In addition, segmentation of the market resulting from competition and therefore a station's focus on a specific target audience influence anglicism use in this context since the stations aim to adapt to their listeners' language use.

In Chapter 7, I looked at how a journalist's immediate professional surrounding bears many polycentric normative forces, and I discussed the major centres of authority at a journalist's workplace and how these shape the use of English linguistic resources on radio. While there are no language policies that regulate anglicism usage on adult contemporary radio, there are various centres of authority that surround the individual journalist, such as the editor, colleagues and professional language used off air, which all shape radio language. What is also relevant here is that even though no official language policies are implemented, there are content rules such as for the length of a piece which partially impact the wordings chosen by a journalist for a radio broadcast. Anglicisms are, however, not generally favoured for being often shorter than their German equivalents since these may cause comprehension problems and, in this case, would additionally have to be explained by the journalist. Despite the various reasons for implementations of anglicisms in radio coverage (see Chapter 8), the use of anglicisms on air is only then effective when these are comprehensible for the target listener. As the results have shown, if comprehensibility cannot be guaranteed, an anglicism is either not used at all, translated, explained directly or made comprehensible through the context in which it is used, which especially applies to novel anglicisms. This demonstrates that the perception of many anglicisms as foreign elements is very much part of the lifeworlds of many German radio journalists and is related to practices of boundary drawing and negotiation, especially in cases where an anglicism appears less frequently in use in the journalists' language worlds. This again iterates the necessity to recognize monolingual ideologies as part of the assemblage of language in analyses of the diffusion of Englishes in localities shaped by both mobility and greater fixity. However, this means not only to acknowledge these as influential normative forces but also to adopt methodological tools into our research designs that allow to explore language perceptions based on structuralist ideologies.

The stations' adult contemporary radio format, which the analysed stations' morning show programmes are subject to, also shapes the language used by radio journalists. Through the radio format, journalists are permanently in contact with American and British popular culture. This is not only the case through the music selection of such stations and journalists' contact with celebrities mainly from English-speaking countries, but the format itself with its structures and presenting styles also functions as a centre of authority. This again shows the structures and boundaries journalists are subject to in their daily working routine.

Not only is the immediate surrounding at a station a relevant shaping factor but also, as was disclosed in Chapter 8, journalists themselves are a centre of authority to their own language use. This highlights the need for future research to include the actual language user in analyses of global Englishes. The chapter shed light on journalists' attitudes towards language usage on radio and how these attitudes differ between age groups amongst journalists. Journalists' personal norms, standards, goals and their experiences and surroundings external to work are recalled here, which all impact the language chosen by journalists in radio coverage. It also became evident that the role journalists see themselves in influences their language usage. Journalists working for the private sector see themselves more as entertainers, whereas journalists of the public service sector show a greater sense of commitment towards contributing to the free shaping of public opinion, at times even by providing critical viewpoints on topics of public interest.

Furthermore, as the analysis of journalists' language attitudes has revealed, semantic and pragmatic reasons are relevant for the use of anglicisms, which gives English linguistic resources many functions on adult contemporary radio. Mainly stylistic purposes are relevant here, such as to create variation in a text and to attract attention. In addition, anglicisms are used by journalists for rhyming purposes and to be more precise in their wordings. Connotations of anglicisms and the images they convey with the listener are also relevant for their use on radio, which includes the use of anglicisms for indexing coolness and modernity. These perceptions, however, depend on the target audience a station wishes to reach. Overall, despite the many stylistic functions of anglicisms on radio, comprehension by the listener, as mentioned above, is prioritized to ensure the effectiveness of journalistic messages on air.

Against the background of increasing sociolinguistic complexity, let me conclude by once more stressing the importance and value of a combined methodological approach to the study of language worlds of speakers for understanding their language practices in times of accelerated globalization. I hope that this book encourages the (socio)linguistic community to widen their perspective when analysing language and that the book provides new impulses for future research to study language as a social practice rather than as linguistic systems. I have tried to show that, despite the increasing effects of processes of spatial and temporal mobility in the social realities of speakers, there are still sedimentation, fixity and boundary maintenance.

By not only looking at the border zones and hotspots of mixing but also at more stable sociolinguistic environments, we find that constructed linguistic boundaries are not always perceived as limitations or constraints to social practices but can themselves become meaningful resources for pursuing communicative aims. This means that there is a vital need to place greater emphasis on discursive practices (such as by the mass media), on the language world of each individual speaker and on how he or she becomes an actor in the constant refashioning and maintaining of boundaries that govern many people's language practices each day. For this, we also need to look in detail at the individual communicative event in which language is practised and shaped by various social and cultural factors. The study of language in society has the capacity to not only produce descriptive accounts of language use but much more to engage with people's language practices to illuminate the complexity of social reality. Understanding our individual language worlds as entangled in cultural and historical contexts as well as in spatial processes is key to understanding language practices, not only for research but also for our everyday social interactions.

Appendices

Table A.1 List of anglicism lexemes.

Rank	Lexeme	Tokens	Lexical field
1	Hit	161	Music/Dance
2	okay	69	General Language
3	Lieblingsmix	62	Music/Dance
4	Mix	62	General Language
5	starten	57	General Language
6	cool	53	General Language
7	live	52	Media/Communication/Entertainment
8	Verkehrsservice	51	Journalism
9	Fan	48	General Language
10	Ticket	44	General Language
11	Morningshow	41	Journalism
12	Lieblingshit	40	Music/Dance
13	Song	39	Music/Dance
14	Musikmix	38	Music/Dance
15	Stop-and-go	35	Transportation/Infrastructure
16	Topthema	34	Journalism
17	Start	33	General Language
18	Job	32	Business/Employment
19	ey	29	General Language
20	hey	29	General Language
21	Hitradio	27	Music/Dance
22	Internet	27	Technology
23	Team	26	General Language
24	Kulthit	24	Music/Dance
25	Film	23	Media/Communication/Entertainment
26	*PS3*-Verkehrsupdate	23	Journalism
27	Handy	22	Technology
28	hi	22	General Language

29	Blitzerservice	20	Journalism
30	*PS3*-Wetterupdate	20	Journalism
31	Regionalreporter	20	Journalism
32	Rundum-Service	20	Journalism
33	Wetterteam	20	Journalism
34	yeah	19	General Language
35	Kids	18	General Language
36	Party	18	Lifestyle/Fashion/Leisure
37	Trainer	18	Sport
38	*F3*-Reporter	17	Journalism
39	Mail	17	Media/Communication/Entertainment
40	App	15	Technology
41	Baby	15	General Language
42	WhatsApp	15	Media/Communication/Entertainment
43	fit	13	Sport
44	online	13	Technology
45	Trainingslager	13	Sport
46	mixen	12	Music/Dance
47	Smartphone	12	Technology
48	Star	12	Lifestyle/Fashion/Leisure
49	Comedy	11	Art/Culture/Education
50	DJ	11	Music/Dance
51	grillen	11	Food
52	testen	11	General Language
53	Wettertrend	11	Journalism
54	Test	10	General Language
55	City	9	Geography
56	Fanmeile	9	Lifestyle/Fashion/Leisure
57	Homepage	9	Media/Communication/Entertainment
58	*PS3*-Blackout	9	General Language
59	wow	9	General Language
60	Blackout	8	General Language
61	Bundestrainer	8	Sport
62	Highlight	8	General Language

(Continued)

Rank	Lexeme	Tokens	Lexical field
63	mailen	8	Media/Communication/Entertainment
64	*P2*-Reporter	8	Journalism
65	Profi	8	General Language
66	*PS1*-Reporter	8	Journalism
67	Public Viewing	8	Lifestyle/Fashion/Leisure
68	rocken	8	Music/Dance
69	Show	8	Media/Communication/Entertainment
70	Stress	8	Medicine
71	up-to-date	8	General Language
72	WLAN	8	Technology
73	Band	7	Music/Dance
74	Ein-Euro-Job	7	Politics
75	Service-Bahn	7	Journalism
76	Waveboard	7	Lifestyle/Fashion/Leisure
77	checken	6	General Language
78	Club	6	General Language
79	Countdown	6	General Language
80	Derby	6	Sport
81	Fußballbundestrainer	6	Sport
82	Interview	6	Journalism
83	News	6	Journalism
84	*P1*-Kinoevent	6	Lifestyle/Fashion/Leisure
85	performen	6	Music/Dance
86	posten	6	Media/Communication/Entertainment
87	*PS2*-Hit	6	Music/Dance
88	sexy	6	Lifestyle/Fashion/Leisure
89	Single	6	General Language
90	stressen	6	Medicine
91	trainieren	6	General Language
92	yay	6	General Language
93	yippie	6	General Language
94	EM-Song	5	Music/Dance
95	Festival	5	Media/Communication/Entertainment

96	Hit-Tipp	5	Music/Dance
97	Livemusik	5	Music/Dance
98	Newcomer	5	Music/Dance
99	*P3*-Radio-App	5	Technology
100	*P3*-Studio-Hotline	5	Media/Communication/Entertainment
101	Reporter	5	Journalism
102	Selfie	5	Media/Communication/Entertainment
103	Servicetipp	5	Journalism
104	sorry	5	General Language
105	Sound	5	Music/Dance
106	Startschuss	5	General Language
107	Top Ten	5	General Language
108	whatsappen	5	Media/Communication/Entertainment
109	Airbag	4	Technology
110	ARD-DeutschlandTrend	4	Journalism
111	Award	4	General Language
112	Bar	4	Food
113	Biker	4	Transportation/Infrastructure
114	Chip(s)	4	Food
115	Cityroller	4	Transportation/Infrastructure
116	Cocktail	4	Food
117	Computer	4	Technology
118	Deal	4	General Language
119	Discounter	4	Business/Employment
120	filmen	4	Media/Communication/Entertainment
121	Gag	4	General Language
122	Grill	4	Food
123	nonstop	4	General Language
124	*P2*-Reporterin	4	Journalism
125	*P3*-Reporter	4	Journalism
126	pink	4	General Language
127	Playlist-Update	4	Music/Dance
128	*PS1*-App	4	Technology
129	*PS3*-Lieblingsmix	4	Music/Dance

(Continued)

Rank	Lexeme	Tokens	Lexical field
130	Reporterin	4	Journalism
131	Spot	4	Media/Communication/Entertainment
132	Update	4	Journalism
133	Wellness	4	Lifestyle/Fashion/Leisure
134	*B3*-Interview	3	Journalism
135	Beat	3	Music/Dance
136	Boxlegende	3	Sport
137	DAB-Empfang	3	Technology
138	DAB-Smartphone	3	Technology
139	Dandy	3	General Language
140	DeutschlandTrend	3	Journalism
141	E-Mail	3	Media/Communication/Entertainment
142	Event	3	Lifestyle/Fashion/Leisure
143	Fahrtest	3	Transportation/Infrastructure
144	Family	3	General Language
145	Fanzone	3	Sport
146	Festivalsommer	3	Media/Communication/Entertainment
147	Flip-Flops	3	Lifestyle/Fashion/Leisure
148	Foul	3	Sport
149	Foulelfmeter	3	Sport
150	happy	3	General Language
151	Kesselchip(s)	3	Food
152	Kick	3	General Language
153	kicken	3	Sport
154	Miss	3	Lifestyle/Fashion/Leisure
155	outen	3	General Language
156	*P1*-Reporter	3	Journalism
157	*P2*-Hit-Tipp	3	Music/Dance
158	Playoff	3	Sport
159	*PS1*-Tischkicker	3	Lifestyle/Fashion/Leisure
160	*PS2*-DJ	3	Music/Dance
161	*PS2*-Reporter	3	Journalism
162	Rock-Pop	3	Music/Dance
163	Singer-Songwriter	3	Music/Dance

164	Sir	3	General Language
165	Snack	3	Food
166	Sommercamp	3	Lifestyle/Fashion/Leisure
167	Sonne-Wolken-Mix	3	General Language
168	Superstar	3	Lifestyle/Fashion/Leisure
169	surfen	3	Media/Communication/Entertainment
170	Terminal	3	Transportation/Infrastructure
171	Trend	3	General Language
172	T-Shirt-Temperaturen	3	General Language
173	Verkehrsupdate	3	Journalism
174	Wags	3	Sport
175	yes	3	General Language
176	80-Cent-Job	2	Politics
177	Action	2	General Language
178	Affenbaby	2	Biology
179	All-you-can-eat-Restaurant	2	Food
180	*B3*-Shop	2	Business/Employment
181	Bachblütenspray	2	Medicine
182	Beamer	2	Technology
183	Bikerparadies	2	Lifestyle/Fashion/Leisure
184	boomen	2	Business/Employment
185	Box	2	Technology
186	Burnout	2	Medicine
187	Cap	2	Lifestyle/Fashion/Leisure
188	Cappy	2	Lifestyle/Fashion/Leisure
189	Charts	2	Music/Dance
190	Coach	2	Sport
191	Cockpit	2	Transportation/Infrastructure
192	Cola	2	Food
193	Curved-TV	2	Technology
194	Date	2	Lifestyle/Fashion/Leisure
195	Design	2	Art/Culture/Education
196	Designhotel	2	Travel/Tourism
197	Display	2	Technology
198	Eco-Lodge	2	Travel/Tourism
199	einchecken	2	General Language

(Continued)

Rank	Lexeme	Tokens	Lexical field
200	Eishockey	2	Sport
201	Elfer-Ticket	2	Sport
202	EU-Türkei-Deal	2	Politics
203	fair	2	General Language
204	Familienevent	2	Lifestyle/Fashion/Leisure
205	Fernsehinterview	2	Journalism
206	Fernsehshow	2	Media/Communication/Entertainment
207	Finalmatch	2	Sport
208	Fitness-Coaching	2	Sport
209	Fußballhit	2	Music/Dance
210	Fußballtrainer	2	Sport
211	Gag-to-go	2	General Language
212	Grillabend	2	Lifestyle/Fashion/Leisure
213	Grillkohle	2	Food
214	Hacksteak	2	Food
215	Hightech	2	Technology
216	Hotspot	2	Technology
217	in	2	Lifestyle/Fashion/Leisure
218	Insider	2	General Language
219	Internetartikel	2	Journalism
220	Internetseite	2	Media/Communication/Entertainment
221	Jeans	2	Lifestyle/Fashion/Leisure
222	Jobcenter	2	Business/Employment
223	Kicker	2	Sport
224	Kinofilm	2	Media/Communication/Entertainment
225	Kult-Comedy	2	Art/Culture/Education
226	Kunstfan	2	Art/Culture/Education
227	Kunsthighlight	2	Art/Culture/Education
228	Lady	2	General Language
229	Laptop	2	Technology
230	Laser	2	Technology
231	Lieblingssong	2	Music/Dance
232	Lieblingsstar	2	Lifestyle/Fashion/Leisure
233	Lift	2	Technology

234	Liveblog	2	Media/Communication/Entertainment
235	Lord	2	Media/Communication/Entertainment
236	Lounge	2	Lifestyle/Fashion/Leisure
237	Manga-Convention	2	Lifestyle/Fashion/Leisure
238	Media-Operations-Volunteer	2	Business/Employment
239	Meeting	2	Business/Employment
240	Megawatt	2	Science
241	Morgenreporterin	2	Journalism
242	Musikchannel	2	Media/Communication/Entertainment
243	Okay	2	General Language
244	Onlinedurchsuchung	2	General Language
245	Outfit	2	Lifestyle/Fashion/Leisure
246	*P2-F2*-Reporterin	2	Journalism
247	*P2*-Public-Viewing	2	Lifestyle/Fashion/Leisure
248	*P3*-Interview	2	Journalism
249	Partynacht	2	Lifestyle/Fashion/Leisure
250	Partystimmung	2	Lifestyle/Fashion/Leisure
251	Pausen-Lounge	2	Lifestyle/Fashion/Leisure
252	Pfefferspray	2	Consumer Goods
253	Playlist	2	Music/Dance
254	Playoff-Halbfinalserie	2	Sport
255	Podcast	2	Media/Communication/Entertainment
256	Pool	2	Lifestyle/Fashion/Leisure
257	Prince	2	General Language
258	*PS2*-App	2	Technology
259	*PS2*-Comedy	2	Art/Culture/Education
260	*PS3*-Hit	2	Music/Dance
261	*PS3*-Reporter	2	Journalism
262	Radargerät	2	Technology
263	Ranking	2	Politics
264	ready	2	General Language
265	relaxt	2	General Language
266	Rock	2	Music/Dance
267	Rockliner	2	Music/Dance

(Continued)

Rank	Lexeme	Tokens	Lexical field
268	SC-Trainer	2	Sport
269	Service-*F3*	2	Journalism
270	shoppen	2	Lifestyle/Fashion/Leisure
271	Shuttlebus	2	Transportation/Infrastructure
272	Sidestep	2	Music/Dance
273	Skateboard	2	Sport
274	SMS	2	Technology
275	SMS-Schreiben	2	Media/Communication/Entertainment
276	Special	2	Journalism
277	Styling-Tipp	2	Lifestyle/Fashion/Leisure
278	testweise	2	General Language
279	thank you	2	General Language
280	Ticketshop	2	Business/Employment
281	Top 3	2	Travel/Tourism
282	Top 8	2	Music/Dance
283	Trainingseinheit	2	Sport
284	T-Shirt	2	Lifestyle/Fashion/Leisure
285	twittern	2	Media/Communication/Entertainment
286	Udo-Song	2	Music/Dance
287	UHD	2	Technology
288	uncool	2	General Language
289	VIP	2	Lifestyle/Fashion/Leisure
290	Virtual-Reality-Gerät	2	Technology
291	Volunteer	2	Business/Employment
292	Volunteer-Center	2	Business/Employment
293	Wahnsinns-App	2	Technology
294	Wellnessurlaub	2	Travel/Tourism
295	Weltliteratur-to-go	2	Art/Culture/Education
296	what	2	General Language
297	WLAN-Hotspot	2	Technology
298	Workshop	2	General Language
299	yep	2	General Language
300	2-Megabit-Anschluss	1	Technology
301	3D-Computereffekt	1	Media/Communication/Entertainment

302	abrocken	1	Music/Dance
303	Achtziger-Power	1	Music/Dance
304	Act	1	Music/Dance
305	a-ha-Hit	1	Music/Dance
306	Airbag-Fahrradhelm	1	Technology
307	Airport-Terminal	1	Transportation/Infrastructure
308	all-inclusive	1	Travel/Tourism
309	all-you-can-eat	1	Food
310	Altglascontainer	1	Transportation/Infrastructure
311	Altrocker	1	Music/Dance
312	always	1	General Language
313	American-Icecream	1	Food
314	amused	1	General Language
315	Animationsfilm	1	Media/Communication/Entertainment
316	Antwort-Mail	1	Media/Communication/Entertainment
317	app-solut	1	General Language
318	Aquaplaning-Unfall	1	Transportation/Infrastructure
319	Arbeits-Blackout	1	General Language
320	ARD-Markencheck	1	Journalism
321	Asthmaspray	1	Medicine
322	Astro-Nerd-Moment	1	General Language
323	Atommanager	1	Business/Employment
324	AUDI-VIP-Shuttle	1	Lifestyle/Fashion/Leisure
325	Außenpool	1	Lifestyle/Fashion/Leisure
326	*B1*-Event	1	Journalism
327	*B1*-Reporterin	1	Journalism
328	Babyduft	1	General Language
329	Babypause	1	General Language
330	Baden-Derby	1	Sport
331	Badeshorts	1	Lifestyle/Fashion/Leisure
332	Bahnmanager	1	Business/Employment
333	Basketballbundesliga	1	Sport
334	Basketballer	1	Sport
335	Basketballmeisterschaft	1	Sport
336	Bass-Boxen-Massage	1	Music/Dance

(Continued)

Rank	Lexeme	Tokens	Lexical field
337	Bayern-Boss	1	Business/Employment
338	Bayernfan	1	Sport
339	beamen	1	General Language
340	Beatbox	1	Music/Dance
341	beatboxfrei	1	Music/Dance
342	Beauty-Druck	1	Lifestyle/Fashion/Leisure
343	Best-of-Five-Serie	1	Sport
344	Biertbox	1	General Language
345	biertboxfrei	1	General Language
346	Bike	1	Transportation/Infrastructure
347	Bike-Saison	1	Lifestyle/Fashion/Leisure
348	Bike-Show	1	Media/Communication/Entertainment
349	Bingo	1	Lifestyle/Fashion/Leisure
350	Bingo-Ausgabe	1	Lifestyle/Fashion/Leisure
351	Boyband	1	Music/Dance
352	boykottieren	1	General Language
353	brain-jogging	1	General Language
354	Bratwurstfan	1	Food
355	bred in Germany	1	General Language
356	BROSE-Manager	1	Business/Employment
357	Bulldog	1	Transportation/Infrastructure
358	Bully	1	Sport
359	Bundesliga-Revierderby	1	Sport
360	Business	1	Business/Employment
361	Busservice	1	Transportation/Infrastructure
362	Captain	1	General Language
363	Car-Sharing-Unternehmen	1	Business/Employment
364	Casting	1	Media/Communication/Entertainment
365	Catering	1	Food
366	Charterflugzeug	1	Transportation/Infrastructure
367	Chatverlauf	1	Media/Communication/Entertainment
368	Check-in	1	Travel/Tourism
369	Check-Team	1	Journalism

370	Clubber	1	Lifestyle/Fashion/Leisure
371	Cocktailtomate	1	Food
372	Comedian	1	Art/Culture/Education
373	Comedy-Show	1	Media/Communication/Entertainment
374	Comedy-Star	1	Lifestyle/Fashion/Leisure
375	Computerklasse	1	Art/Culture/Education
376	Computersystem	1	Technology
377	Computertechnik	1	Technology
378	Computervirus	1	Technology
379	Container	1	Transportation/Infrastructure
380	Containerterminal	1	Transportation/Infrastructure
381	Cornrows	1	Lifestyle/Fashion/Leisure
382	correct	1	General Language
383	Co-Trainer	1	Sport
384	Couch	1	Consumer Goods
385	covern	1	Music/Dance
386	Cowboy	1	General Language
387	DAB Plus	1	Technology
388	DAB-Digitalradio	1	Technology
389	Dancefloor	1	Lifestyle/Fashion/Leisure
390	DEB-Team	1	Sport
391	designen	1	Art/Culture/Education
392	Designer	1	Art/Culture/Education
393	Deutsch-Pop	1	Music/Dance
394	Deutschrocker	1	Music/Dance
395	Dinner	1	Food
396	Discounter-Produkt	1	Consumer Goods
397	Disneyfilm	1	Media/Communication/Entertainment
398	dissen	1	General Language
399	DNA-Probe	1	Science
400	DNA-Test	1	Science
401	Doping-Enthüllungen	1	Sport
402	Dopingtest	1	Sport
403	Dos und Don'ts	1	General Language
404	Double	1	Sport

(Continued)

Rank	Lexeme	Tokens	Lexical field
405	Downhill	1	Sport
406	downloaden	1	Technology
407	Drink	1	Food
408	Drogendealer	1	General Language
409	Dschungelbuch-Film	1	Media/Communication/Entertainment
410	DVBT2-Siegel	1	Technology
411	DVD	1	Technology
412	Edge LED	1	Technology
413	Ed-Sheeran-Remix	1	Music/Dance
414	eingrooven	1	Music/Dance
415	Einlauf-Kids	1	Sport
416	Eishockeymeister	1	Sport
417	Eishockeynationalmannschaft	1	Sport
418	E-Jugend-Team	1	Sport
419	EM-Eröffnungsparty	1	Lifestyle/Fashion/Leisure
420	EM-Grillgut	1	Food
421	EM-Start	1	Sport
422	EM-Touch	1	Food
423	Endspurt	1	Politics
424	Eröffnungsparty	1	Lifestyle/Fashion/Leisure
425	Escort-Service	1	Business/Employment
426	exactly	1	General Language
427	Expertenteam	1	Biology
428	Facebook-Account	1	Media/Communication/Entertainment
429	Facebook-Fan	1	Media/Communication/Entertainment
430	Facebook-Lieblings-Posting	1	Media/Communication/Entertainment
431	Fairness	1	Sport
432	Fanartikel	1	Consumer Goods
433	Fan-Elf	1	Sport
434	Fanfest	1	Lifestyle/Fashion/Leisure
435	Fanparty	1	Lifestyle/Fashion/Leisure
436	Fan-Trainingslager	1	Sport
437	Farbfestival	1	Lifestyle/Fashion/Leisure

438	FCA-Trainer	1	Sport
439	FC-Fan	1	Sport
440	FC-Reporter	1	Journalism
441	Featuring	1	Music/Dance
442	Ferienhit	1	Music/Dance
443	Fernsehcomedian	1	Media/Communication/Entertainment
444	Fernsehteam	1	Media/Communication/Entertainment
445	Festivalkoch	1	Food
446	Fetzenparty	1	Lifestyle/Fashion/Leisure
447	Filmaufnahme	1	Media/Communication/Entertainment
448	Filmhandlung	1	Media/Communication/Entertainment
449	Filmmaterial	1	Media/Communication/Entertainment
450	Final Four	1	Sport
451	Finalshow	1	Media/Communication/Entertainment
452	First Lady	1	Politics
453	Fischfan	1	General Language
454	Fitness	1	Sport
455	flashen	1	Media/Communication/Entertainment
456	Flohshampoo	1	Medicine
457	Flower-Power-Generation	1	Art/Culture/Education
458	Flüchtlings-Deal	1	Politics
459	Free-WLAN	1	Technology
460	Freitags-Feeling	1	General Language
461	Freitagsrock	1	Music/Dance
462	Freitagsstart	1	General Language
463	Fremdschäm-Spezialreporter	1	Journalism
464	Friendzone	1	General Language
465	Frühjahrsshow	1	Media/Communication/Entertainment
466	Full-HD	1	Technology
467	Fußballfan	1	Sport
468	Fußballparty	1	Lifestyle/Fashion/Leisure

(Continued)

Rank	Lexeme	Tokens	Lexical field
469	Fußballprofi	1	Sport
470	Fußballstar	1	Lifestyle/Fashion/Leisure
471	Gag-Autor	1	General Language
472	Galadinner	1	Lifestyle/Fashion/Leisure
473	Gangsterkomödie	1	Media/Communication/Entertainment
474	Gartenparty	1	Lifestyle/Fashion/Leisure
475	Geburtstagseinladungsticket	1	General Language
476	Geschmackscheck	1	Food
477	Gin	1	Food
478	Glamour	1	Lifestyle/Fashion/Leisure
479	Glückwunschmail	1	Media/Communication/Entertainment
480	Golfplatz	1	Sport
481	Golfwägelchen	1	Sport
482	goodbye	1	General Language
483	Grillbike	1	Food
484	Grillköhle	1	General Language
485	Grillwetter	1	General Language
486	Grillwiese	1	Lifestyle/Fashion/Leisure
487	Gute-Laune-Hit	1	Music/Dance
488	Gute-Laune-to-go	1	General Language
489	Haarshampoo	1	Consumer Goods
490	Haarspray	1	Consumer Goods
491	Haie-Fan	1	Sport
492	Halbzeitsnack	1	Food
493	Hammerparty	1	Lifestyle/Fashion/Leisure
494	Hammer-Start	1	General Language
495	Hand-Biker	1	Transportation/Infrastructure
496	Hand-Entertainment	1	General Language
497	Handy-Ampel	1	Technology
498	happy birthday	1	General Language
499	Happy End	1	General Language
500	Hardcore-Fan	1	Sport
501	Hardware	1	Technology

502	Hashtag	1	Media/Communication/Entertainment
503	HbbTV	1	Technology
504	HD	1	Technology
505	HD-Livestream	1	Technology
506	HDMI	1	Technology
507	HDR	1	Technology
508	HDTV	1	Technology
509	Head-down-Gesellschaft	1	General Language
510	hello	1	General Language
511	Hippie-Blümchen	1	Lifestyle/Fashion/Leisure
512	Hipster-Namen	1	Music/Dance
513	Hispanic	1	Art/Culture/Education
514	Hit-Lounge	1	Journalism
515	Hitparade	1	Music/Dance
516	Hobby	1	Lifestyle/Fashion/Leisure
517	Hollywood-Größe	1	Lifestyle/Fashion/Leisure
518	Hollywoodstar	1	Lifestyle/Fashion/Leisure
519	holy moly	1	General Language
520	Holzkohlegrill	1	Food
521	Homegrown-Rechts-Terrorismus	1	Politics
522	Homegrown-Terror-Rechts	1	Politics
523	Hotelmarkt-Report	1	Business/Employment
524	Hotline	1	Media/Communication/Entertainment
525	Imagefaktor	1	Lifestyle/Fashion/Leisure
526	in action	1	General Language
527	Independent Folkrock	1	Music/Dance
528	Indie-Folkrock-Szene	1	Music/Dance
529	Inlineskate	1	Sport
530	Internetanbieter	1	Business/Employment
531	Internetausfall	1	Technology
532	Internetbewertung	1	Media/Communication/Entertainment
533	Internetbox	1	Technology
534	Internet-Decke	1	Media/Communication/Entertainment

(Continued)

Rank	Lexeme	Tokens	Lexical field
535	Internetforum	1	Media/Communication/Entertainment
536	Internetgeschwindigkeit	1	Technology
537	Internetverbot	1	General Language
538	interviewen	1	Journalism
539	Intranet	1	Media/Communication/Entertainment
540	Irgendwie-wird-das-Wetter-schon-Kompetenzteam	1	Journalism
541	IT-Fachleute	1	Business/Employment
542	It-Girl	1	Lifestyle/Fashion/Leisure
543	IT-System	1	Technology
544	Jeansjacke	1	Lifestyle/Fashion/Leisure
545	jetten	1	Transportation/Infrastructure
546	Jobsuche	1	Business/Employment
547	Jobticket	1	Transportation/Infrastructure
548	Jobverlust	1	Business/Employment
549	Jodel-Cam	1	Technology
550	Joint	1	General Language
551	Journalistenfilm	1	Media/Communication/Entertainment
552	Jubel-Training	1	Sport
553	Kaffee-Light	1	Food
554	Kaffee-Zero	1	Food
555	Karaoke-Bar	1	Lifestyle/Fashion/Leisure
556	Karaoke-Happening	1	Lifestyle/Fashion/Leisure
557	Katastrophen-App	1	Technology
558	Katastrophenfilm	1	Media/Communication/Entertainment
559	Katy-Perry-Song	1	Music/Dance
560	Katzenbaby	1	Biology
561	Ketchup	1	Food
562	kickern	1	Lifestyle/Fashion/Leisure
563	Kickers-Fan	1	Sport
564	Kiddie	1	General Language
565	Kinderfilm	1	Media/Communication/Entertainment

566	King	1	General Language
567	Klo-Flatrate	1	General Language
568	Koch-Tutorial	1	Media/Communication/Entertainment
569	Konkurrenzteam	1	Sport
570	K-O-Phase	1	Sport
571	Langzeitjob	1	Business/Employment
572	laser-gestützt	1	Technology
573	LED-Armband	1	Technology
574	LED-Leuchte	1	Technology
575	Lieblingsfestival	1	Media/Communication/Entertainment
576	Lift-Dinger	1	Technology
577	Link	1	Technology
578	Liveact	1	Music/Dance
579	Liveversion	1	Music/Dance
580	Lunch	1	Food
581	Luxus-Wellness	1	Lifestyle/Fashion/Leisure
582	made in Germany	1	General Language
583	Mail-Schreiben	1	Media/Communication/Entertainment
584	Mainstream	1	General Language
585	Markencheck	1	Journalism
586	Marketingtrick	1	Business/Employment
587	Mega-Hit-Tipp	1	Music/Dance
588	Megastar	1	Lifestyle/Fashion/Leisure
589	Meistertrainer	1	Sport
590	Merchandising-Artikel	1	Consumer Goods
591	Metal-Fan	1	Music/Dance
592	Minijob	1	Business/Employment
593	Mister	1	General Language
594	mitfilmen	1	Media/Communication/Entertainment
595	Mixed-Zone	1	Sport
596	Model	1	Lifestyle/Fashion/Leisure
597	Monatsticket	1	Transportation/Infrastructure
598	Moonwalk	1	Music/Dance
599	Morgenshow	1	Journalism

(Continued)

Rank	Lexeme	Tokens	Lexical field
600	Mountainbike	1	Sport
601	Musical	1	Music/Dance
602	Musikevent	1	Lifestyle/Fashion/Leisure
603	Muttertags-Song	1	Music/Dance
604	neonpink-orange	1	General Language
605	Neumanager	1	Business/Employment
606	Nicht-Bayernfan	1	Sport
607	Nonstop-Jodelgesang	1	Music/Dance
608	Number-One-Hit	1	Music/Dance
609	Nummer-1-Hit	1	Music/Dance
610	Nummer-1-Hit-Tag	1	Music/Dance
611	OLED	1	Technology
612	Onlinereiseportal	1	Travel/Tourism
613	Onlineshop	1	Business/Employment
614	Open-Air	1	Media/Communication/Entertainment
615	Open-Air-Bühne	1	Media/Communication/Entertainment
616	Open-Air-Konzert	1	Media/Communication/Entertainment
617	Organic Cotton	1	Consumer Goods
618	*P1*-Star	1	Lifestyle/Fashion/Leisure
619	*P1*-Team	1	Journalism
620	*P2*-Team	1	Journalism
621	*P2*-Wunsch-Hit-Vatertag	1	Music/Dance
622	*P3*-EM-Song	1	Music/Dance
623	*P3*-Jodel-Cam	1	Technology
624	Pampers	1	Consumer Goods
625	Party-Aspekt	1	Lifestyle/Fashion/Leisure
626	Partykanone	1	Lifestyle/Fashion/Leisure
627	Patchworkfamilie	1	General Language
628	PC	1	Technology
629	Pitch-Access	1	Sport
630	Playoff-Finalrunde	1	Sport
631	Playoff-Halbfinale	1	Sport
632	PMI	1	Technology

633	Politshow	1	Politics
634	Polizei-E-Mail	1	Media/Communication/Entertainment
635	Poloshirt	1	Lifestyle/Fashion/Leisure
636	Ponyhof	1	Lifestyle/Fashion/Leisure
637	Pop	1	Music/Dance
638	Popcorn	1	Food
639	Popstar	1	Lifestyle/Fashion/Leisure
640	Pornofilm-Milieu	1	Media/Communication/Entertainment
641	Post	1	Media/Communication/Entertainment
642	President	1	Politics
643	Presse-Container	1	Journalism
644	Pressing	1	Sport
645	Private Viewing	1	Lifestyle/Fashion/Leisure
646	Profi-Fußballern	1	Sport
647	Profi-Karaoke-Performer	1	Music/Dance
648	*PS1*-Fußball-Update	1	Journalism
649	*PS1*-Party	1	Lifestyle/Fashion/Leisure
650	*PS1*-Reporterin	1	Journalism
651	*PS1*-Team	1	Journalism
652	*PS1*-Tickethotline	1	Media/Communication/Entertainment
653	*PS2*-Comedystar	1	Lifestyle/Fashion/Leisure
654	*PS2*-Reporterin	1	Journalism
655	*PS3*-Reporterin	1	Journalism
656	Public-Viewing-Arena	1	Lifestyle/Fashion/Leisure
657	public-viewing-mäßig	1	Lifestyle/Fashion/Leisure
658	Public-Viewing-Ort	1	Lifestyle/Fashion/Leisure
659	Public-Viewing-Party	1	Lifestyle/Fashion/Leisure
660	Public-Viewing-Termin	1	Lifestyle/Fashion/Leisure
661	Pulli	1	Lifestyle/Fashion/Leisure
662	pushen	1	Politics
663	Push-Nachricht	1	Technology
664	Push-Up-Nachricht	1	Technology
665	Radarfalle	1	Technology

(Continued)

Rank	Lexeme	Tokens	Lexical field
666	Radio-Blogger	1	Media/Communication/Entertainment
667	Rapper	1	Music/Dance
668	rauskicken	1	Sport
669	Reaktionstest	1	General Language
670	Reality-Format	1	Media/Communication/Entertainment
671	Recall	1	Media/Communication/Entertainment
672	Recycling-Betrieb	1	Transportation/Infrastructure
673	Regenradar	1	Technology
674	Regenschirm-App	1	Technology
675	Reisebloggerin	1	Media/Communication/Entertainment
676	reloaded	1	General Language
677	Remix	1	Music/Dance
678	Reporterarbeit	1	Journalism
679	Restticket	1	Media/Communication/Entertainment
680	Revierderby	1	Sport
681	Riesen-Bläser-Combo	1	Music/Dance
682	Riesenhit	1	Music/Dance
683	Riesenparty	1	Lifestyle/Fashion/Leisure
684	Rock-Erlebnis	1	Music/Dance
685	Rockermilieu	1	General Language
686	Rockfestival	1	Media/Communication/Entertainment
687	Rockhymne	1	Music/Dance
688	rockig	1	Music/Dance
689	Rocklegende	1	Music/Dance
690	Rockmusik	1	Music/Dance
691	Rockmusiker	1	Music/Dance
692	RTL-Interview	1	Journalism
693	Rundum-Sorglos-Wellnessurlaub	1	Travel/Tourism
694	Saisonendspurt	1	Sport
695	Salat-Hit	1	Music/Dance
696	Satellitenterminal	1	Transportation/Infrastructure

697	Schau-aufs-Handy	1	General Language
698	Schinkensandwich	1	Food
699	Schlagerstar	1	Music/Dance
700	Schluss-Gag	1	General Language
701	Schulcomputer	1	Technology
702	Schülerticket	1	Transportation/Infrastructure
703	Security	1	General Language
704	Semesterticket	1	Transportation/Infrastructure
705	Server	1	Technology
706	Service	1	General Language
707	Service-Redaktion	1	Journalism
708	Service-S-Bahn	1	Journalism
709	Service-*T3*	1	Journalism
710	Set	1	Consumer Goods
711	Shampoo	1	Consumer Goods
712	Shetland-Sheep-Dog	1	Biology
713	shit happens	1	General Language
714	Shoppinglustiger	1	Lifestyle/Fashion/Leisure
715	Showbusiness	1	Business/Employment
716	Siggi-Pop	1	General Language
717	Sight-Sleeping-Hotel	1	Travel/Tourism
718	Smartphone-Akku	1	Technology
719	Smartphone-App	1	Technology
720	Smartphone-Application	1	Technology
721	Smartphone-Besitzer	1	General Language
722	Smiley	1	Media/Communication/Entertainment
723	Snare	1	Music/Dance
724	Social-Monika	1	General Language
725	Solidaritätsshow	1	Media/Communication/Entertainment
726	Sommerhit	1	Music/Dance
727	Sommerhit-Alarm	1	Music/Dance
728	Sommer-Open-Air	1	Media/Communication/Entertainment
729	Songremix	1	Music/Dance
730	Sonnenschein-App	1	Technology

(Continued)

Rank	Lexeme	Tokens	Lexical field
731	Sonnen-Wolken-Mix	1	General Language
732	Soul-Pop-Stimme	1	Music/Dance
733	Soundcheck	1	Music/Dance
734	spacig	1	General Language
735	Spielfilm	1	Media/Communication/Entertainment
736	splendid	1	General Language
737	Sportfan	1	Sport
738	Sportreporter	1	Journalism
739	Sportreporter-Legende	1	Journalism
740	Spray	1	Consumer Goods
741	Spurt	1	General Language
742	Star-Auflauf	1	Lifestyle/Fashion/Leisure
743	Star-DJ	1	Music/Dance
744	Starfriseur	1	Lifestyle/Fashion/Leisure
745	Stargeiger	1	Music/Dance
746	Starmoderator	1	Journalism
747	Startaufstellung	1	Sport
748	Starterfeld	1	Sport
749	Startgeld	1	Sport
750	Startlöcher	1	General Language
751	Start-Ziel-Sieg	1	Sport
752	Statement	1	Politics
753	Staucam	1	Technology
754	Steak	1	Food
755	strange	1	General Language
756	Stream	1	Technology
757	Streber-Fan	1	General Language
758	Stretch-Format	1	General Language
759	stylen	1	Lifestyle/Fashion/Leisure
760	Styling	1	Lifestyle/Fashion/Leisure
761	stylisch	1	Lifestyle/Fashion/Leisure
762	Sunblogger	1	General Language
763	supercool	1	General Language
764	Surfbrett	1	Sport

765	switchen	1	General Language
766	Tablet	1	Technology
767	Tages-Special	1	General Language
768	Task-Force	1	General Language
769	Teambus	1	Transportation/Infrastructure
770	Teamchef	1	Sport
771	Teamquartier	1	General Language
772	Teddybär	1	Consumer Goods
773	Tennisclub	1	Lifestyle/Fashion/Leisure
774	Terminstress	1	Medicine
775	Tester	1	General Language
776	Testnachricht	1	Media/Communication/Entertainment
777	Testsieger	1	Consumer Goods
778	Testspiel	1	Sport
779	Tickethotline	1	Media/Communication/Entertainment
780	Toaster	1	Technology
781	top	1	General Language
782	Top-DJ	1	Music/Dance
783	Topfrühlingstag	1	General Language
784	Topjournalist	1	Journalism
785	Topkakerlakenexporteur	1	Business/Employment
786	Toplage	1	General Language
787	topmodern	1	Transportation/Infrastructure
788	toppen	1	General Language
789	Traditionsclub	1	Sport
790	Trailer	1	Media/Communication/Entertainment
791	Trail-Fahren	1	Sport
792	Trainerin	1	Sport
793	Trainerstab	1	Sport
794	Trainerwechsel	1	Sport
795	Training	1	Sport
796	Trainingsplatz	1	Sport
797	Trainingszentrum	1	General Language
798	Trambahnhaltestelle	1	Transportation/Infrastructure

(Continued)

Rank	Lexeme	Tokens	Lexical field
799	Tri-Material-Coin	1	Technology
800	Trip	1	Travel/Tourism
801	Triple	1	Sport
802	try and error	1	General Language
803	Tweet	1	Media/Communication/Entertainment
804	Twitter-Account	1	Media/Communication/Entertainment
805	Udo-Hit	1	Music/Dance
806	Ultra Surround	1	Technology
807	ultracool	1	General Language
808	Ultra-HD	1	Technology
809	USB	1	Technology
810	Videoclip-Teil	1	Media/Communication/Entertainment
811	Video-Livestream	1	Technology
812	VIP-Beauftragter	1	Lifestyle/Fashion/Leisure
813	VIP-Bereich	1	Lifestyle/Fashion/Leisure
814	VIP-Tribüne	1	Lifestyle/Fashion/Leisure
815	Warm-up-Familienfest	1	Lifestyle/Fashion/Leisure
816	Web	1	Technology
817	Webcam	1	Technology
818	wegfaden	1	General Language
819	Wellnessbereich	1	Lifestyle/Fashion/Leisure
820	Wellnesshotel	1	Travel/Tourism
821	Wellnesslandschaft	1	Lifestyle/Fashion/Leisure
822	Wellnessoase	1	Lifestyle/Fashion/Leisure
823	Welthit	1	Music/Dance
824	Werbeclip	1	Media/Communication/Entertainment
825	Wettercam	1	Technology
826	win win win	1	General Language
827	Wives and Girlfriends	1	Sport
828	WLAN-Besitzer	1	Technology
829	WLAN-Netz	1	Technology
830	WLAN-Zugang	1	Technology

831	Wunsch-Hit-Vatertag	1	Music/Dance
832	XXL-Wochenende	1	General Language
833	yeeha	1	General Language
834	Yippie-und-Juhu-Tante	1	General Language
835	Youngster	1	Sport
836	Zeichentrickfilm	1	Media/Communication/Entertainment
837	Zeitungsinterview	1	Journalism
838	zurückwhatsappen	1	Media/Communication/Entertainment

Note: The same pseudonyms as used in the main text were applied for public services stations (*PS1*, *PS2*, *PS3*) and private stations (*P1*, *P2*, *P3*) in this list. Furthermore, the names of public service broadcasters (*B1*, *B2*, *B3*) as well as of towns (*T1*, *T2*, *T3*) and federal states (*F1*, *F2*, *F3*) in the respective broadcasting areas of each of the stations were additionally pseudonymized. Anglicisms which are unique for an individual station and could not be pseudonymized are not included in this list.

Table A.2 List of catachrestic and non-catachrestic anglicism bases.

Rank	Base anglicism	n/c	Tokens	(S/E/L) (D) (*) (**)	German near-equivalents in context
1	Hit	n	297	(S)	Schlager, Gassenhauer; Knaller
2	Mix	n	175	(S)	Mischung
3	Service	n/c	111	(S/L) (*)	Dienst, Dienstleistung
4	Reporter	n	91	(S) (D)	Berichterstatter
5	Fan	n	81	(S)	Anhänger; Verehrer, Liebhaber; Begeisterter
6	Morningshow	n	78	(S)	Morgensendung, Morgenprogramm (Unterhaltungsprogramm)
7	Team	n	78	(S)	Mannschaft; Gruppe; Truppe
8	okay	n	69	(S/L) (D)	gut, in Ordnung
9	live	n/c	63	(S/E) (D) (*)	selbst, persönlich; direkt; in echt
10	Update	n	62	(S/E)	Meldung, Nachricht, Bericht; Aktualisierung
11	cool	n	57	(S/E)	brillant, großartig, genial; lässig, gelassen; gut; ätzend (uncool); angesagt
12	starten	n	57	(S) (D)	aufmachen, beginnen, anlaufen, abfliegen, aufbrechen, losziehen, abheben, loslegen, anfangen; einschalten
13	Ticket	n	56	(S/E)	Eintrittskarte, Karte; Fahrkarte, Bordkarte; Parkschein
14	Song	n	52	(E)	Lied
15	Job	n	48	(S)	Stelle, Position, Arbeitsplatz; Beruf, Arbeit; Arbeits-(Fahrkarte)
16	Party	n	45	(E)	Feier, Fete
17	Start	n/c	45	(S) (D) (*)	Eröffnung, Auftakt; Ausgangs-(Aufstellung); Anfang, Beginn; Antritts-(Geld)
18	top	n	45	(S/E)	Spitzen-(Frühlingstag, Kakerlakenexporteur, Lage, Journalist), super-; Haupt-(Thema); ausgezeichnet, bestens, brillant
19	Trainer	n	42	(S) (D)	Übungsleiter

20	Trend	n	41	(S)		Entwicklung, Prognose, Tendenz; in Mode
21	Internet	c	39			
22	Profi	n	38	(S/E)	(**)	Experte, Fachmann; Berufssportler; Berufs-(Fußballern)
23	Film	n	37	(S) (D)		Streifen; Video
24	Stop-and-go	n	35	(S)		stockender/zähfließender Verkehr
25	App	c	32			
26	Star	n	30	(S/E) (D)		Berühmtheit, Sternchen; Ass
27	ey	n	29	(S/E)		Mensch!, Alter!; sag mal
28	hey	n	29	(S/E)		hallo; Mensch!; sag mal
29	Award	n	27	(S/L)		Auszeichnung, Preis; Preisverleihung; Preisträger
30	Handy	n	24	(S) (D)	(**)	Mobiltelefon
31	Show	n	24	(S/E)		Sendung; Vorführung, Vorstellung; Schau-(Geschäft)
32	hi	n	22	(S)		hallo
33	Baby	n	20	(E) (D)		Säugling; Junges; Schätzchen, Liebling
34	Comedy	n	20	(E/L)		Spaß(-Sendung); Kabarett, Spaßsendung
35	Mail	c	20			
36	Training	n	20	(E) (D)		Übungs-(Einheiten, Platz, Lager), Schulungs-(Zentrum), Übung
37	Kids	n	19	(S)		Kinder
38	Smartphone	c	19			
39	Test	n	19	(S) (D)		Probe, Versuch; Kontrolle, Prüfung; Untersuchung; Erprobung
40	*yeah*	n	19	(E)		ja!
41	Blackout	n	18	(S)		Aussetzer
42	DJ	c	18			
43	online	c	17			
44	Hotline	c	15			
45	Interview	n	15	(E) (D)		Befragung
46	WhatsApp	c	15			
47	Festival	n	14	(E/L)		Fest, Musikfest, Festspiel
48	Grill	n	14	(S) (D)		Bratrost
49	Public Viewing	c	14			
50	City	n	13	(S)		Stadtzentrum, Innenstadt

(Continued)

Rank	Base anglicism	n/c	Tokens	(S/E/L) (D) (*) (**)	German near-equivalents in context
51	Event	n	13	(S)	Veranstaltung, Ereignis
52	fit	n	13	(S) (D)	gesund, in Form, munter
53	WLAN	c	13		
54	mixen	n	12	(E)	mischen
55	Rock	c	12		
56	Wellness	c	12		
57	grillen	c	11		
58	testen	n	11	(S) (D)	ausprobieren, kontrollieren, überprüfen
59	Computer	c	10		
60	Highlight	n	10	(S)	Höhepunkt, Attraktion
61	Derby	c	9		
62	Gag	n	9	(E)	Spaß, Witz
63	Homepage	c	9		
64	rocken	n/c	9	(S/E) (D) (*)	begeistern; schaukeln
65	Stress	n	9	(S/E) (D)	Ärger; Druck, Belastung, Anstrengung
66	wow	n	9	(E)	toll!; Mensch!, Mann!
67	checken	n	8	(S/E)	kapieren; durchgucken, prüfen, überprüfen; anmelden (einchecken)
68	Club	n	8	(S) (D)	Diskothek; Verein
69	DAB	c	8		
70	mailen	c	8		
71	Special	n	8	(S/E)	Sonderbericht, Sonderausgabe; (Tages)-Extra
72	up-to-date	n	8	(S)	auf dem Laufenden, auf dem neuesten Stand
73	Band	n	7	(S)	Musikgruppe, Gruppe
74	Biker	n	7	(S)	Motorradfahrer, Kradfahrer; Radfahrer
75	Check	n	7	(S)	Prüfung, Probe, Prüfungs-(Team)
76	Chip(s)	c	7		
77	Deal	n	7	(S)	Abmachung, Vereinbarung, Abkommen
78	Playoff	c	7		
79	Pop	c	7		
80	Spray	c	7		
81	VIP	c	7		

82	Waveboard	c	7			
83	yippie	n	7	(E)	hurra!	
84	Camp	n	6	(S)	Lager	
85	Center	n	6	(E)	Zentrum	
86	Countdown	c	6			
87	Foul	n	6	(S/E) (D)	Regelwidrigkeit, Unsportlichkeit; Straf-(Elfmeter)	
88	News	n	6	(S)	Nachrichten	
89	performen	n	6	(E)	darbieten, auftreten	
90	Playlist	n	6	(S)	Wiedergabeliste	
91	posten	c	6			
92	sexy	n	6	(S) (D)	attraktiv	
93	Single	n	6	(S/E) (D)	Alleinstehender, Lediger; Platte	
94	Snack	n	6	(S)	Happen, Imbiss	
95	Sound	n	6	(E)	Klang, Tonqualität	
96	Terminal	n	6	(S)	Abfertigungsgebäude; Umschlagplatz	
97	trainieren	n	6	(E/L) (D)	üben; betreuen	
98	whatsappen	c	6			
99	*yay*	n	6	(S)	juhu!	
100	Airbag	c	5			
101	Bar	n	5	(S) (D)	Lokal, Kneipe; Theke	
102	Cam	c	5		short for: Webcam	
103	Discounter	c	5			
104	filmen	c	5			
105	Kicker	n	5	(S) (**)	Tischfußball; Fußballspieler	
106	Lounge	n	5	(S)	Aufenthaltsbereich, Gesellschaftsraum; Ecke	
107	Newcomer	n	5	(L)	Anfänger, Neuling	
108	nonstop	n	5	(S)	ununterbrochen	
109	pink	c	5			
110	Selfie	c	5			
111	Shop	n	5	(S)	Laden	
112	sorry	n	5	(S)	Entschuldigung	
113	to-go	n	5	(S)	zum Mitnehmen	
114	Top Ten	n	5	(S)	besten zehn	
115	T-Shirt	c	5			
116	Bike	n	4	(S)	Motorrad; Fahrrad	
117	Box	n	4	(S) (D)	Lautsprecher; Gerät	

(Continued)

Rank	Base anglicism	n/c	Tokens	(S/E/L) (D) (*) (**)	German near-equivalents in context
118	Cocktail	n	4	(S)	Mischgetränk
119	Container	n	4	(E) (D)	Behälter
120	Design	c	4		
121	E-Mail	c	4		
122	Hockey	c	4		
123	Hotspot	c	4		
124	kicken	n	4	(E)	spielen (Fußball), bolzen, (raus)werfen
125	Manager	n	4	(L) (D)	Chef, Leiter
126	Open-Air	n	4	(S/L)	Freiluftkonzert, Freiluft-(Konzert), Freilicht-(Bühne)
127	Radar	c	4		
128	SMS	n	4	(D)	Kurznachricht
129	Spot	c	4		
130	Volunteer	n	4	(S)	Freiwilliger
131	all-you-can-eat	n	3	(L)	Büffet
132	Beat	n	3	(S/E)	Rhythmus, Schlag
133	Dandy	n	3	(S)	Lackaffe
134	Family	n	3	(S)	Familie
135	Fitness	c	3		
136	Flip-Flops	c	3		
137	happy	n	3	(S/E)	glücklich, zufrieden
138	HD	c	3		
139	Jeans	c	3		
140	Kick	n/c	3	(S/E) (*)	(Fußball-)Spiel; Nervenkitzel
141	Lift	n	3	(S) (D)	Aufzug, Höhenverstell-(Dinger)
142	Miss	n	3	(S)	Schönheitskönigin
143	outen	c	3		
144	Pool	n	3	(S)	Schwimmbecken
145	Remix	c	3		
146	Report	n	3	(E)	Bericht
147	Rocker	c	3		
148	Shampoo	n	3	(S) (D)	Haarwaschmittel; (Haar)waschmittel
149	Shuttle	n	3	(S/E)	Pendel-(Bus); Pendelfahrzeug
150	Singer-Songwriter	n	3	(L)	Liedermacher
151	Sir	c	3		

Appendices 231

152	Spurt	c	3			
153	Steak	c	3			
154	Stream	c	3			
155	stressen	n	3	(S/E) (D)	anstrengen, schaffen	
156	Styling	n	3	(S)	Zurechtmachen, Aufbrezel-(Tipps)	
157	surfen	c	3			
158	Wags	n	3	(S)	Spielerfrauen	
159	*yes*	n	3	(E)	ja	
160	Account	n	2	(E)	Konto	
161	Act	n	2	(S)	Künstler, Interpret; Auftritt	
162	Action	n	2	(S)	(spannende) Handlung; (spannende) Aktivitäten	
163	Basketball	c	2			
164	Beamer	n	2	(S) (**)	Projektor	
165	Bingo	c	2			
166	Blog	c	2			
167	Blogger	c	2			
168	boomen	n	2	(E)	brummen	
169	Burnout	c	2			
170	Business	n	2	(E)	Geschäft	
171	Cap	n	2	(S)	Schildmütze	
172	Cappy	n	2	(S) (**)	Schildmütze	
173	Channel	n	2	(E)	Kanal	
174	Charts	n	2	(S)	Schlagerparade	
175	Clip	c	2			
176	Coach	n	2	(S)	Übungsleiter	
177	Coaching	c	2			
178	Cockpit	n	2	(S) (D)	Pilotenkanzel	
179	Cola	c	2			
180	Comedian	n	2	(L)	Komiker	
181	Convention	n	2	(L)	Zusammenkunft, Treffen, Versammlung	
182	Curved-TV	c	2			
183	Date	n	2	(S)	Verabredung	
184	Dinner	n	2	(S/E)	Abendessen; Bankett	
185	Display	n	2	(E)	Bildschirm	
186	DNA	n	2	(E)	DNS	
187	Doping	c	2			
188	Eco-Lodge	n	2	(S)	Öko-Ferienhaus	

(Continued)

Rank	Base anglicism	n/c	Tokens	(S/E/L) (*) (D) (**)	German near-equivalents in context
189	fair	n	2	(S) (D)	anständig, gerecht
190	Golf	c	2		
191	Hightech	n	2	(S)	Hochtechnologie
192	Hollywood	c	2		
193	in	n	2	(S)	angesagt, in Mode, modern
194	Insider	n	2	(S)	Eingeweihter
195	IT	c	2		
196	Lady	n	2	(E)	Dame
197	Laptop	c	2		
198	Laser	c	2		
199	LED	c	2		
200	Lord	c	2		
201	Match	n	2	(E)	Spiel
202	Media-Operations-Volunteer	c	2		
203	Meeting	n	2	(S)	Besprechung
204	Okay	n	2	(S) (D)	Einverständnis, Einwilligung, Zustimmung, Genehmigung
205	Outfit	n	2	(S)	Aufmachung
206	Podcast	c	2		
207	*Prince*	n	2	(E)	(englischer) Prinz
208	Ranking	n	2	(S)	Rangliste
209	*ready*	n	2	(E)	bereit
210	relaxt	n	2	(E)	entspannt
211	shoppen	n	2	(S)	einkaufen
212	Sidestep	n	2	(S)	Seitenschritt
213	Skateboard	c	2		
214	Talk	n	2	(S)	Gespräch
215	*thank you*	n	2	(E)	danke
216	twittern	c	2		
217	UHD	c	2		
218	Virtual-Reality	c	2		
219	Watt	c	2		
220	Web	c	2		
221	*what*	n	2	(E)	was
222	Workshop	n	2	(S)	Arbeitskreis; Übungskurs
223	*yep*	n	2	(E)	ja

224	Airport	n	1	(S)		Flughafen
225	all-inclusive	c	1			
226	*always*	n	1	(E)		immer
227	American-Icecream	n	1	(S)		amerikanische Eiscreme
228	*amused*	n	1	(S)		amüsiert
229	Application	c	1			
230	Aquaplaning	n	1	(E)		Wasserglätte
231	Basketballer	c	1			
232	beamen	c	1			
233	Beatbox	c	1			
234	Beauty	n	1	(E)		Schönheit
235	Best-of-Five	c	1			
236	Bit	c	1			
237	Boss	n	1	(S)		Vorstandsvorsitzender
238	Boyband	c	1			
239	boykottieren	n	1	(L)		meiden
240	Brain-Jogging	n	1	(S)		Gehirn-Übungen
241	Bulldog	n	1	(S) (D)		Zugmaschine
242	Bully	c	1			
243	*Captain*	n	1	(S)		Kapitän
244	Car-Sharing	c	1			
245	Casting	n	1	(S)		Auswahlverfahren
246	Catering	c	1			
247	Charter	n	1	(L) (D)		Miet-(Flugzeug)
248	Chat	c	1			
249	Check-in	c	1			
250	Clubber	n	1	(S)		Vereinsmitglied
251	Combo	n	1	(S)		Ensemble
252	Cornrows	c	1			
253	*correct*	n	1	(E)		richtig
254	Couch	n	1	(S) (D)		Sofa
255	covern	c	1			
256	Cowboy	n	1	(E) (D)		Kuhhirt
257	Dancefloor	n	1	(S)		Tanzfläche
258	Dealer	n	1	(E)		(Drogen-)Händler
259	designen	n	1	(E)		gestalten, entwerfen
260	Designer	c	1			
261	dissen	n	1	(S)		beschimpfen
262	Dos und Don'ts	c	1			

(Continued)

Rank	Base anglicism	n/c	Tokens	(S/E/L) (D) (*) (**)	German near-equivalents in context
263	Double	c	1		
264	Downhill	n	1	(E)	Abfahrt
265	downloaden	n	1	(S)	herunterladen
266	Drink	n	1	(S)	(alkoholisches) Getränk
267	DVBT	c	1		
268	DVD	c	1		
269	Edge LED	c	1		
270	Entertainment	n	1	(E)	Unterhaltung
271	Escort-Service	c	1		
272	*exactly*	n	1	(L)	genau
273	faden	n	1	(E)	(aus)klingen
274	Fairness	n	1	(E)	Sportgeist
275	Featuring	c	1		
276	Feeling	n	1	(E)	Gefühl
277	Final Four	c	1		
278	First Lady	c	1		
279	flashen	n	1	(S)	begeistern, elektrisieren
280	Flatrate	n	1	(S)	Pauschale
281	Flower-Power	c	1		
282	Free-WLAN	n	1	(S)	kostenloses WLAN
283	Friendzone	n	1	(S)	Freundeskreis
284	Full-HD	c	1		
285	Gangster	n	1	(E)	Bandit, Verbrecher
286	Gin	c	1		
287	Glamour	c	1		
288	*goodbye*	n	1	(S)	auf Wiedersehen
289	grooven	c	1		
290	Happening	n	1	(E)	Ereignis
291	happy birthday!	n	1	(S)	alles Gute zum Geburtstag!
292	Happy End	n	1	(S)	glückliches Ende
293	Hardcore	c	1		
294	Hardware	c	1		
295	Hashtag	c	1		
296	HbbTV	c	1		
297	HDMI	c	1		
298	HDR	c	1		
299	HDTV	c	1		
300	*hello*	n	1	(E)	hallo

301	Hippie	c	1			
302	Hipster	c	1			
303	Hispanic	n	1	(S)	Lateinamerikaner	
304	Hobby	n	1	(S) (D)	Steckenpferd, Zeitvertreib	
305	holy moly!	n	1	(S)	Heiliger Strohsack!	
306	Image	n	1	(S)	Ansehen(sfaktor)	
307	in action	n	1	(E)	in Aufruhr, aufgeregt	
308	Independent Folkrock	c	1			
309	Indie-Folkrock	c	1			
310	Inlineskate	c	1			
311	interviewen	n	1	(L) (D)	befragen	
312	Intranet	c	1			
313	It-Girl	c	1			
314	jetten	n	1	(E)	fliegen	
315	Joint	n	1	(S)	Marihuanazigarette	
316	Ketchup	c	1			
317	kickern	c	1	(**)		
318	Kiddie	n	1	(L)	Kind	
319	King	n	1	(S)	König	
320	K-O	c	1			
321	light	n	1	(E)	leicht	
322	Link	c	1			
323	Lunch	n	1	(S)	Mahlzeit, Mittagessen	
324	made in Germany	n	1	(S) (D)	hergestellt in Deutschland	
325	Mainstream	n	1	(S)	breite Masse	
326	Marketing	n	1	(E)	Vermarktung	
327	Merchandising	c	1			
328	Metal	c	1			
329	Mister	n	1	(L)	Herr	
330	Mixed-Zone	c	1			
331	Model	n	1	(S)	Fotomodell, Mannequin	
332	Moonwalk	c	1			
333	Mountainbike	c	1			
334	Musical	c	1			
335	Nerd	c	1			
336	Number-One	n	1	(E)	Nummer 1	
337	OLED	c	1			
338	Organic Cotton	n	1	(E)	Bio-Baumwolle	

(Continued)

Rank	Base anglicism	n/c	Tokens	(S/E/L) (D) (*) (**)	German near-equivalents in context
339	Pampers	n	1	(E) (D)	Windel
340	Patchwork	c	1		
341	PC	c	1		
342	Performer	n	1	(L)	Künstler
343	Pitch-Access	n	1	(S)	Spielfeldzugang
344	PMI	c	1		
345	Pony	c	1		
346	Popcorn	c	1		
347	Post	c	1		
348	Posting	c	1		
349	Power	n	1	(L)	Pep, Schwung
350	*President*	n	1	(E)	Präsident
351	Pressing	c	1		
352	Pulli	c	1	(**)	
353	pushen	n	1	(S)	vorantreiben
354	Rapper	c	1		
355	Reality	c	1		
356	Recall	c	1		
357	Recycling	n	1	(S)	Abfallverwertung
358	reloaded	n	1	(S)	neu aufgelegt
359	Sandwich	n	1	(D)	Schnitte, Stulle
360	Security	n	1	(S)	Sicherheitspersonal
361	Server	c	1		
362	Set	n	1	(S)	Garnitur
363	Shetland-Sheep-Dog	c	1		
364	Shirt	n	1	(E)	Hemd
365	shit happens	n	1	(S)	dumm gelaufen
366	Shopping	n	1	(E)	Einkaufs-
367	Shorts	n	1	(S)	(Bade-)Hose
368	Smiley	c	1		
369	Snare	n	1	(S)	Schnarrtrommel
370	Soul	c	1		
371	*splendid*	n	1	(S)	ausgezeichnet
372	Starter	n	1	(S)	Teilnehmer
373	Statement	n	1	(S)	Äußerung, Kommentar
374	strange	n	1	(S)	komisch
375	Stretch	n	1	(E)	Lang-(Format)

376	stylen	n	1	(S)		zurechtmachen
377	Surround	c	1			
378	switchen	n	1	(E)		wechseln
379	Tablet	c	1			
380	Task-Force	n	1	(S)		Arbeitsgruppe
381	Teddy	c	1			
382	Tester	n	1	(E) (D)		Prüfer
383	Toaster	c	1			
384	toppen	n	1	(S)		übertreffen, übertrumpfen
385	Touch	n	1	(S)		Note
386	Trail	n	1	(S)		Wanderweg(-Fahren)
387	Trailer	n	1	(E)		Vorschau
388	Tram	n	1	(S) (D)		Straßenbahn
389	Tri-Material-Coin	c	1			
390	Trip	n	1	(S)		Ausflug
391	Triple	c	1			
392	try and error	n	1	(S)		Versuch und Irrtum
393	Tutorial	n	1	(L)		Anleitung
394	Tweet	c	1			
395	USB	c	1			
396	Warm-up	n	1	(E)		Aufwärm-(Familienfest)
397	win win win	n	1	(S)		gewinnen, gewinnen, gewinnen
398	Wives and Girlfriends	n	1	(E)		Spielerfrauen
399	XXL	n	1	(L)		Riesen-(Wochenende)
400	*yeeha*	n	1	(E)		oh ja!
401	Youngster	n	1	(S)		Junior

Note: Table A.2 lists all anglicism bases found in the radio corpus except for one anglicism base which was unique for an individual station and could not be pseudonymized. Each anglicism is marked as c (for catachrestic) and n (for non-catachrestic) according to their catachrestic or non-catachrestic nature. The table additionally depicts the frequency of each base type (number of tokens). Diachronic development is marked with the letter (D), the relative length of each anglicism in context in comparison to the German semantic near-equivalent which could have been used optionally by radio journalists is marked with either (S) for shorter, (E) for equal or (L) for longer than the equivalent. Catachrestic/non-catachrestic splits are indicated with one asterisk (*), while pseudo-anglicisms are marked with two asterisks (**). All single-word codeswitches found in the corpus are set in italics. Novel creations were excluded from this analysis since these bear neither M- nor I-implicatures. In addition, derivations where in the process of base extraction the base would have changed grammatical category were excluded from the catachrestic/non-catachrestic analysis.

Notes

Chapter 1

1 All English translations of examples from the radio corpus are my own.
2 I use the term 'modernity' both in the sense of a modern way of life and for the epoch of modernity in this book. To avoid ambiguity, I will refer to the era of Modernity by using a capital *M*.

Chapter 2

1 Wallerstein also defines a fifth dimension of *transformational* TimeSpace, which focuses on significant changes or ruptures caused by an individual event and is therefore not relevant for this discussion.
2 Following reunification, the West German broadcasting system was also implemented in the Eastern states of Germany. This means that journalistic practices and styles were aligned with West German standards (Goldhammer 1995).
3 Arbeitsgemeinschaft der Landesmedienanstalten in der Bundesrepublik Deutschland, 'Jahrbuch 2015/2016', https://www.die-medienanstalten.de/fileadmin/user_upload/die_medienanstalten/Publikationen/Jahrbuch/Jahrbuch_2015-2016.pdf, accessed 8 April 2023.

Chapter 3

1 Without going into detail here about the discussion around the problems attached to the concept of 'native speaker' (see Love and Ansaldo 2010; Saraceni 2015), it shall be sufficient to say that asking proficient speakers of English for verification is not necessarily a satisfactory method since it is not only time-consuming, but also entirely dependent on each person's language repertoire. While using reference works as a first step of identification of such pseudo-cases allows for a basic classification, large English-language online corpora are useful to verify if words that are potential pseudo-anglicisms are used regularly by proficient speakers of English in the same sense as used by speakers of German or not.

2   In his theory of presumptive meanings, Levison (2000) develops the concept of I- and M-implicatures to highlight stable pragmatic meanings. I-implicatures stand for informativeness and, according to Levison, are one of three types of conversational implicatures. An utterance conveying I-implicatures is, so to say, the standard way to express something and therefore describes a stereotypical situation. This differs from M-implicatures (of manner), which are described as something that is said in an abnormal way and therefore is not the standard phrasing and conveys additional pragmatic meaning.

Chapter 4

1   Arbeitsgemeinschaft der Landesmedienanstalten in der Bundesrepublik Deutschland, 'Jahrbuch 2015/2016', https://www.die-medienanstalten.de/fileadmin/user_upload/die_medienanstalten/Publikationen/Jahrbuch/Jahrbuch_2015-2016.pdf, accessed 8 April 2023.
2   ARD, 'Hörfunk 2017', https://www.ard.de/download/449540/Hoerfunknutzung_bundesweit_ma_2017_II.pdf, accessed 7 April 2019.
3   ARD, 'Finanzen der ARD', http://www.ard.de/home/die-ard/fakten/finanzen-der-ard/Finanzen_der_ARD/346640/index.html, last modified 1 September 2017.
4   See decision BVerfGE 74, 297/350f.; 83, 238/298 of the German Federal Constitutional Court.
5   See section II, article 11, *Interstate Treaty on Broadcasting and Telemedia (Interstate Broadcasting Treaty)*, 20th Amendment, in effect 1 September 2017.
6   See decision BVerfGE 73, 118/159 of the German Federal Constitutional Court.
7   The term 'culture', according to the Interstate Broadcasting Treaty, comprises 'theatre plays, music, television plays, television films and radio plays, fine arts, architecture, philosophy, literature and cinema' (see section I, article 2, *Interstate Treaty on Broadcasting and Telemedia (Interstate Broadcasting Treaty)*, 20th Amendment, in effect 1 September 2017).
8   See section II, article 11, *Interstate Treaty on Broadcasting and Telemedia (Interstate Broadcasting Treaty)*, 20th Amendment, in effect 1 September 2017.
9   Shoemaker and Reese's model was originally developed in the first edition of their book: Shoemaker, P. J. and S. D. Reese (1991), *Mediating the Message: Theories of Influences on Mass Media Content*, White Plains, NY: Longman.
10 Against the background of accelerated globalization and the internationalization of the media, it is also important to note that media systems in each locality should not only be considered as confined to the jurisdiction of a certain nation-state. Instead, it is necessary to adopt a more 'transcultural' conception of media systems as also transgressing constructed national and cultural boundaries (see Hepp and Coulpry 2009).

11 As part of the ethical clearance for the case study, the Research Ethics Committee at the University of Galway required the protection of the identities of participants in the qualitative interviews. Since participants in this project partially are figures in the public eye who have unique roles within small journalistic teams of the morning show at their individual station (e.g. a station's morning show hosts, news presenters and editors), the names of stations were additionally pseudonymized to guarantee participants' anonymity.

12 Station imaging segments containing no spoken content for more than 2 seconds were cut out to avoid distortion of the frequency of anglicisms.

13 All statements made by the participants of this research project on the usage of anglicisms in adult contemporary radio content express their personal opinions only and therefore cannot be taken as official positions or statements of the stations where they are employed.

14 Names and other characteristics that would allow for identification of the interviewees in this study are not disclosed to ensure anonymity. I received informed consent of all participants prior to the individual interviews.

Chapter 5

1 See Kultusministerkonferenz (2011), *Empfehlungen der Kultusministerkonferenz zur Stärkung der Fremdsprachenkompetenz*, https://www.kmk.org/fileadmin/Dateien/veroeffentlichungen_beschluesse/2011/2011_12_08-Fremdsprachenkompetenz.pdf, accessed 14 June 2020.

2 Journalists differentiate between two types of news topics. *Soft news* mainly concerns human interest stories such as on celebrities, lifestyle and fashion, while *hard news* refers to stories that cover, for example, international affairs, economy and politics.

Chapter 6

1 Sagmeister-Brandner (2008) considers those words as anglicisms that appear foreign to the audience. However, in contrast to the present study on radio in Germany, she also includes certain Greek or Latinate terms such as *Atom* (atom) as anglicisms, which are said to have experienced an increase in usage through the influence of English on German.

Chapter 8

1 *Kradfahrer* is a shortening of *Kraftradfahrer*, which comes originally from German bureaucratic and military jargon.

References

Adler, M. (2004), 'Form und Häufigkeit der Verwendung von Anglizismen in deutschen und schwedischen Massenmedien', PhD thesis, Jena: Friedrich Schiller University Jena.

Aikhenvald, A. (2007), 'Grammars in Contact: A Cross-Linguistic Perspective', in A. Aikhenvald and R. M. W. Dixon (eds), *Grammars in Contact: A Cross-Linguistic Typology*, 1–66, Oxford: Oxford University Press.

Allenbacher, P. K. (1999), *Anglizismen in der Fachlexik*, Frankfurt am Main: Neue Wissenschaft.

Andersen, G. (2015), 'Pseudo-Borrowings as Cases of Pragmatic Borrowing: Focus on Anglicisms in Norwegian', in C. Furiassi and H. Gottlieb (eds), *Pseudo-English: Studies on False Anglicisms in Europe*, 123–44, Berlin: De Gruyter Mouton.

Anderson, B. (2016), *Imagined Communities: Reflections on the Origin and Spread of Nations*, revised edn, London: Verso.

Appadurai, A. (1996), *Modernity at Large: Cultural Dimensions of Globalization*, Minneapolis: University of Minnesota Press.

Appadurai, A. (2000), 'Grassroots Globalization and the Research Imagination', *Public Culture*, 12 (1): 1–19.

Auer, P. (2022), '"Translanguaging" or "Doing Languages"? Multilingual Practices and the Notion of "Codes"', in J. MacSwan (ed), *Multilingual Perspectives on Translanguaging*, 126–53, Bristol: Multilingual Matters.

Backus, A. (2001), 'The Role of Semantic Specificity in Insertional Codeswitching: Evidence from Dutch-Turkish', in R. Jacobson (ed), *Codeswitching Worldwide II*, 125–54, Berlin: Mouton de Gruyter.

Barad, K. (2007), *Meeting the Universe Halfway: Quantum Physics and the Entanglement of Matter and Meaning*, Durham: Duke University Press.

Bauer, R. A. (1958), 'The Communicator and the Audience', *Journal of Conflict Resolution*, 2 (1): 67–77.

Baum, B. (2016), 'Sprache als Marke von Radioformaten: Versuch eines zielgruppenfokussierten Stationality-Tunings von Nachrichten- und Moderationstexten des Saarländischen Rundfunks', PhD thesis, Saarbrücken: Universität des Saarlandes.

Bauman, R. and C. L. Briggs (2003), *Voices of Modernity: Language Ideologies and the Politics of Inequality*, Cambridge: Cambridge University Press.

Becker, F. (2006), 'Wirklichkeit oder Phantasma?', in A. Stephan and J. Vogt (eds), *America on My Mind: Zur Amerikanisierung der deutschen Kultur nach 1945*, 51–73, München: Wilhelm Fink Verlag.

Bell, A. (1991), *The Language of News Media*, Oxford: Blackwell.
Betz, W. (1959), 'Lehnwörter und Lehnprägungen im Vor- und Frühdeutschen', in F. Maurer and F. Stroh (eds), *Deutsche Wortgeschichte*, 127–47, Berlin: De Gruyter.
Beuge, P. (2019), *Was ist gutes Deutsch? Eine qualitative Analyse laienlinguistischen Sprachnormwissens*, Berlin: De Gruyter.
Bezemer, J. and K. Cowan (2021), 'Exploring Reading in Social Semiotics: Theory and Methods', *Education 3–13*, 49 (1): 107–18.
Bhatia, V. K. (2014), *Worlds of Written Discourse: A Genre-Based View*, London: Bloomsbury Academic.
Blommaert, J. (1990), 'Review of: Thomason and Kaufman: Language Contact, Creolization, and Genetic Linguistics', *Journal of Pragmatics*, 14: 813–17.
Blommaert, J. (2005), *Discourse: A Critical Introduction*, New York: Cambridge University Press.
Blommaert, J. (2006), 'Language Policy and National Identity', in T. Ricento (ed), *An Introduction to Language Policy: Theory and Method*, 238–54, Malden, MA: Blackwell.
Blommaert, J. (2010), *The Sociolinguistics of Globalization*, Cambridge: Cambridge University Press.
Blommaert, J. (2013), *Ethnography, Superdiversity and Linguistic Landscapes: Chronicles of Complexity*, Bristol: Multilingual Matters.
Blommaert, J. and D. Jie (2020), *Ethnographic Fieldwork: A Beginner's Guide*, 2nd edn, Blue Ridge Summit: Multilingual Matters.
Blommaert, J., S. Leppänen and M. Spotti (2012), 'Endangering Multilingualism', in J. Blommaert, S. Leppänen, P. Pahta and T. Räisänen (eds), *Dangerous Multilingualism*, 1–21, London: Palgrave Macmillan.
Blommaert, J. and B. Rampton (2011), 'Language and Superdiversity', *Diversities*, 13 (2): 1–21.
Bolton, K. (2013), 'World Englishes, Globalisation, and Language Worlds', in N.-L. Johannesson, G. Melchers and B. Björkman (eds), *Of Butterflies and Birds, of Dialects and Genres: Essays in Honour of Philip Shaw*, 227–52, Stockholm: Stockholm University.
Braun, A. (2018), 'Approaching Wordplay from the Angle of Phonology and Phonetics – Examples from German', in S. Arndt-Lappe, A. Braun, C. Moulin and E. Winter-Froemel (eds), *Expanding the Lexicon*, 173–202, Berlin: De Gruyter.
Breed, W. (1955), 'Social Control in the Newsroom: A Functional Analysis', *Social Forces*, 33 (4): 326–35.
Brennen, B. (2017), *Qualitative Research Methods for Media Studies*, 2nd edn, New York: Routledge.
Bryant, L. R. (2011), *The Democracy of Objects*, Ann Arbor: Open Humanities Press.
Buchholz, A. (2017), 'Morningshow/Frühsendung', in W. von La Roche and A. Buchholz (eds), *Radio-Journalismus: Ein Handbuch für Ausbildung und Praxis im Hörfunk*, 11th edn, 301–6, Wiesbaden: Springer VS.

Burger, H. and M. Luginbühl (2014), *Mediensprache: Eine Einführung in Sprache und Kommunikationsformen der Massenmedien*, 4th edn, Berlin: De Gruyter Mouton.

Busse, U. (1993), *Anglizismen im Duden: Eine Untersuchung zur Darstellung englischen Wortguts in den Ausgaben des Rechtschreibdudens von 1880-1986*, Tübingen: Niemeyer.

Busse, U. (1996), 'Neologismen: Der Versuch einer Begriffsbestimmung', in M. Gellerstam, J. Järborg, S.-G. Malmgren, K. Norén, L. Rogström and C. Röjder Papmehl (eds), *EURALEX '96: Proceedings. Part 2*, 645-58, Göteborg: Göteborg University, Department of Swedish.

Busse, U. (2008), 'Some Comments on the Dictionary of European Anglicisms and Some Suggestions for Its Second Edition Exemplified by the Entry Kids', in R. Fischer (ed), *Anglicisms in Europe: Linguistic Diversity in a Global Context*, 274-98, Newcastle upon Tyne: Cambridge Scholars Publishing.

Busse, U. and B. Carstensen (1993), *Anglizismen-Wörterbuch: Der Einfluss des Englischen auf den deutschen Wortschatz nach 1945. Band 1, A - E*, Berlin: De Gruyter.

Busse, U. and B. Carstensen (1994), *Anglizismen-Wörterbuch: Der Einfluss des Englischen auf den deutschen Wortschatz nach 1945. Band 2, F - O*, Berlin: De Gruyter.

Busse, U. and B. Carstensen (1996), *Anglizismen-Wörterbuch: Der Einfluss des Englischen auf den deutschen Wortschatz nach 1945. Band 3, P - Z*, Berlin: De Gruyter.

Busse, U. and M. Görlach (2002), 'German', in M. Görlach (ed), *English in Europe*, 13-36, Oxford: Oxford University Press.

Canagarajah, S. (2013), *Translingual Practice: Global Englishes and Cosmopolitan Relations*, Abingdon: Routledge.

Canagarajah, S. (2018a), 'Translingual Practice as Spatial Repertoires: Expanding the Paradigm beyond Structuralist Orientations', *Applied Linguistics*, 39 (1): 31-54.

Canagarajah, S. (2018b), 'The Unit and Focus of Analysis in Lingua Franca English Interactions: In Search of a Method', *International Journal of Bilingual Education and Bilingualism*, 21 (7): 805-24.

Canagarajah, S. (2020), 'English as a Resource in a Communicative Assemblage: A Perspective from Flat Ontology', in C. J. Hall and R. Wicaksono (eds), *Ontologies of English*, 295-314, Cambridge: Cambridge University Press.

Canagarajah, S. (2021), 'Rethinking Mobility and Language: From the Global South', *The Modern Language Journal*, 105 (2): 570-82.

Canagarajah, S. and V. Minakova (2022), 'Objects in Embodied Sociolinguistics: Mind the Door in Research Group Meetings', *Language in Society*, 1-32.

Caronia, L. and L. Mortari (2015), 'The Agency of Things: How Spaces and Artefacts Organize the Moral Order of an Intensive Care Unit', *Social Semiotics*, 25 (4): 401-22.

Carstensen, B. (1965), *Englische Einflüsse auf die deutsche Sprache nach 1945*, Heidelberg: Winter.

Carstensen, B. (1980), 'Semantische Scheinentlehnungen des Deutschen aus dem Englischen', in W. Viereck (ed), *Studien zum Einfluß der englischen Sprache auf das Deutsche*, 77–99, Tübingen: Günter Narr Verlag.

Clyne, M. (2003), *Dynamics of Language Contact: English and Immigrant Languages*, Cambridge: Cambridge University Press.

Cotter, C. (2010), *News Talk: Investigating the Language of Journalism*, Cambridge: Cambridge University Press.

Creese, A. and A. Blackledge (2011), 'Separate and Flexible Bilingualism in Complementary Schools: Multiple Language Practices in Interrelationship', *Journal of Pragmatics*, 43 (5): 1196–1208.

Crisell, A. (1986), *Understanding Radio*, London: Methuen.

Culler, J. (1986), *Ferdinand de Saussure*, revised edn, Ithaca, NY: Cornell University Press.

Curran, J. (2002), *Media and Power*, London: Routledge.

Dahl, P. (1983), *Radio: Sozialgeschichte des Rundfunks für Sender und Empfänger*, Hamburg: Rowohlt.

Davies, M. (2008), 'The Corpus of Contemporary American English (COCA): 560 Million Words, 1990–Present', available online: https://www.english-corpora.org/coca/.

Deleuze, G. and F. Guattari (1987), *A Thousand Plateaus: Capitalism and Schizophrenia*, Minneapolis: University of Minnesota Press.

Demont-Heinrich, C. (2020), 'New Global Music Distribution System, Same Old Linguistic Hegemony?', in O. Boyd-Barrett and T. Mirrlees (eds), *Media Imperialism: Continuity and Change*, 199–211, Lanham, MD: Rowman and Littlefield.

Díaz, J. A. R. (2019), 'The Semantics and Functions of Anglicisms and Germanisms in Present-Day Advertising Written Peninsular Spanish: A Comparison', *Lebende Sprachen*, 64 (1): 23–46.

Dovchin, S. (2020), *Language, Social Media and Ideologies: Translingual Englishes, Facebook and Authenticities*, Cham: Springer.

Duckworth, D. (1977), 'Zur terminologischen und systematischen Grundlage der Forschung auf dem Gebiet der englisch-deutschen Interferenz', in H. Kolb and H. Lauffer (eds), *Sprachliche Interferenz*, 36–56, Tübingen: Niemeyer.

Duden, Das Fremdwörterbuch (2015), 11th edn, Der Duden in zwölf Bänden, Berlin: Dudenverlag.

Duden, Das Herkunftswörterbuch: Etymologie der deutschen Sprache (2014), 5th edn, Der Duden in zwölf Bänden, Berlin: Dudenverlag.

Duden, Die Deutsche Rechtschreibung (2013), 26th edn, Der Duden in zwölf Bänden, Berlin: Dudenverlag.

Dudenverlag (n.d.), *Duden Online*, available online: http://www.duden.de (accessed 1 July 2020).

Dunger, H. (1882), *Wörterbuch von Verdeutschungen entbehrlicher Fremdwörter*, Leipzig: Teubner.

Duszak, A. (2004), 'Globalisation as Interdiscursivity: On the Spread of Global Intertexts', in A. Duszak and U. Okulska (eds), *Speaking from the Margin: Global English from a European Perspective*, 117–32, Frankfurt am Main: Peter Lang.

D'warte, J. (2014), 'Linguistic Repertoires: Teachers and Students Explore Their Everyday Language Worlds', *Language Arts*, 91 (5): 352–62.

'DWDS – Digitales Wörterbuch der deutschen Sprache' (n.d.), available online: https://www.dwds.de/ (accessed 1 July 2020).

Eide, M. and G. Knight (1999), 'Public/Private Service: Service Journalism and the Problems of Everyday Life', *European Journal of Communication*, 14 (4): 525–47.

Elsen, H. (2011), *Neologismen: Formen und Funktionen neuer Wörter in verschiedenen Varietäten des Deutschen*, 2nd edn, Tübingen: Narr.

Ermarth, M., ed. (1993), *America and the Shaping of the German Society 1945–1955*, Providence: Berg.

Esser, F. (1998), *Die Kräfte hinter den Schlagzeilen: Englischer und deutscher Journalismus im Vergleich*, Freiburg: K. Alber.

Estel, B. (2014), *Weder Demokratie noch Freiheit: Zur Herrschaft des Guten in Deutschland*, Münster: MV-Verlag.

European Commission (2017), 'Strengthening European Identity through Education and Culture', communication paper COM(2017) 673, Strasbourg.

Fairclough, N. (1995), *Media Discourse*, London: Arnold.

Fairclough, N. (2006), *Language and Globalization*, Abingdon: Routledge.

Fairclough, N. (2010), *Critical Discourse Analysis: The Critical Study of Language*, 2nd edn, Harlow: Longman.

Faulstich, W. (2006), '"Amerikanisierung" als kultureller Mehrwert', in A. Stephan and J. Vogt (eds), *America on My Mind: Zur Amerikanisierung der deutschen Kultur nach 1945*, 153–71, München: Wilhelm Fink Verlag.

Fiedler, S. (2017), 'Phraseological Borrowing from English into German: Cultural and Pragmatic Implications', *Journal of Pragmatics*, 113: 89–102.

Fiedler, S. (2022), '"Mit dem Topping bin ich auch fein"–Anglicisms in a German TV cooking show', *Espaces Linguistiques*, 4.

Field, F. (2002), *Linguistic Borrowing in Bilingual Contexts*, Amsterdam: John Benjamins.

Fink, H., L. Fijas and D. Schons (1997), *Anglizismen in der Sprache der Neuen Bundesländer: Eine Analyse zur Verwendung und Rezeption*, Frankfurt am Main: Peter Lang.

Fitzgerald, R. (2006), 'Radio: Language', in E. K. Brown (ed), *Encyclopedia of Language & Linguistics*, 348–54, Amsterdam: Elsevier.

Fjaestad, B. and P. G. Holmlov (1976), 'The Journalist's View', *Journal of Communication*, 2: 108–14.

Flügge, M. (2009), *Spannungsfeld Auftrag – Konvergenz: Der öffentlich-rechtliche Rundfunk in Deutschland*, Berlin: Univ.-Verl. der TU Berlin.

Fowler, R. (1991), *Language in the News: Discourse and Ideology in the Press*, London: Routledge.

Furiassi, C. (2010), *False Anglicisms in Italian*, Monza: Polimetrica.

Galinsky, H. (1963), 'Stylistic Aspects of Linguistic Borrowing: A Stylistic and Comparative View of American Elements in Modern German, and British English', *Jahrbuch für Amerikastudien*, 8: 98–135.

Gans, H. (1979), *Deciding What's News*, New York: Pantheon Books.

Gerhards, M. and H. Stümpert (2017), 'Formate für Begleitprogramme', in W. von La Roche and A. Buchholz (eds), *Radio-Journalismus: Ein Handbuch für Ausbildung und Praxis im Hörfunk*, 11th edn, 353–62, Wiesbaden: Springer VS.

Gerritsen, M., C. Nickerson, A. van Hooft, F. van Meurs, U. Nederstigt, M. Starren and R. Crijns (2007), 'English in Product Advertisements in Belgium, France, Germany, the Netherlands and Spain', *World Englishes*, 26 (3): 291–315.

Glahn, R. (2002), *Der Einfluß des Englischen auf gesprochene deutsche Gegenwartssprache: Eine Analyse öffentlich gesprochener Sprache am Beispiel von 'Fernsehdeutsch'*, 2nd edn, Frankfurt am Main: Peter Lang.

Goldhammer, K. (1995), *Formatradio in Deutschland*, Berlin: Wissenschaftsverlag Volker Spiess.

Görlach, M. (1994), 'A Usage Dictionary of Anglicisms in Selected European Languages', *International Journal of Lexicography*, 7 (3): 223–46.

Görlach, M. (2003), *English Words Abroad*, Amsterdam: John Benjamins.

Gottlieb, H. (2015), 'Danish Pseudo-Anglicisms: A Corpus-Based Analysis', in C. Furiassi and H. Gottlieb (eds), *Pseudo-English: Studies on False Anglicisms in Europe*, 61–98, Berlin: De Gruyter Mouton.

Gottlieb, H. (2020), *Echoes of English: Anglicisms in Minor Speech Communities – with Special Focus on Danish and Afrikaans*, Berlin: Peter Lang.

Grundy, P. (2020), *Doing Pragmatics*, 4th edn, New York: Routledge.

Gundlach, H. (2010), 'Analyse des publizistischen Wettbewerbs: Untersuchung des publizistischen Wettbewerbs anlässlich des geplanten Telemedienangebots NDR Online – Niedersachsen Regional', Hamburg: NDR.

Gutberlet, B. I. (2007), *Die 50 größten Lügen und Legenden der Weltgeschichte*, Bergisch Gladbach: Ehrenwirth.

Haas, M. H., U. Frigge and G. Zimmer (1991), *Radio-Management: Ein Handbuch für Radio-Journalisten*, München: Ölschläger.

Habermas, J. (1981), *Theorie des kommunikativen Handelns*, Frankfurt am Main: Suhrkamp.

Hall, S. (2013), 'The Work of Representation', in S. Hall, J. Evans and S. Nixon (eds), *Representation*, 2nd edn, 1–47, Los Angeles; Milton Keynes: SAGE; The Open University.

Hamelink, C. J. (1983), *Cultural Autonomy in Global Communications: Planning National Information Policy*, New York: Longman.

Haspelmath, M. (2009), 'Lexical Borrowing: Concepts and Issues', in M. Haspelmath and U. Tadmor (eds), *Loanwords in the World's Languages: A Comparative Handbook*, 35–54, Berlin: De Gruyter Mouton.

Haugen, E. (1949), 'Problems of Bilingualism', *Lingua*, 2: 271–90.

Haugen, E. (1950), 'The Analysis of Linguistic Borrowing', *Language*, 26: 210–31.

Heine, B. and T. Kuteva (2008), 'Constraints on Contact-Induced Linguistic Change', *Journal of Language Contact*, 2 (1): 57–90.

Hepp, A. (2005), 'Medienkultur', in A. Hepp, F. Krotz and C. Winter (eds), *Gobalisierung der Medienkommunikation*, 137–63, Wiesbaden: VS Verlag für Sozialwissenschaften.

Hepp, A. and N. Coulpry (2009), 'What Should Comparative Media Research Be Comparing? Towards a Transcultural Approach to "Media Cultures"', in D. K. Thussu (ed), *Internationalizing Media Studies: Impediments and Imperatives*, 32–47, New York: Routledge.

Hesmondhalgh, D. (2019), *The Cultural Industries*, 4th edn, Thousand Oaks, CA: SAGE.

Hjarvard, S. (2004), 'The Globalization of Language: How the Media Contribute to the Spread of English and the Emergence of Medialects', *Nordicom Review*, 25 (1–2): 75–98.

Hoffmann-Riem, W. (1991), *Rundfunkrecht neben Wirtschaftsrecht: Zur Anwendbarkeit des GWB und des EWG-V auf das Wettbewerbsverhalten öffentlich-rechtlichen Rundfunks in der dualen Rundfunkordnung*, Baden-Baden: Nomos.

Holdcroft, D. (1998), 'Structuralism in Linguistics', in *Routledge Encyclopedia of Philosophy*, London: Routledge, available online: https://www.rep.routledge.com/articles/thematic/structuralism-in-linguistics/v-1.

Horkheimer, M. and T. W. Adorno (1972), 'The Culture Industry: Enlightenment as Mass Deception', in *Dialectic of Enlightenment*, 120–67, New York: Herder & Herder.

Hunt, J. W. (2019), 'Anglicisms in German: Tsunami or Trickle?', in A. Koll-Stobbe (ed), *Informalization and Hybridization of Speech Practices: Polylingual Meaning-Making across Domains, Genres, and Media*, 25–58, Frankfurt am Main: Peter Lang.

Hutchby, I. (2001), 'Technologies, Texts and Affordances', *Sociology*, 35 (2): 441–56.

Iedema, R. (2003), 'Multimodality, Resemiotization: Extending the Analysis of Discourse as Multi-Semiotic Practice', *Visual Communication*, 2 (1): 29–57.

Ivankova, N. and S. Stick (2011), 'Students' Persistence in a Distributed Doctoral Program in Educational Leadership in Higher Education', in J. W. Creswell and V. L. Plano Clark (eds), *Designing and Conducting Mixed Methods Research*, 2nd ed, 301–34, Los Angeles: SAGE.

James, A. (2009), 'Theorising English and Globalisation: Semiodiversity and Linguistic Structure in Global English, World Englishes and Lingua Franca English', *Apples – Journal of Applied Language Studies*, 3 (1): 79–92.

Kachru, B. B. (1985), 'Standards, Codification and Sociolinguistic Realism: The English Language in the Outer Circle', in R. Quirk and H. G. Widdowson (eds), *English in the World: Teaching and Learning the Language and Literatures*, 11–30, Cambridge: Cambridge University Press.

Kachru, B. B. (1994), 'Englishization and Contact Linguistics', *World Englishes*, 13 (2): 135–54.

Kellner, H. and H.-G. Soeffner (2002), 'Cultural Globalization in Germany', in P. L. Berger and S. P. Huntington (eds), *Many Globalizations: Cultural Diversity in the Contemporary World*, 119–45, New York: Oxford University Press.

Kerswill, P. and E. Torgersen (2017), 'London's Cockney in the Twentieth Century: Stability or Cycles of Contact-Driven Change?', in R. Hickey (ed), *Listening to the*

Past: Audio Records of Accents of English, 85–113, Cambridge: Cambridge University Press.

Kleinsteuber, H. J. (2012), *Radio: Eine Einführung*, Wiesbaden: VS Verlag für Sozialwissenschaften.

Klosa-Kückelhaus, A. and S. Wolfer (2020), 'Considerations on the Acceptance of German Neologisms from the 1990s', *International Journal of Lexicography*, 33 (2): 150–67.

Kluge, F. and E. Seebold (2011), *Etymologisches Wörterbuch der deutschen Sprache*, 25th edn, Berlin: De Gruyter.

Knospe, S. (2014), *Entlehnung oder Codeswitching? Sprachmischungen mit dem Englischen im deutschen Printjournalismus*, Frankfurt am Main: Peter Lang.

Knospe, S. (2015), 'Pseudo-Anglicisms in the Language of the Contemporary German Press', in C. Furiassi and H. Gottlieb (eds), *Pseudo-English: Studies on False Anglicisms in Europe*, 99–122, Berlin: De Gruyter Mouton.

Kortmann, B. and C. Langstrof (2012), 'Varieties of English: Regional Varieties of British English', in A. Bergs and L. Brinton (eds), *English Historical Linguistics: An International Handbook*, 1928–50, Berlin: De Gruyter Mouton.

Kortmann, B. and E. W. Schneider, eds. (2004), *A Handbook of Varieties of English: A Multimedia Reference Tool*, Berlin: Mouton de Gruyter.

Kress, G. R. (2010), *Multimodality: A Social Semiotic Approach to Contemporary Communication*, London: Routledge.

Kress, G. R. and T. van Leeuwen (2001), *Multimodal Discourse: The Modes and Media of Contemporary Communication*, London: Arnold.

Kubota, R. (2016), 'The Multi/Plural Turn, Postcolonial Theory, and Neoliberal Multiculturalism: Complicities and Implications for Applied Linguistics', *Applied Linguistics*, 37 (4): 474–94.

Kubota, R. (2020), 'Promoting and Problematizing Multi/Plural Approaches in Language Pedagogy', in S. M. C. Lau and S. van Viegen (eds), *Plurilingual Pedagogies: Critical and Creative Endeavors for Equitable Language in Education*, 303–21, Cham: Springer International.

Kubota, R. and E. R. Miller (2017), 'Re-examining and Re-envisioning Criticality in Language Studies: Theories and Praxis', *Critical Inquiry in Language Studies*, 14 (2–3): 129–57.

Kuhn, T. S. (2012), *The Structure of Scientific Revolutions*, 4th edn, Chicago: University of Chicago Press.

Kuppens, A. H. (2013), 'Cultural Globalization and the Global Spread of English: From "Separate Fields, Similar Paradigms" to a Transdisciplinary Approach', *Globalizations*, 10 (2): 327–42.

Labov, W. (1972), *Sociolinguistic Patterns*, Philadelphia: University of Pennsylvania Press.

Labov, W. (1982), *The Social Stratification of English in New York City*, Washington, DC: Center for Applied Linguistics.

Lee, J. S. (2014), 'English on Korean Television', *World Englishes*, 33 (1): 33–49.

Léglise, I. and C. Chamoreau, eds. (2013), *The Interplay of Variation and Change in Contact Settings*, Amsterdam: John Benjamins.

Leibniz-Institut für Deutsche Sprache (2006ff), 'Neologismenwörterbuch', *OWID – Online Wortschatz- Informationssystem deutsch*, available online: http://www.owid.de/wb/neo/start.html (accessed 1 July 2020).

Lengenfelder, W. G. (2017), 'Verpackungselemente', in W. von La Roche and A. Buchholz (eds), *Radio-Journalismus: Ein Handbuch für Ausbildung und Praxis im Hörfunk*, 11th edn, 385–91, Wiesbaden: Springer VS.

Levinson, S. C. (2000), *Presumptive Meanings: The Theory of Generalized Conversational Implicature*, Cambridge, MA: MIT Press.

Li, W. (2011), 'Moment Analysis and Translanguaging Space: Discursive Construction of Identities by Multilingual Chinese Youth in Britain', *Journal of Pragmatics*, 43 (5): 1222–35.

Li, W. (2018), 'Translanguaging as a Practical Theory of Language', *Applied Linguistics*, 39 (1): 9–30.

Lievrouw, L. A. (2014), 'Materiality and Media in Communication and Technology Studies: An Unfinished Project', in T. Gillespie, P. J. Boczkowski and K. A. Foot (eds), *Media Technologies: Essays on Communication, Materiality, and Society*, 21–51, Cambridge, MA: MIT Press.

Lilienthal, V. (1991), 'Zählbare Erfolge … nur hören tut man nichts: Die Dualisierung im Hörfunk', *Weiterbildung und Medien*, 3: 14–17.

Lim, L. and U. Ansaldo (2016), *Languages in Contact*, Cambridge: Cambridge University Press.

Love, N. and U. Ansaldo (2010), 'The Native Speaker and the Mother Tongue', *Language Sciences*, 32 (6): 589–93.

Lüdtke, A., I. Marßolek and A. von Saldern, eds. (1996), *Amerikanisierung: Traum und Alptraum im Deutschland des 20. Jahrhunderts*, Stuttgart: Franz Steiner.

Maase, K. (1996), 'Amerikanisierung von unten: Demonstrative Vulgarität und kulturelle Hegemonie in der Bundesrepublik der 50er Jahre', in A. Lüdtke, I. Marßolek and A. von Saldern (eds), *Amerikanisierung: Traum und Alptraum im Deutschland des 20. Jahrhunderts*, 291–313, Stuttgart: Franz Steiner.

Maase, K. (1997), 'Amerikanisierung der Gesellschaft', in K. Jarausch and H. Siegrist (eds), *Amerikanisierung und Sowjetisierung in Deutschland 1945–1970*, 219–42, Frankfurt am Main: Campus Verlag.

MacKenzie, I. (2012), 'Fair Play to Them: Proficiency in English and Types of Borrowing', in C. Furiassi, V. Pulcini and F. Rodríguez González (eds), *The Anglicization of European Lexis*, 27–42, Amsterdam: John Benjamins.

MacSwan, J. (2020), 'Translanguaging, Language Ontology, and Civil Rights', *World Englishes*, 39 (2): 321–33.

Mair, C. (2013), 'The World System of Englishes: Accounting for the Transnational Importance of Mobile and Mediated Vernaculars', *English World-Wide*, 34: 253–78.

Martin, E. (2006), *Marketing Identities through Language: English and Global Imagery in French Advertising*, Basingstoke: Palgrave Macmillan.

Matras, Y. (2007), 'The Borrowability of Structural Categories', in Y. Matras and J. Sakel (eds), *Grammatical Borrowing in Cross-Linguistic Perspective*, Berlin: Mouton de Gruyter.

Matras, Y. (2009), *Language Contact*, Cambridge: Cambridge University Press.

Matras, Y. (2013), 'Languages in Contact in a World Marked by Change and Mobility', *Revue française de linguistique appliquée*, 18 (2): 7–13.

Mattelart, A. (1983), *Transnationals and the Third World: The Struggle for Culture*, South Hadley, MA: Bergin and Garvey.

McQuail, D. (2010), *McQuail's Mass Communication Theory*, 6th edn, London: SAGE.

Mediendaten Südwest (n.d.), 'Radionutzung im Tagesverlauf 2016', available online: http://www.mediendaten.de/mediendaten/hoerfunk/radionutzung/ (accessed 5 March 2016).

Merminod, G. and M. Burger (2020), 'Narrative of Vicarious Experience in Broadcast News: A Linguistic Ethnographic Approach to Semiotic Mediations in the Newsroom', *Journal of Pragmatics*, 155: 240–60.

Montgomery, M. (2007), *The Discourse of Broadcast News: A Linguistic Approach*, London: Routledge.

Morley, D. (2006), 'Globalisation and Cultural Imperialism Reconsidered: Old Questions in New Guises', in J. Curran and D. Morley (eds), *Media and Cultural Theory*, 30–43, London: Routledge.

Muysken, P. (1981), 'Halfway between Quechua and Spanish: The Case for Relexification', in A. Highfield and A. Valdman (eds), *Historicity and Variation in Creole Studies*, 52–78, Ann Arbor: Karoma.

Myers-Scotton, C. (1993), *Duelling Languages: Grammatical Structure in Codeswitching*, Oxford: Clarendon.

Nederveen Pieterse, J. (2009), *Globalization and Culture: Global Mélange*, 2nd edn, Lanham, MD: Rowman and Littlefield.

Nowottnick, M. (1989), *Jugend, Sprache und Medien: Untersuchungen von Rundfunksendungen für Jugendliche*, Berlin: De Gruyter.

Onysko, A. (2004), 'Anglicisms in German: From Iniquitous to Ubiquitous?', *English Today*, 20 (1): 59–64.

Onysko, A. (2007), *Anglicisms in German: Borrowing, Lexical Productivity, and Written Codeswitching*, Berlin: De Gruyter.

Onysko, A. (2016), 'Modeling World Englishes from the Perspective of Language Contact', *World Englishes*, 35 (2): 196–220.

Onysko, A. and E. Winter-Froemel (2011), 'Necessary Loans – Luxury Loans? Exploring the Pragmatic Dimension of Borrowing', *Journal of Pragmatics*, 43 (6): 1550–67.

Otheguy, R., O. García and W. Reid (2015), 'Clarifying Translanguaging and Deconstructing Named Languages: A Perspective from Linguistics', *Applied Linguistics Review*, 6 (3): 281–307.

Otsuji, E. and A. Pennycook (2010), 'Metrolingualism: Fixity, Fluidity and Language in Flux', *International Journal of Multilingualism*, 7 (3): 240–54.

Oxford University Press (n.d.), *OED Online*, available online: http://www.oed.com (accessed 1 July 2022).
Peiser, W. (2000), 'Setting the Journalist Agenda: Influences from Journalists' Individual Characteristics and from Media Factors', *Journalism and Mass Communication Quarterly*, 77 (2): 243–57.
Pennycook, A. (2003), 'Global Englishes, Rip Slyme, and Performativity', *Journal of Sociolinguistics*, 7 (4): 513–33.
Pennycook, A. (2007), *Global Englishes and Transcultural Flows*, Abingdon: Routledge.
Pennycook, A. (2017), 'Translanguaging and Semiotic Assemblages', *International Journal of Multilingualism*, 14 (3): 269–82.
Pennycook, A. (2020a), 'Pushing the Ontological Boundaries of English', in C. J. Hall and R. Wicaksono (eds), *Ontologies of English*, 355–67, Cambridge: Cambridge University Press.
Pennycook, A. (2020b), 'Translingual Entanglements of English', *World Englishes*, 39 (2): 222–35.
Pennycook, A. and E. Otsuji (2015), *Metrolingualism: Language in the City*, London: Routledge.
Pennycook, A. and E. Otsuji (2017), 'Fish, Phone Cards and Semiotic Assemblages in Two Bangladeshi Shops in Sydney and Tokyo', *Social Semiotics*, 27 (4): 434–50.
Perrin, D. (2013), *The Linguistics of Newswriting*, Amsterdam: John Benjamins.
Perrin, D. (2017), 'Language in the Media: The Process Perspective', in K. Bedijs and C. Maaß (eds), *Manual of Romance Languages in the Media*, 263–89, Berlin: De Gruyter.
Pfalzgraf, F. (2009), 'Linguistic Purism in the History of the German Language', in G. Horan, N. Langer and S. Watts (eds), *Landmarks in the History of the German Language*, 137–68, Frankfurt am Main: Peter Lang.
Pfitzner, J. (1978), *Der Anglizismus im Deutschen: Ein Beitrag zur Bestimmung seiner stilistischen Funktion in der heutigen Presse*, Stuttgart: Metzler.
Phillipson, R. (1992), *Linguistic Imperialism*, Oxford: Oxford University Press.
Phillipson, R. (2009), *Linguistic Imperialism Continued*, New York: Routledge.
Picone, M. D. (1996), *Anglicisms, Neologisms and Dynamic French*, Amsterdam: John Benjamins.
Pietikäinen, S. (2016), 'Critical Debates: Discourse, Boundaries and Social Change', in N. Coupland (ed), *Sociolinguistics: Theoretical Debates*, 263–81, Cambridge: Cambridge University Press.
Piller, I. (2001), 'Identity Constructions in Multilingual Advertising', *Language in Society*, 30: 153–86.
Piller, I. (2003), 'Advertising as a Site of Language Contact', *Annual Review of Applied Linguistics*, 23: 170–83.
Piller, I. (2016), 'Herder: An Explainer for Linguists', *Language on the Move* [blog], 4 March, available online: https://www.languageonthemove.com/herder-an-explainer-for-linguists/ (accessed 9 December 2021).

Plaisance, P. L. and E. A. Skewes (2003), 'Personal and Professional Dimensions of Newswork: Exploring Links between Journalists' Values and Roles', *Journalism and Mass Communication Quarterly*, 20 (4): 833–48.

Plümer, N. (2000), *Anglizismus, Purismus, sprachliche Identität: Eine Untersuchung zu den Anglizismen in der deutschen und französischen Mediensprache*, Frankfurt am Main: Peter Lang.

Pool, I. de S. and I. Shulman (1959), 'Newsmen's Fantasies, Audiences, and Newswriting', *Public Opinion Quarterly*, 23 (2): 145–58.

Poplack, S. (1993), 'Variation Theory and Language Contact: Concepts, Methods and Data', in D. R. Preston (ed), *American Dialect Research*, 251–86, Amsterdam: John Benjamins.

Preston, P. (2008), *Making the News: Journalism and News Cultures in Europe*, New York: Routledge.

Pulcini, V., C. Furiassi and F. Rodríguez González (2012), 'The Lexical Influence of English on European Languages: From Words to Phraseology', in C. Furiassi, V. Pulcini and F. Rodríguez González (eds), *The Anglicization of European Lexis*, 1–26, Amsterdam: John Benjamins.

Ritzer, G. (2019), *The McDonaldization of Society: Into the Digital Age*, 9th edn, Thousand Oaks, CA: SAGE.

Ross, P. (2014), 'Were Producers and Audiences Ever Separate? Conceptualizing Media Production as Social Situation', *Television & New Media*, 15 (2): 157–74.

Rumpf, W. (2007), *Music in the Air: AFN, BFBS, Ö3, Radio Luxemburg und die Radiokultur in Deutschland*, Berlin: LIT Verlag.

Sagmeister-Brandner, S. (2008), *Breaking News: So kommen englische Wörter ins Radio und Fernsehen: Eine empirische Studie österreichischer Nachrichten zwischen 1967–2004*, Frankfurt am Main: Peter Lang.

Sandford, J. (1997), 'Television in Germany', in J. A. Coleman and B. Rollet (eds), *Television in Europe*, 49–60, Exeter: Intellect Books.

Sankoff, G. (2002), 'Linguistic Outcomes of Language Contact', in J. K. Chambers, P. Trudgill and N. Schilling-Estes (eds), *The Handbook of Language Variation and Change*, 638–68, Oxford: Blackwell.

Saraceni, M. (2015), *World Englishes: A Critical Analysis*, London: Bloomsbury Academic.

Schaefer, S. J. (2019), 'Anglicisms in German Media: Exploring Catachrestic and Non-Catachrestic Innovations in Radio Station Imaging', *Lingua*, 221: 72–88.

Schaefer, S. J. (2021a), 'Hybridization or What? A Question of Linguistic and Cultural Change in Germany', *Globalizations*, 18 (4): 667–82.

Schaefer, S. J. (2021b), 'English on Air: Novel Anglicisms in German Radio Language', *Open Linguistics*, 7: 569–93.

Schaefer, S. J. (2022), 'Global Englishes and the Semiotics of German Radio – Encouraging the Listener's Visual Imagination through Translingual and Transmodal Practices', *Frontiers in Communication*, 7: 780195.

Schatz, H., N. Immer and F. Marcinkowski (1989), 'Der Vielfalt eine Chance? Empirische Befunde zu einem zentralen Argument für die "Dualisierung" des Rundfunks in der Bundesrepublik Deutschland', *Rundfunk und Fernsehen*, 37 (1): 5–24.

Schelper, D. (1995), 'Anglizismen in der Pressesprache der BRD, der DDR, Österreichs und der Schweiz: Eine vergleichende, typologische und chronologische Studie', PhD thesis, Quebec: Université Laval.

Schiller, H. I. (1968), 'The Use of American Power in the Post-Colonial World', *The Massachusetts Review*, 9 (4): 631–50.

Schiller, H. I. (1976), *Communication and Cultural Domination*, White Plains, NY: International Arts and Sciences Press.

Schiller, H. I. (1989), *Culture, Inc.*, New York: Oxford University Press.

Schneider, B., K. Schönbach and D. Stürzebecher (1993), 'Journalisten im vereinigten Deutschland: Strukturen, Arbeitsweisen und Einstellungen im Ost-West-Vergleich', *Publizistik*, 38 (3): 353–82.

Schneider, E. W. (2007), *Postcolonial English: Varieties around the World*, Cambridge: Cambridge University Press.

Schreier, D., M. Hundt and E. W. Schneider, eds. (2020), *The Cambridge Handbook of World Englishes*, Cambridge: Cambridge University Press.

Scollon, R. (2008), 'Discourse Itineraries: Nine Processes of Resemiotization', in V. Bhatia, J. Flowerdew and R. H. Jones (eds), *Advances in Discourse Studies*, 233–44, London: Routledge.

Scollon, R. and S. W. Scollon (2004), *Nexus Analysis: Discourse and the Emerging Internet*, London: Routledge.

Sharma, B. K. (2012), 'Beyond Social Networking: Performing Global Englishes in Facebook by College Youth in Nepal', *Journal of Sociolinguistics*, 16 (4): 483–509.

Shingler, M. and C. Wieringa (1998), *On Air: Methods and Meanings of Radio*, London: Arnold.

Shi-xu (2023), 'A Culturalist Approach to Discourse', in J. P. Gee and M. Handford (eds), *The Routledge Handbook of Discourse Analysis*, 2nd edn, 39–52, London: Routledge.

Shoemaker, P. J. and S. D. Reese (2014), *Mediating the Message in the 21st Century: A Media Sociology Perspective*, New York: Routledge.

Shulman, L. S. (1986), 'Those Who Understand: Knowledge Growth in Teaching', *Educational Researcher*, 15 (2): 4–14.

Silverstein, M. (1985), 'Language and the Culture of Gender: At the Intersection of Structure, Usage and Ideology', in E. Mertz and R. Parmentier (eds), *Semiotic Mediation: Sociocultural and Psychological Perspectives*, 219–59, New York: Academic Press.

Silverstein, M. (1996), 'Monoglot "Standard" in America: Standardization and Metaphors of Linguistic Hegemony', in D. L. Brenneis and R. K. S. Macaulay (eds), *The Matrix of Language: Contemporary Linguistic Anthropology*, 284–306, Boulder, CO: Westview Press.

Şimon, S. (2016), 'Necessary and Luxury English Loanwords in Some Romanian Online Newspapers and Magazines', in D. Dejica, G. Hansen, P. Sandrini and I. Para (eds), *Language in the Digital Era: Challenges and Perspectives*, 29–36, Warsaw: De Gruyter Open.

'Sketch Engine' (n.d.), available online: https://www.sketchengine.eu (accessed 1 July 2020).

Slembrouck, S. (2021), 'The Various Guises of Translanguaging and "Its Volatile Exchange Rates"', Presentation at Sociolinguistics Symposium 23, Hong Kong.
Slembrouck, S. (2022), 'The Various Guises of Translanguaging and Its Theoretical Airstrip', *Journal of Multilingual and Multicultural Development*, (published online ahead of print 5 December).
Smakman, D., H. Korzilius, F. van Meurs and E. van Neerven (2009), 'English Words and Phrases in Radio Commercials in the Netherlands: Their Use and Effects', *ESP across Cultures*, 6: 107–28.
Spitzmüller, J. (2005), *Metasprachdiskurse: Einstellungen zu Anglizismen und ihre wissenschaftliche Rezeption*, Berlin: De Gruyter.
Stephan, A. (2006), 'Culture Clash?', in A. Stephan and J. Vogt (eds), *America on My Mind: Zur Amerikanisierung der deutschen Kultur nach 1945*, 29–50, München: Wilhelm Fink Verlag.
Tagliavini, C. and R. Meisterfeld (1998), *Einführung in die romanische Philologie*, 2nd edn, Tübingen: Francke.
Tesch, G. (1978), *Linguale Interferenz: Theoretische, terminologische und methodische Grundfragen zu ihrer Erforschung*, Tübingen: TBL-Verlag Narr.
Thomason, S. G. (2010), 'Contact Explanations in Linguistics', in R. Hickey (ed), *The Handbook of Language Contact*, 29–47, Oxford: Wiley-Blackwell.
Thomason, S. G. (2001), *Language Contact*, Edinburgh: Edinburgh University Press.
Thomason, S. G. and T. Kaufman (1988), *Language Contact, Creolization, and Genetic Linguistics*, Berkeley: University of California Press.
Thoms, G., D. Adger, C. Heycock and J. Smith (2019), 'Syntactic Variation and Auxiliary Contraction: The Surprising Case of Scots', *Language*, 95 (3): 421–55.
Tolson, A. (2006), *Media Talk: Spoken Discourse on TV and Radio*, Edinburgh: Edinburgh University Press.
Tomlinson, J. (1991), *Cultural Imperialism*, Baltimore: Johns Hopkins University Press.
Trudgill, P. (1974), *The Social Differentiation of English in Norwich*, Cambridge: Cambridge University Press.
Tuchman, G. (1978), *Making News: A Study in the Construction of Reality*, New York: Free Press.
van Coetsem, F. (2000), *A General and Unified Theory of the Transmission Process in Language Contact*, Heidelberg: Winter.
van Dijk, T. A. (1988), *News as Discourse*, Hillsdale, NJ: L. Erlbaum.
van Dijk, T. A. (1999), 'Critical Discourse Analysis and Conversation Analysis', *Discourse & Society*, 10 (4): 459–60.
van Dijk, T. A. (2008), *Discourse and Context: A Socio-cognitive Approach*, Cambridge: Cambridge University Press.
van Dijk, T. A. (2015), 'Critical Discourse Analysis', in D. Tannen, H. E. Hamilton and D. Schiffrin (eds), *The Handbook of Discourse Analysis*, 2nd edn, 466–85, Malden, MA: Wiley Blackwell.

van Hout, T. (2011), 'Sourcing Business News: A Case Study of Public Relations Uptake', in B. Franklin and M. Carlson (eds), *Journalists, Sources, and Credibility*, 107–26, New York: Routledge.

van Hout, T. (2015), 'Between Text and Social Practice: Balancing Linguistics and Ethnography in Journalism Studies', in J. Snell, S. Shaw and F. Copland (eds), *Linguistic Ethnography*, 71–89, London: Palgrave Macmillan.

Viereck, W. (1986), 'The Influence of English on German in the Past and in the Federal Republic of Germany', in W. Viereck and W.-D. Bald (eds), *English in Contact with Other Languages*, 107–28, Budapest: Akadémiai Kiadó.

Walker, J. A. and M. Meyerhoff (2023), 'Complementation and the Creole Continuum in the Eastern Caribbean', *World Englishes*, 42 (1): 9–26.

Wallerstein, I. (1998), 'The Time of Space and the Space of Time: The Future of Social Science', *Political Geography*, 17 (1): 71–82.

Weaver, D. H. and G. C. Wilhoit (1991), *The American Journalist: A Portrait of U.S. News People and Their Work*, 2nd edn, Bloomington: Indiana University Press.

Weaver, D. H., R. A. Beam, B. J. Brownlee, P. S. Voakes and G. C. Wilhoit (2007), *The American Journalist in the 21st Century: U.S. News People at the Dawn of a New Millennium*, New York: Lawrence Erlbaum.

Weinreich, U. (1953), *Languages in Contact*, citations from 9th printing, 1979, The Hague: Mouton.

Weischenberg, S. (2004), *Journalistik: Medienkommunikation: Theorie und Praxis Band 1: Mediensysteme – Medienethik – Medieninstitutionen*, 3rd edn, Wiesbaden: VS Verlag für Sozialwissenschaften.

Weischenberg, S., M. Löffelholz and A. Scholl (1998), 'Journalism in German', in D. H. Weaver (ed), *The Global Journalist: Newspeople around the World*, 229–56, Cresskill, NJ: Hampton.

Willett, R. (1989), *The Americanization of Germany, 1945–49*, London: Routledge.

Winford, D. (2003), *An Introduction to Contact Linguistics*, Malden, MA: Blackwell.

Winford, D. (2007), 'Some Issues in the Study of Language Contact', *Journal of Language Contact*, 1 (1): 22–40.

Winter-Froemel, E., A. Onysko and A. Calude (2014), 'Why Some Non-Catachrestic Borrowings Are More Successful than Others: A Case Study of English Loans in German', in A. Koll-Stobbe and S. Knospe (eds), *Language Contact Around the Globe: Proceedings of the LCTG3 Conference*, 119–44, Frankfurt am Main: Peter Lang.

Wright, S. (2012), 'Language Policy, the Nation and Nationalism', in B. Spolsky (ed), *The Cambridge Handbook of Language Policy*, 59–78, Cambridge: Cambridge University Press.

Yang, W. (1990), *Anglizismen im Deutschen: Am Beispiel des Nachrichtenmagazins Der Spiegel*, Tübingen: Niemeyer.

Zenner, E., D. Speelman and D. Geeraerts (2012), 'Cognitive Sociolinguistics Meets Loanword Research: Measuring Variation in the Success of Anglicisms in Dutch', *Cognitive Linguistics*, 23 (4): 749–92.

Index

adult contemporary radio
    characteristics of language 14–19,
        84–5, 119
    format 8, 13–14, 17, 108–10, 119,
        124–5, 145–7, 156, 164–5,
        169–70, 195–8
affordances 9–10, 66, 86, 176, 179
Americanization 27, 32–6, 38–9, 107, 123–4
Anderson, B. 5–6
anglicisms 3, 45, 51–4, 67
    borrowing 49–50, 54, 106
    codeswitching 55–7, 67, 69–70,
        111–15, 125, 188
    conceptual transmissions 52, 56
    frequency 92–3, 106–7, 132–49, 160,
        196
    hybrid 54–6, 68–9, 71, 106–7, 159, 189
    modernity 35, 143, 148, 178–85, 191,
        198
    pseudo 55–6, 106, 158–9, 161, 188–9
    stylistic functions 67, 112, 184–5,
        187–9, 191–2, 198
Appadurai, A. 28–31, 119
appropriation 3, 26, 54, 106, 183, 190
assemblage 9–12, 59, 64–6, 80–1, 84–7, 99,
    113–14, 162–3, 180–1, 195, 197
asymmetrical hybridization 38–9, 101–10,
    123–5, 127, 177–8, 195–6
audio clips 115–18, 124

Blommaert, J. 1, 7, 9, 23–8, 42, 65, 79,
    83–5, 106
Bolton, K. 19, 42
broadcasting landscape 36–8, 72, 128,
    141–4
broadcasting regulation 73–5, 128, 141–4
broadcasting system 12, 36–8, 72–5, 82–3,
    127

Calude, A. 94–5
Canagarajah, S. 2, 11, 24–5, 43, 65–6, 81
capitalism 28, 46

catachrestic/non-catachrestic anglicisms
    57–8, 67, 93–7, 129–30, 144–5
    brevity 94–5, 166–9, 197
    diachronic development 58, 96–7,
        145–9
    lexical fields 95–6, 119–123, 125, 195
    semantic reasons 95, 179–81, 185–9,
        191–2, 198
centres of authority 26–7, 80–1, 83–7, 194
    competition and segmentation 147–8,
        196–7
    global/cultural environment 123–5,
        195–6
    journalist 190–1, 198
    workplace 165, 169–70, 197–8
comedy *see under* radio genres
commercialization 37–8, 102, 131–2
communicative intent 121–3, 182–4,
    191–2
competition 72–5, 127, 131–2, 136–44,
    147–9, 196–7
comprehensibility 110–18, 156–61, 167–9,
    192, 197–8
connotation 160, 162–3, 179–81, 185–7,
    198
contact linguistics 3, 45–51, 58–61, 66–71,
    193, 195
creation 55–7, 68, 71
critical discourse analysis (CDA) 10–11,
    78–80
cultural authenticity 70–1, 113–18, 124
cultural flows 8–9, 24, 28–31
    imbalance 28–30, 35–6, 38–9, 102–9,
        115, 119, 125, 195–6

de Saussure, F. 47
Deleuze, G. 80

editorial supervision 75–6, 153–4, 169
emblematic function 70–1, 112–15, 125
emic perspective 51, 66–7, 71, 195
Esser, F. 83

Fairclough, N. 10–11, 26, 78–9
flat ontology 65–6, 71, 80–1, 83–5, 99
format radio 12–13, 37–8, 74–5, 137–8

global Englishes 2, 23, 27
global/cultural environment *see under* centres of authority
globalization 1, 11–12, 23–36, 101–10, 124
groupings of influences 83–6, 99–100, 127
Guattari, F. 80

Haspelmath, M. 56
hegemony 107, 118
Herderian triad 46
Hesmondhalgh, D. 74, 128
homogenization 27–34, 38–9
host talk *see under* radio genres
human agency 65, 79–80, 84, 174
Hutchby, I. 9
hybridity 4–5, 28–31, 40, 107
hybridization 1–2, 28–35, 38–9, 83, 107

imagined audience 77, 127–9
imperialism 30
    cultural 28, 31, 35–6, 103, 124
    linguistic 28, 31

Jie, D. 7
journalistic terminology 102, 162–3, 170

Kachru, B. B. 2–3
Kress, G. R. 10–11, 78–80
Kubota, R. 40

language attitudes 174–8, 190–2, 198
language–culture nexus 27–8, 48
language perceptions 42, 53–4, 60, 66, 68, 104–5, 107, 123, 178–92, 197
language world 19–20, 42–3, 45, 58, 64–7, 71, 86–8, 97–8, 123–5, 130–1, 147, 154, 170, 174–8, 190–1, 195–9
Lievrouw, L. A. 9
lifeworld–system duality 42–3
lingua franca 103–6, 113–15

linguistic boundaries 5–7, 14, 42–3, 56–9, 65–71, 193, 197–9
    crossing 158–9
    maintenance 109, 130, 162–3
    negotiation 111–12, 167–9, 190, 192

Maase, K. 32, 34
markedness
    formal 52–3, 91
    pragmatic 67, 96–7, 121, 145–9, 180–1
material ecology 18, 64–5, 129, 163
materiality 10, 59, 65, 113–14, 174
    medium 9, 15–16, 18, 86, 95, 160, 169, 194
Matras, Y. 56, 61, 69–70
Media Language Model 64, 80–1, 83–7, 194
methodological pluralism 3, 194
Miller, E. R. 40
mobility paradigm 2, 4–5, 8, 64, 193
monolingual bias 43, 58
monolingual ideology 6–7, 25, 41, 46–7, 66, 197
monolithic orientation 1–3, 5–7, 19–20, 40–3, 51, 59–60
morning show 13–14, 78, 89, 130, 136–9, 158, 164–5
multimodality 10, 79–80

national languages 5–6, 46–7, 108
nationalism 31, 46–7
nation-state 6–7, 29–31, 46–7
Nederveen Pieterse, J. 28–31, 38, 107
neologism 68
news *see under* radio genres
novel anglicisms 55–7, 67–71, 169, 197
    creation 56–7, 67–9, 156, 158–61
    identification 91–2
    incipient borrowing 56, 67–71, 156–8

Onysko, A. 52–5, 57–8, 67, 69, 94–5, 133–4, 145, 186
orders of indexicality 26–7, 83, 86, 170

paradigmatic gap 2–3, 6, 45, 65–6, 86, 98–9, 193–4
paradigmatic parallelism 2–3, 193
paradigmatic shift 2, 5, 39–40, 64
Pennycook, A. 2, 10, 24, 27–9, 105
polycentricity 27, 80–1, 83, 85–6, 127, 195

pop music 8, 17, 104–5, 110–13, 124–5, 163–4, 180–1
   lexical fields 119, 121, 195–6
popular culture 16–17, 28, 34–5, 124–5, 156, 195, 197
poststructuralist linguistics 20, 40–2, 45, 65–6
Preston, P. 81–2

qualitative interviews 8, 87–8, 95, 97–8, 195

radio genres 13, 90, 93
   comedy 136, 158–9, 189
   communicative aims 15–16, 156–61, 164–5, 170
   conventions 15–19, 159–60, 164–5, 170
   host talk 16, 136, 164–5, 170
   news 15–16, 74, 122, 135–6, 153
   service 136, 157–8
   station imaging 13, 16–18, 87, 93, 144–9, 159–61, 166–7
      anglicism frequency 135, 196
      lexical fields 120–2, 125
reconceptualization of language 1–3
Reese, S. D. 78, 82, 173
resemiotization 26, 106, 177–8
rhizome 80–1, 85–6, 173, 194
role perceptions 77–8, 173, 176, 191, 198
routine practices 71, 162–70, 176, 197–8

Saussurean synchrony 24, 47
scales 25–7, 65, 84–6, 99, 110, 170, 195–6
scapes 29
   linguascapes 29, 35, 118
   mediascapes 35, 119, 125
   technoscapes 35, 119
Schiller, H. I. 28, 33
sedimentation 198
   journalistic practices 14, 16, 64, 174
   language resources 54, 65, 68, 71, 97, 111, 190
   social structures 80–1, 85
segmentation 74, 110, 128–9, 132, 147–9, 196–7
service *see under* radio genres
Shoemaker, P. J. 78, 82, 173
Slembrouck, S. 42–3

social semiotics 11, 78–80
socially grounded spatial approach 3, 64–6, 99, 193–4
sociolinguistics of mass media 9–12, 80, 193–4
sociolinguistics of mobility 1, 5, 24–7, 42, 45, 64, 71, 83–4, 109, 193–4
spatial approach 11, 64–5, 80, 83, 95, 98–9
spatial ecology 64–5, 85, 174
spatial repertoire 14, 64–6, 84–6, 98–100, 108–9, 174
station image 18, 121–3, 136–44, 147–8, 174, 196–7
station imaging *see under* radio genres
structuralist linguistics 24, 45–7, 51, 64–7
structuralist perspective 5–6, 9, 42–3, 45–8, 54, 58–61, 64–7, 87, 99, 190, 197

target audience 8, 128–32, 147, 196–7
text–context binary 11, 49, 59–60, 65, 78–80, 99, 195
theory–practice gap 40–3, 45, 64–6, 99
Thomason, S. G. 47–9, 60
TimeSpace 25–6, 30–1
transcultural flows 2, 24, 104–5, 118–21, 125
transfer processes 48–52, 71, 92
translanguaging 25, 113–14
translingualism 24–5, 43
   practice 14, 83, 85–6, 111, 164
transmodality 10–11
   practice 14–15, 17–18, 83, 85–6, 113–15, 163–4, 170, 174, 194
   transcriptions 17–18, 112, 114, 163, 180

van Coetsem, F. 49–50, 58–9
van Dijk, T. A. 11, 78–9
van Leeuwen, T. 10–11, 78–9

Wallerstein, I. 25, 30–1
Weischenberg, S. 73, 75–6, 82, 154, 168
Winter-Froemel, E. 57–8, 94–5, 145, 186
wordplay 158–61
workplace *see under* centres of authority
World Englishes 2–3, 9, 193

www.ingramcontent.com/pod-product-compliance
Lightning Source LLC
Chambersburg PA
CBHW071815300426
44116CB00009B/1321